GOOD MORNING,
MR. SH*TTYBOTTOM

35 Years in the Life of an Expat Adman

John Fuery

Table of Contents

For Mum and Dad who made all this possible but sadly couldn't stick around long enough to read about it.

'It's only advertising, no one gets killed.'

−Anon

Author's Note

Hope you've not blown a hole in your bank balance in the belief you might have bought some insightful 'wow, I never knew *that!*' travelogue or fact-packed history of advertising. My book contains nothing more weighty than a series of personal recollections cherry-picked from a career spent in ad agencies across Africa, Asia, Europe, and the Middle East.

While each and every one of the stories contained herein is true, almost all of the names of the agencies and people I worked with or met along the way have had to be changed. Several of these modifications have been made to spare people problems caused by my raking up things they'd either hoped others had long forgotten or would rather not remember themselves.

Others have been forced on me by the economic reality that sales of this book are unlikely to cause sleepless nights for the likes of Dan Brown or E.L. James. With many former colleagues and friends possessed of considerably thinner skins and far deeper pockets than my own, and the absurdly high legal fees needed to defend lawsuits, I'm sure you'll understand my position.

Where names have been changed, they are denoted by single quotation marks on their first appearance in the text. In making such changes,

I've tried to stick as closely to the sort of wordings I and my colleagues used to use for agencies where we worked together or acquaintances we shared. So while no one with the name 'Despond' ever worked at 'Sceptre'/'Septic', I did know someone of the same name around that time. Ditto the global creative director I had lunch with at CPU. While he wasn't actually called 'Roger Thornhill', the man did seem to me to be a bit of a prick, and aeroplanes did indeed play a sizeable role in his life.

Where the titles of agency staffers or other advertising terminologies appear in the main text, I first use the full title (e.g. senior account director) followed by the acronym (e.g. SAD) on every page of the book thereafter.

John Fuery

Roscommon, Ireland

September, 2018

Prologue

Saturday, August 17, 2013

The inevitable effects of ageing and the steady decline in demand for my freelance skills had finally begun to kick in. Seeing the writing – not mine for once – on the wall, my wife, Belle, and I decided to up sticks and eke out our twilight years in Europe. And where better to do just that than the place my mum and dad used to call home – Roscommon in the west of Ireland.

But first, a brief history lesson...

By the mid 16th century, English rule over the Irish was consolidated in Dublin. Anyone unfortunate enough to live outside the new parliament's limits (i.e. everyone who wasn't English) was dismissed as being 'beyond the pale'.

A rocky, relentlessly rainy location where few things grow and only cow and sheep shit can be said to prosper, Roscommon's home in Connaught Province was the pale beyond the pale. So much so that, in 1654, Cromwell had no hesitation in ordering Ireland's millions of hungry peasants to go to 'hell or to Connacht' (sic).

When the potato famine struck in 1845, the area was one of the hardest hit, accounting for just under a third of the million souls whose lives were lost. Still, having spent many happy childhood holidays playing with my uncle Jimmy's dogs by the River Shannon, it remains my favourite of all the places I've been fortunate enough to be able to visit. Well, at least it is on those rare days when it's not pissing down with rain.

Fast forward 168 years, five months, and one interminable, 26-hour door-to-door journey via Istanbul later. Having finally arrived in Roscommon to start our new lives, Belle and I were decanted outside Gleesons' Guesthouse by our taxi driver. Although we'd spent the previous 12 years enjoying their hospitality during pre-Christmas breaks, we were touched when owners Eamon and Mary showed us to their best room.

Such preferential treatment initially seemed a little puzzling when we discovered President Obama's head of the CIA, John Brennan, was a fellow guest. While no relative of mine, the über spy was, bizarrely, a cousin of a cousin, and was staying in the hotel with his 92-year-old dad, a schoolfriend of my own father. VVVIP he might have been, but Mr. B couldn't have been nicer when I braved being gunned down in the breakfast buffet to say 'hi' to his father and him the next morning.

The reasoning behind Gleesons' egalitarian room allocations had finally become apparent the previous evening when I'd caught sight of two men in black surreptitiously talking into their cuffs in the hotel courtyard below our room. It was then that my still jetlag-befuddled brain had cottoned on that the pair were just two of the small army of well-trained killing machines that accompanied the CIA big cheese at all times. From there, it was but the tiniest of leaps to work out why it was us and not J. Brennan, Esquire who wound up lording it up in the hotel's prize digs.

Should a crazed lunatic sidle past the guards and get close enough to lob a bomb through Gleesons' front window, Belle and I were expendable, whereas Obama's chief intelligence advisor was not.

It's at times like this that the clichés really do kick into overdrive and your whole life really does flash past your eyes.

All those failures at once, it's all a bit too much to take. As we're about to discover…

BOOK ONE:

Climbing up the Greasy Pole

'What's to learn?'

–Agency senior account director reacting to a younger colleague's desire to quit her job because she didn't seem to be 'learning anything'.

Chapter One

The bay frae Stewpit Strit

Given my eventual choice of career and insatiable wanderlust, it will probably come as no surprise that my first job was a media role that involved plenty of travel. I was a paperboy with Mr. Franklin's newsagents at the top of Harris Road in Coventry. The only time in recorded history that an employer has kept my details 'on file' and actually contacted me when a 'suitable vacancy arose', my hiring there remains a personal human resources first.

As Mr. F memorably said of the various deliveries I was to make as he slung the heavy canvas bag over my shoulder before my first round: 'Like the *News of The World* says, John, all human life is here. Well, perhaps not at 22 Grant Road. But then they take the *Daily Mail*.'

The best thing about this particular 'job' was being able to read – for free – copies of bloodthirsty comics like the *Victor* and the *Hotspur*. Showing how Britain had apparently single-handedly won World War Two with an army consisting of some 15 soldiers, new issues of each comic were garishly illustrated punches to youthful stomachs. The only fly in this vast expanse of creamy ointment was that the customers expected their papers to be delivered on time and with their pages still virgin fresh and uncreased.

It was from these eager weekly readings that I quickly picked up my – to this day – very rudimentary grasp of conversational German and Japanese. Frustratingly, the various colleagues and clients I later met from those countries remained mystifyingly unappreciative of my mastery of conversational icebreakers such as *Donner und Blitzen! Kamerad! Gott in Himmel!* and *Banzai!*

Happily, with puberty fast approaching and licensing laws in the early 1970s being rather laxer than they are today, it wasn't very long before I gravitated to employment of a more adult kind. And so it was I happily took a job behind the sort of bar I would never in a million years have spent quite so much time in front of later in life.

My bartending 'career' began not long after my 17th birthday and lasted roughly one year. It eventually ended with my sensational, Ziggy Stardust-like (in my mind anyway) retirement shortly before the day I became legally entitled to drink.

My first taste of serving rather than swilling pints came at Coombe Abbey Working Men's Club at the bottom of nearby Binley Road. Still hopelessly inexperienced in the ways of the world, my naiveté was ruthlessly exploited by the club's members (or 'old jacks' as us young pups behind the bar scornfully called them).

In those far-off days, third-rate entertainers who couldn't carry a tune or joke in a bucket didn't watch their dreams wither and die during auditions for the *X-Factor* or *Britain's Got Talent*. No, they signed up with the West Midlands' equivalent of Woody Allen's theatrical agent Broadway Danny Rose. Before they knew it, these talentless turns found their weekends eaten up with 'starring' roles in weekend entertainment cavalcades at working men's clubs the length and breadth of middle England.

And weekends at 'the Coombe' didn't get any hotter than when the club president stopped dragging and started cracking his knuckles in readiness to draw the Saturday night tombola.

The most irritating of the rabble of tormentors who'd made it their mission to make my life behind the club's bar a misery was a permanently pissed Glaswegian called 'Jimmy'. With getting 'stimmin' on tombola night a particular highlight, Jimmy's great pleasures seemed to be as lifeless as the brown teeth that jostled messily for squatters' rights in his gob.

Another of his favourite pastimes involved barking out the most elaborate possible litany of drinks for his friends as he headed to the bar during between-draw breaks. 'Whisky pep! Guinness and black! M&B! Wha's M&B? Meyeld ay bittur! Are yew frae Stewpit Strit er whut, sun?' ran the predictable refrain.

A city skyline array of drinks balanced precariously on a tray, Jimmy would invariably produce an Everest-sized assortment of grubby coppers and tarnished silver coins from his trouser pocket. The scrapheap of shrapnel tinkling merrily in his shaky hands our Great Scot would then begin meticulously counting out the amount needed to pay for his round. Just as he neared the total, he would sigh theatrically, dump the change back in his pocket, and produce a couple of greasy notes from his wallet.

It was a close-run thing as to who detested Jimmy the most: the staff smiling at him through gritted teeth or the angry boozers behind him whose gimlet stares were boring holes in his back.

Whatever satisfaction Lord Jim derived from unnecessarily inconveniencing everyone else was only the first of what he doubtless thought as being a generously stocked bag of tricks. Foaming tankards (actually old-fashioned handled nonik tumblers) of ale served, money taken, and change pocketed – never, ever minus a drink for the staff – Jimmy would pause and turn like Peter Falk's *Columbo*.

Having spotted an attempt on the life of one of his pints or halves, the eagle-eyed 'tec would begin minutely scrutinizing the 'collars', or heads, on top of each glass. His right eye screwed up as if it held a jeweller's loupe, our discerning drinker would inevitably find fault with at least one of the assorted beers. 'D'yez thank ye cud sqwiz a debble whiskey un thur, sun?' Jimmy would ask, much to the merriment of whatever pals had arrived to assist with the triumphant carrying off of his order.

Towards the end of my time at the Coombe, I'd had enough of Jimmy's thigh-slapping attempts at my belittlement to last me a lifetime. As my final shift was to be a Saturday night, I resolved to extract a little payback.

Rather than attempt to dodge serving the man – as did almost everyone who'd spent any time behind the bar – I rushed forwards to greet Mr. Barrel of Laughs like a long-lost friend. Beers painstakingly assayed, Jimmy did his usual thing of tipping his mates a wink before he started stage two of his hijinks.

Chums duly alerted that their sides were in danger of splitting with an excess of merriment, Jimmy predictably began offering expert critiques of the various drinks that made up his round.

Jimmy, it goes without saying didn't miss a trick.

Goodness me, if he didn't remark on how the sizeable shortfall in the head of one particular beer had left sufficient space for a double-sized measure of premium-grade Scotch. Grabbing the offending pint, I walked over to the optics at the back of the bar and pressed the glass against the Coombe's most expensive – O.K. only – single malt twice in quick succession.

'That'll be £1.30p extra (well, it was the early 1970s) for the double Scotch, please,' I said as I plonked the freshly fortified pint in front of the now plainly gobsmacked gobshite. Struck dumb by the sight of the most expensive drink he would probably ever buy, Jimmy's face was a picture Edvard Munch would have been proud to paint. 'Aye, he gut you thur, Jahmy!' said one of the pissed-up patrons at the bar to our by now very pissed-off one-man pictish army.

***

The remainder of my career at the bar was spent at another working men's watering hole called the Stoke Ex-Servicemen's Club (SESC) in Ball Hill, about a mile from where I lived. After being almost totally flattened (literally coventrated) by Luftwaffe bombs during World War Two, Coventry had miraculously emerged from the ashes like the phoenix on its city crest. By the time the 1970s began, Cov had achieved a level of once undreamt-of prosperity on the back of Britain's then thriving motor trade.

With left-leaning union firebrands like my then best friend Pat Fox's dad, Bruce, calling their members out on the flimsiest of premises, the city's car factories were a hotbed of toxic labour relations.

'You won't get me. I'm part of the Union!' as the chorus on The Strawbs' atypical hit of the time had it. The fact that strike-worthy offences included production line managers regularly having to wake slumbering union members who should have been hard at work didn't bode well for the future.

Although happy to leverage their collective bargaining power to feather their own nests, none of the 'working men' I served gave a shit about the welfare of those pulling their pints. One night towards the end of my stint at SESC, I lead a bunch of disaffected bar staff in giving the old jacks a taste of their own medicine.

The moment we chose to strike – literally – was the eagerly awaited Saturday night tombola rollover during August Bank Holiday weekend 1973. For the first and only time, the usual between-draw rush for drinks, unfunny comic gurning, and tuneless massacres of 'hits' like *Una Paloma Blanca* held no terror for us.

No, tonight I was to step forward like a Ball Hill version of Lech Walesa and tell the baying ranks of thirsty old jacks that we'd downed towels. There would, I was to announce, be no further drinks served until such time as Joe, the SESC's aptly named bar steward, agreed to sit down and discuss our pay and conditions.

The evening's initial session of tombola all over, bar the post-game grumbling, the first wave of what would soon become tsunami of thirsty punters crashed up against the club bar.

'Whisky pep!' shouted one.

'Two pints of M&B!' screamed a second.

'Three halves of lager tops!' banshee-wailed a third.

Faster than you could say 'the milky bars are on me', the entire length of the 60-foot bar was three deep with drinkers brandishing empty glasses and shouting out exactly how they wanted them to be refilled. The only thing the anxious rabble was missing was a set of Mobs'R'Us flaming torches.

Answer and action from the various Tolpuddle Bartyrs manning the pumps and optics came there none.

As quickly as it had risen to a crescendo, the babble of voices fell silent. As always happens in such cases, one voice quickly signalled its owner's intention to exert some kind of rule on the mob. 'What's going on here, then, lads?' said Albert, the club secretary and a keen imbiber of the club's disgusting sludge-textured mild.

'We're sick and tired of being paid crap money and the abysmal way you and the rest of the members here treat us,' said I. 'Despite having tried to raise our concerns with you and Joe several times, you've never made the slightest effort to listen to or address our grievances. As a result, we've been left with no other option than to take a leaf out of your members' books and withdraw our labour.'

The Mexican wave of outrage that rippled through the throng gave way to dark mutterings about who'd died and left these little scrotes in charge.

'I think you and I had better visit Joe's office for a chat, young John,' said Albert. This was not good news, as my freshly minted antagonist was a brick shithouse of a bloke and considerably less mild of temperament than the slop he drank. In the end, he and Joe simply fired me, paid me off, and told me to never, ever darken the door of their club again.

When I ran into a couple of my former SESC colleagues a few weeks later, they said that they had been told of my on-the-spot dismissal and decided to return to work. Can't say I really blamed them. Still, the look of outrage on the faces of the assembled crowd when presented with the shitty end of the stick for a change was wondrous to behold. Amusingly, the only barman who didn't join our impromptu industrial action later pitched up at the agency where I worked in Bahrain just as my time there was nearing its end. Needless to say, he didn't contribute to my leaving present.

***

The summer of 1974 saw me leave secondary

school with two A levels. A continued career in the hospitality industry looking unlikely, I'd next to no idea as to what to do with the rest of my life. Looking on the bright side, I had secured myself places on the American Studies courses at both Hull and Warwick universities for October 1975. The only problem now was how to fill the 15 or so months before I ventured out into the big bad world.

Still reeling from the aftermath of then UK Prime Minister Ted Heath's recent miner's-strike-fuelled three-day week, Coventry was no longer the cornucopia of easily accessible jobs it formerly had been. Soon, an even less palatable Tory leader would ensure that full employment here was soon relegated to the 'Remember When' pages of the local paper.

As the concept of 'gap years' was then limited to a few trust-funded Tabithas and Tarquins from the soppy south, there seemed little chance I would ever get the chance to travel the world. One day, I found myself reading a recruitment ad from the 'vibrant entity' that was Coventry District Council (CDC). A couple of weeks later, I was in front of a panel of council panjandrums and lying through my teeth about why I relished 'building my future' as part of this 'paragon of local government excellence'.

Although too many years, beers, and spliffs

have robbed me of total recall of this particular interview, I do remember asking about the possibility of a job in communications or PR. Naturally, a gossamer-light 20- to 30-minute grilling was all it took for the various time servers who saw me to know my strengths and interests far better than I did myself. Peering mole-like across the desk, one panel member proceeded to map out a career path I had absolutely no interest in taking up and even less intention of sticking with for any length of time.

A few weeks later, in early October 1974, I became one of the two office juniors employed chasing debts in CDC's Outside Collection (OC) Department. Despite the olive-drab-walled anonymity of the office and the institutionalized grey pallor of most of those imprisoned inside it, OC was not without its occasional brighter moments. If the following comes across as being ungrateful, it's not meant to be. We all have to start somewhere, right?

In overall charge of OC was a rather forbidding old-school gentleman with the unlikely moniker of 'Tom LePetomaine' – 'TLP' to his friends and 'Tom LePompous' to everyone else. Tom – sorry, *Mr.* LePetomaine; early on, he 'reprimanded' me for having the temerity to use his first name – was one of those puffed-up types who always seem to end up as council jobsworths. Assuming they've not yet been replaced by automatons, I would imagine the TLPs of this world continue to lord it over a new generation of junior serfs like myself to this day.

Still, impossibly ancient even then, Tom is now almost certainly safely entombed in some dusty, seldom-opened filing cabinet in the sky. As a result, I'm sure he won't be Ouija-boarding his lawyers if we all give a rousing yell of 'Well, whaddya know! If it isn't Tom, Tom, Tommy, the Tomster!'

Having sometimes tried to shove chippy youngsters down the rocky road towards a Brighter Future© at agencies myself, the years have made me more sympathetic towards Tom. But Lord, he didn't make it easy for himself.

A plum lodged irretrievably somewhere between his arse and his oesophagus, Tommy Boy laboured under the massive misapprehension that his every utterance packed a gravitas that extended far beyond OC's office walls. His habit of brusquely announcing, 'LePetomaine speaking,' every time he picked up the phone is one abiding memory of him that 40-odd years have failed to erode.

Drunk with what little actual power he possessed, TLP seized every opportunity to underline his grand poohbah title for anyone – staff or debtor – unfortunate enough to enter his orbit. As the office skivvy, I was routinely assigned menial tasks that only the lowliest specimens of CDC's pond life were deemed incapable of fucking up. Trips to the council stationery department – presumably an early CDC prototype of today's 'naughty step' – were a regular occurrence.

Determined to make my sentence at OC pass as quickly as I could, I used to stretch these trips out for as long as was humanly possible. One day, while dawdling aimlessly along a corridor, I was horrified to bump into TLP as he and his ever-present pile of life-wrecking buff folders came barrelling around a corner. 'Fuery!' he bellowed, 'what on earth are you doing here? Shouldn't you still be at your post? Have you been relieved already?'

'No, Mr. LePetomaine, but if you'll excuse me, I've a feeling I'm about to be,' I said, quickening my pace and striding rather more purposefully towards the gents' toilet.

By far, the worst of the mundane drudgeries tossed my way was having to open letters and packages in CDC's mailroom. Normally, this would have been a doddle, but with the IRA's bombing of the mainland UK then reaching its 1970s zenith, even innocuous-looking packages represented a potential threat.

While the above may sound a tad drama-queenish on my part, the risks were actually far more real than one might think. In the space of eight days in November 1974, I came ascloseasthis to getting blown up in two bombings. The first occurred on Thursday, November 14, 1974, when a group of us were drinking at a city centre pub called The Penny Black.

Pints interrupted by a surprisingly subdued **WHUMPH!** almost every drinker inside the taproom ran out onto the street to see what had happened. Lying a few yards from the pub's front door was a steaming pile of charred meat, which, it eventually turned out, comprised the earthly remains of one James McDade.

It seems Mr. McD had been trying to commemorate the anniversary of the last major IRA-initiated explosion in Coventry some 40 years earlier by flattening the city's central telephone exchange. If the resultant detonation hadn't quite blown the failed terrorist all the way to kingdom come, it had at least propelled him the quarter of a mile to the doors of The Penny Black.

Less diligent in his handling of explosives than was perhaps advisable, the late and largely unlamented Mr. McD might now have been little more than a tiny footnote in the history of the Troubles. Tragically, many historians believe the authorities' blanket banning of marches commemorating McDade's death led directly to the horrific Birmingham pub bombings that occurred exactly one week later.

The following Wednesday, some mates and I went to see Jethro Tull at the Birmingham Odeon. Before the show had started, we'd spent a pleasant couple of hours drinking in a pub called the Tavern in the Town. The next evening, I was horrified to turn on the TV to discover that the Tavern was one of the two pubs destroyed by IRA bombs.

Had the concert taken place just 24 hours later, my friends and I could well have ended up amongst the 21 people killed. Even had we survived, our shared Irish backgrounds might have resulted in our being dragooned into the group of six blameless paddies the West Midlands Police subsequently fitted up for the deaths.

But enough of chastening truths and back to my unwelcome stint in CDC's post room. Every Thursday morning, I'd reluctantly dilly-dally my way up to the third floor for my three or four hours of mindless grind. The only bright spot was getting to sit next to Maxine – to my then erection-obsessed adolescent mind very probably the hottest office junior in Coventry city centre.

Despite my hormones doing loop-de-loops, I never summoned up the courage to invite this goddess of the post room for post-work drinks at the nearby Golden Cross – my local since about age 15. All too soon, my elaborate Watney's Red Barrel-fuelled fantasies were dashed when Maxine was replaced by a spotty male with a quavery, high-pitched voice called Enda.

The next time I encountered the divine Miss M was when her name appeared in the court reports in the evening paper. It seemed that poor old Maxi had been afflicted with *stickyfingeritis* and had been caught stealing cash from the envelopes we'd been opening. Given a stern talking to by a local magistrate, she'd been lucky to escape with probation.

***

The only time I can ever recall the Tomster cracking anything that could be considered as being within the same postcode as a smile was Tuesday, February 11, 1975. For those of you with an especially shaky grasp of history, this was, of course, the day that saw Maggie Thatcher 'romp home' in the Tory leadership contest. In doing so, she began an inexorable march towards 11 years of probably the most divisive premiership the UK has ever had to suffer. 'Now we'll see things start getting done,' said our delighted leader to everyone in the office. And once she and her party got elected in May 1979, get things done Thatcher did indeed begin to do.

Within a few years of her entering Downing Street, Thatcher and her droogs had annihilated the car industry on which almost every family in Coventry was dependent for their livelihoods. With no work for those whose income sustained its shops and pubs, my hometown quickly became a wasteland even the German bomber pilots who'd targeted it 30 years earlier might have marvelled at.

By the early 1980s, local band The Specials would be lamenting this once happy, confident city's unwanted reputation as a 'ghost town'.

Other members of the OC team who heard TLP's stirring speech that day almost certainly included his departmental number two, a rather more amiable old cove called 'Jim Newsome'. Wounded in the war – or so legend had it – Jim walked with a stick, liked a drink or four, and always seemed to have a twinkle in his eye – after lunch, anyway.

There was a lot to be said for lunchtime boozing back then. It was a pleasurable habit which was, if not exactly encouraged, then tolerated rather than sternly frowned upon as now. As unforgiving as he was with those whose poor judgement or luck had seen them fall behind on their council rents or rates, Jim was always unfailingly patient with juniors like me.

Then there were the spear carriers who made up the numbers in the OC office. 'First man with spear' was a fidget-riven wreck of a man called 'Jeff Kirkham'. I turned out that poor old JK had just returned to work after three months enforced leave following a nervous breakdown. A haunted look in his eyes, the poor bastard used to peck away at his typewriter with two fingers as his workmates cruelly poked fun at his car crash of a home life.

The most frequent and vociferous of JK's tormentors were the various retired ex-coppers who served as OC's bailiffs. More Gene Cunt than Gene Hunt, all four were as happy as pigs in shit with CDC's generous topping-up of their police pensions with large monthly stipends. After all, what more pleasant way to while away those dreary pre-daytime telly mornings and afternoons than by first knocking on, and occasionally later kicking down, various debtors' doors? And all without having to go to the bother of trying to fasten uniform buttons over your now alarmingly prodigious gut.

While almost all of these Cro-Magnon ex-coppers exhibited levels of sexism and racism that was – even in those unenlightened times – truly off-the-scale, the wheel of karma did occasionally dish them up some just desserts. Caught ogling one especially violent habitual jailbird's rather comely common-law-wife, a former plod called 'Ray McInnes' received a pretty serious looking black eye. While the angry blue-black bruises faded as the weeks wore on, McInnes' resultant nickname never did. He remained 'Sugar Ray' for the remainder of my time at BD.

Bundled into the back of an unmarked police car for nothing more serious than walking home from my bar job at Coombe Abbey late one night, I'd experienced Coventry coppers' awfulness first-hand. Devotees of then popular cop show, *The Sweeney*, many police officers of that era fantasised they were Jack Regan-style mavericks for whom the law was merely a minor irritant.

Sporting a cheesy nylon car coat and those *faux*-leather backless driving gloves that were standard issue for TV cops of the time, the only laws my chief tormentor was flouting involved good taste. Clad in a safari-suit-style buttoned leather jacket fresh from the remainder racks at Man at C&A, his sidekick was guilty of violating several fashion statutes himself.

Fearful of inadvertently causing the couple who'd hired the still underage me as a barman to face charges, I'd kept *schtum* in the face of some patently idiotic questioning. The most ludicrous of the several 'offences' I was accused of was a burglary whose scene I'd have had to sprint two miles across a golf course to escape. If I was innocent of the charge, one of the clichéd good cop/bad cop double act asked, how come the bottom of my trousers were soaking wet? Resisting the urge to break down and sob it was 'a fair cop', I pointed out that the dampness might have been the result of an evening's worth of sustained rainfall.

After two hours of such back-and-forth bull-shitting, the West Midlands' Holmes and Watson reluctantly conceded they had no grounds on which to hold me, and no option other than to let me go.

When my dad heard about what had happened the following day, he wanted to head straight down to the cop shop and register a formal complaint. Having heard plenty of horror stories about the fate befalling many of those entering police stations in the UK at that time, I begged him to leave things be. Given the rough justice awaiting Irish people who found themselves on the wrong end of the long arm of the law back then, I remain forever grateful he let the matter drop.

***

One of the things I was expressly forbidden from doing after clambering aboard the good ship OC was interviewing the poor fuckers who'd wound up in hock to CDC. Desperate to break the relentless grind of my deskbound life, I was, of course, down at the interview counters 'assessing' debtors' circumstances every chance I got. Despite CDC's Soviet-like crushing of the merest glimmer of anything that smacked of initiative, desperate understaffing meant blind eyes were frequently turned towards such infringements.

Jim Newsome was far from being unique in seeing the value of a brace of strong midday stiffeners when it came to getting through the afternoon. Disappointingly, my salary rarely stretched to more than a couple of post-payday lunchtime pints. As a result, when everyone else abandoned of the office at 1:00 pm, I spent the next hour conducting illicit trawls of OC's copious stacks of debtors' files.

Stored inside a row of six or seven four-drawer-high institutional steel grey filing cabinets were hundreds of buff folders. Each and every one of them was grim to the brim with sick-making stories that would have filled series after series for 21st century TV misery merchants like Jeremy Kyle.

Human nature being human nature, inquisitiveness quickly got the better of me, and I soon began searching the drawers for names I might recognise. The horrific early discovery that a former schoolmate's step-sister had been repeatedly raped by her father stopped me looking up friends and acquaintances for the remainder of my time at CDC.

With Coventry's post-prosperity decline accelerating by the day, the number of genuinely pitiful individuals becoming ensnared in OC's bad books was one of my home town's few remaining growth industries.

The one debtor every OCer did bend over backwards to try and interview was 'Mrs. Walsh', a vivacious redhead in her early 30s. While she probably had queues of potential soulmates stretching around the block, the youthful Mrs. W had made a cardinal error. She'd chosen to get hitched to a world-class dirtbag from one of Coventry's scummiest sink estates. On the few times I interviewed her, I found it incredibly dispiriting to see how poor choices had ended up suffocating someone so presumably formerly full of life.

Having spent years happily banging up suspects on the flimsiest of grounds in order to hit the pub at early doors, OC's motley band of bailiffs were predictably less compassionate. The callousness with which the former rozzers recounted the sex acts they vainly envisaged performing on (rather than with) any vaguely attractive woman sucked into their orbit was utterly pathetic. Oft-repeated *bon mots* such as 'I'd like to slip her a length next time she comes up short with her payments!' were par for the course.

With words and phrases like 'arrears' and 'behind' part of OC's *lingua franca*, the potential for smutty double entendres was almost endless. Each new crudity was inevitably rewarded with levels of merriment not heard since Oscar Wilde split his fellow members' sides in London's Albemarle Club some 80 years earlier. With their thigh-slapping mirth likely to shake you off the pavement and deposit you in front of speeding traffic, passing their homes during showings of 1970s laff-fests like *On the Buses* was not advisable.

On the wrong side of the fence were the debtors whose arrival downstairs caused everyone to become suddenly and inexplicably busy. Foremost amongst this group was a grime-encrusted old Yorkshireman called 'Martin Shires'. The mystery of why Mr. S had not been stopped from running up a Mount Eiger-sized pile of unpaid CDC bills ranked with the whereabouts of the recently vanished Lord Lucan. Nowadays, the tormented fucker's obvious inability to cope would almost certainly propel him to the head of the queue for what little counselling might still be available. Four-and-a-half decades ago, it merely earned him a court order to try and haul himself out of the ocean of debt in which he was drowning at a rate of 50p a week.

Every Monday morning without fail, Mr. S would trudge to OC's interview desk for his weekly humiliation. Once arrived in this ninth circle of debtor's hell, he would summon up whatever dignity he could muster and make his latest tiny dent in his ginormous liabilities. Typically, these payments would consist of unimaginably icky small-denomination coins that looked as though they had been picked up from the bottom of a urinal. Like every other OCer, I – to my eternal shame – did everything I could to avoid touching his little pile of God-knows-what-contagion-laden coinage.

If Mr. S was offended by the inconsiderate way I cruelly hammered yet another unnecessary dent into his dignity, he demonstrated consider-ably more grace than I ever could by never once complaining. He simply dropped his coins in the envelope offered him, slid his amends across the counter, collected his receipt, and was gone for another week.

One Monday, it was nearer to 5:00 pm than 10:00 am when an even more dreadful-looking than usual Mr. S arrived to pay his weekly penance. 'Are you OK, Mr. Shires? I asked him. 'Nay, lad, I'm not. On Saturday night, I'd had just about enough and swallowed half a bottle of aspirin followed by four cans of Newky Brown.'

Mr. S was only saved because another resident of his sheltered accommodation found his unconscious body on the floor and frantically dialled 999 to summon help. A few years later, I got to know a guy who drove an ambulance for a living. When I told him the story of Mr. S's unsuccessful suicide bid, the man simply gave a disinterested shrug. 'The first time me and my mates are despatched to deal with someone who's tried to top themselves, we'll put the pedal to the metal and do everything possible to try and save them. After a few repeat calls involving the same person at the same address, we stick well within the speed limit and don't even bother to put the siren on.'

This isn't to say the victims of OC's callousness were limited to those on the debtors' side of the interview/cashier's desk. The aforementioned Jeff Kirkham was a case in point. Here was someone who should never have been put into a situation where he was required to deal with people who were every bit as fragile as he was.

After spunking my entire month's Luncheon Vouchers at the local sandwich shop one weekday, I returned to the office to while away a pleasant hour immersed in that week's *NME*. Instead, I found Jeff alone at his desk, face down on the typewriter and wracked with sobs.

As anyone with half a heart would have done, I asked him if there was anything I could do to help. Between the tears, he told me that he hated and simply couldn't handle the kind of tasks he was expected to perform any more. It turned out that the only reason he'd come back to a job that had obviously played a major role in his breakdown was that his sick pay had run out.

Jeff's lack of suitability when it came to talking to people who were almost literally drowning in debt became most horribly apparent the day I interviewed a very upset pensioner called 'Mrs. Boswell'. The old dear confided that she and her equally elderly invalided husband had committed the cardinal crime of falling a couple of hundred quid behind in their rates.

In its infinite wisdom, CDC had sent the Boswells a document known as a distraint warrant that authorized OC's bailiffs to call on the couple and collect the money they owed. Despite my best attempts to reassure her that arrangements could be made to clear or maybe even write off their debt, poor Mrs. B was in floods of tears. Unable to accept the word of an office junior that she and her other half would be spared the modern-day equivalent of Newgate Prison, she sobbingly begged to talk to someone more experienced.

At my wit's end, I told the unfortunate woman to hang on and sprinted upstairs to the office in search of help. While undoubtedly a decent bloke, Jeff was the last person one would wish to turn to when dealing with someone so clearly distressed. Unfortunately, JK's was the only game in town in the centre of Coventry that particular afternoon. After giving him a quick overview of the old lady's circumstances and case, he and I hurried back downstairs to the interview desk.

Seeing someone older and presumably more senior, Mrs. B let out an almost audible sigh of relief. Listening surprisingly patiently to an almost verbatim repeat of what I'd just told him, Jeff imperiously raised a hand as if urging the old dear to 'Listen. To. The. Voice. Of. Calm. And. Reason.'

'This is just a distraint warrant, Mrs. Boswell. There's really no need to worry about yourself and your husband being arrested or thrown out of your home and onto the street!' Jeff began brightly. 'No, what this document actually means is simply that officers of the court in the form of bailiffs from this office are legally empowered to knock on your front door and request admittance.

'Once you and your husband have allowed

them to enter, they can retrieve from your dwelling goods and chattels to the value of the £217 you owe.' Whilst impressive, JK's seamless segue into legalese succeeded only in unleashing yet another torrent of tears from our by now very traumatized old lady.

***

Buried far back in the stationery cupboard, common decency was a value not especially highly prized in the OC of the mid 1970s. Whatever empathy for others I myself may have possessed, I wasn't prepared to surrender for a career in local government. My unwillingness to do so almost certainly contributed to my being summoned upstairs to CDC's grimly impersonal personnel office in the spring of 1975. The other reason for my being carpeted? To answer LePompous' – fully justified – gripes about my 'attitude' and seeming 'total lack of ambition'.

Not yet having had all of the humanity (TLP), compassion (the ex-cops/bailiffs), and consideration (JK) sucked out of me, I was caught bang to rights. Just months away from starting Hull University's American Studies course, I had zilch desire to let OC slowly corrupt whatever finer qualities I hadn't already despoiled by myself. That said, I will happily plead *mea culpa* to the Tomster's charge that my sense of get-up-and-go had rarely ever (let's be balls-to-the-wall honest here, never,

ever) left neutral. Knowing that I would be taking the train to pastures new come summer's end, the prospect of a future spent rotting away in CDC was one best dumped in life's dustbin.

Of course, come the day I was ushered in front of the three-man personnel panel, I kept my true intentions deep below the surface. At the end of the day, jobs – even shitty, intellectually stifling ones like my stint at CDC – were very hard to come by back then. If you were honest (i.e. dense) enough to even hint you were off the moment something better came along, a future on the wrong side of OC's interview desk became a very real possibility.

Putting on my best confused-adolescent act, I told the panel of would-be Torquemadas that I needed more time before I could make any kind of definitive decision about my future. When the inquisitor in chief began lowering his standard-is-sue half-moon glasses to better look down his nose at me, I feared the jig was up. Happily, one stern ticking-off about 'bucking up my ideas' later, I was free to go. Pulling up my metaphorical socks, I scuttled back to OC. Once back behind my desk, I kept my head down and my tail bushy and saw out the remainder of my sentence like any good con.

Chapter Two

Look, no tie. I'm creative

Like un-cringeworthy clothes, halfway-decent jobs were in absurdly short supply in the Britain of aircraft carrier-wide kipper ties and 747-high platform shoes. And few job hunts were harder than the one facing would-be wordsmiths like myself after I left uni in the summer of 1978. Having earlier thrown my arms up in the air in surrender and given up on the journalistic front (more of which later), I'd set my sights on a career as an advertising copywriter.

I was in for a long, hard slog.

And please don't think that I'm complaining. If advertising was a horribly hard field to enter 40 years ago, one dreads to think of the hassles facing anyone starting out in today's era of odious unpaid internships. Saddled with insanely large debts and chucked without a lifebelt into an uncaring sea of employers offering zero-hour contracts, jobseekers and graduates today have it about a zillion times worse.

The first Monday after the end of Hull University 's 1978 summer term, three friends and I took the bus to the city's main Department of Health and Social Security (DHSS)* office and signed on. Determined to transition seamlessly from a cushy existence in academia to the relentless dreariness of subsistence on the dole, we waited until the afternoon to do so.

'Welcome to the great ranks of the unemployed,' said the smiling – doubtless former Hull Uni undergraduate – government stooge behind the counter.

***

Despite the business having provided me with a good living for most of my life, advertising was not my first choice of career – journalism was.

While still at school, I'd developed a lifelong love of words and language. Regrettably, my initial post-A-Level attempts to gain a job as a journalist with the local rag, the *Coventry Evening Telegraph*, (CET) fell on stony ground.

Although the *CET* logo-embossed letter that arrived a few days after my unsolicited application for an entry-level reporter's job seemed ripe with promise, the reply I received from editor, 'Martin Munton' was negativity writ large.

Essentially an unnecessarily brusque brush off, Mr. M's reply was full of irrelevant pontifications

---

* Rebranded as the Department of Works and Pensions in 2001 in another futile example of the UK government's regular rearranging of the deck chairs on the Titanic.

about the sacredness of accuracy and integrity. Quite what his words had to do with my no-frills enquiry remains a mystery to this day. Whatever impact he may have intended, our Mart's hectoring wasn't going to inspire a previously enthusiastic school leaver to join him on the barricades in the battle for truth and impartiality.

Shortly thereafter, Munton's own rather slapdash attitude to the holy grail of factuality became glaringly apparent in his regular weekly record review of the 'platters that matter!' This particular week, my ex-potential employer wrote a glowing hosanna to 1970s band Slade's cover of former Loving Spoonful singer John Sebastian's *Darling Be Home Soon.* Ironically, Mr. Accuracy and Integrity had incorrectly identified the song as having been written by Johann Sebastian Bach.

My crusading prose bound for the bottom of editors' bins rather than readers' birdcages, I promptly junked my journalistic pretensions and began thinking about breaking into advertising. Damned by Orwell as the 'rattling of a stick in a swill bucket' and hailed by Rosser Reeves 'as the art of moving an idea from one man's head into another', the ad biz certainly sounded intriguing. Let's be honest here, spending one's days hitting a galvanized metal container with a piece of wood also sounds like a lot more fun than actually working for a living. Jesus, the guys who dreamt up the 'musical' *Stomp* have been clanging bin lids together since 1991 had even received an Olivier Award for their efforts.

With iconic campaigns such as the Cadbury's Smash aliens appearing during almost every TV ad break, the mid 1970s were something of a Golden Age for British advertising. And the more I learned about the business, the more I wanted to be one of the men and women who wrote and art-directed the ads.

With my American Studies degree at Hull set to occupy most of the next three years, my copywriting ambitions had been put on the back burner until the spring of 1978. As a result, it wasn't until the grim prospect of the end of my course loomed into sight that I began making serious efforts to try and break into the ad biz.

The annual university 'milk round' of potential graduate employers usually made in students' final years seemed like an obvious place to start. Frustratingly, the four or five top ad agencies involved in this exercise had already snapped up their annual allotment of fresh blood from the likes of Oxford and Cambridge long before visiting Hull.

There was nothing for it but to put pen to paper and watch the copying and postage costs set up base camp for what was sure to be a ruinously expensive climb. Having endured the misery of being on DHSS handouts for six months or so, I fully sympathise with many of those whom papers like the *Daily Fail* routinely lambast as the scum of the earth.

One of the main aims of social security has always been to support claimants while they search for work. As I had my heart set on a career in advertising and agencies did not refund expenses, every trip down to London for interviews had to paid for out of my own pocket. With the Humber Bridge not set to open until June 1981, return journeys usually required a minimum of two full days to complete.

Despite my best attempts to request a one- or two-day deferment of my signing on date each time I had to travel out of town, the callous bastards at the DHSS kept terminating my benefit payments. Each time they did so, I was forced to repeat the whole degrading rigmarole of having to make a new appointment and sign on again.

Of even less help than the DHSS was a former housemate called 'Tim', who once stole and cashed my weekly giro while I was attending an interview in Manchester. With no refunded expenses to fall back on, this was a massive kick in the teeth when I needed it least. Thank God the current-day concept of Universal Credit and its resultant weeks-long waiting period was still a wishful twinkle in some minor functionary's eye or I'd have been in real trouble.

Determined to follow a career path I was passionately interested in, I was forced to run up a huge debt at the Bank of Mum and Dad. Having made up my grant with money they could ill afford to sacrifice, my folks unselfishly came through for me time and time again.

Quaint as it may seem today, in the 1970s, the odd potential employer *would* remember how tough starting out had been and send you back a letter of encouragement. Despite their not always being able to offer interviews or jobs, the fact that such contacts took the time to offer a few supportive words was always heartening. When I was in a position to repay the favour, I later always did my best to take time to encourage anyone who contacted me for advice about a career in advertising.

***

Refunded interview expenses from better-heeled potential employers proved to be an excellent source of top-ups for my anaemic-looking bank balance. Although companies nowadays would probably have HR/personnel managers who covered candidates' interview exes sectioned under the Mental Health Act, some employers back then did do their best for potential hires. For a few post-uni months, swapping notes with friends as to which companies splashed the cash to applicants proved a very effective way of staying afloat financially.

Cover letter and c.v. dashed off and interview (hopefully) granted, it was always worth trying to shoehorn interviews with expenses-paying companies and non-expenses-paying ad agencies into one trip. Any corporate hand-outs were a real lifeline when you consider the derisory amount the DHSS of the late 1970s used to pay out in basic benefits. After rent, I was left with roughly £10 to last me the full week between signing on sessions.

While I had (and still have) sod all interest in – or aptitude for – computer programming, software developers were invariably the most willing and unquestioning refunders. Best of all, this being a field that was as wet behind the ears as I was myself, there seemed to be an awful lot of them competing for talent. This was, of course, manna from heaven for a newly impoverished ex-student like myself.

One of my abiding memories of this time is an interview I was given in Brighton by American Express. Never having visited the city and with friends at the local uni, I was only too happy to attend. I promptly headed for the M62 and hitched my way down to the South Coast.

Programming aptitude tests in those days were a Gordian knot of 'If you've answered 'yes' to more than seven questions in section one, skip sections two and three and move directly to the questions in section four subsection C (iii).' After almost certainly making a complete pig's ear of Amex' test, I was astonished to find myself selected for a roundtable interview.

Before proceedings began, the interviewer asked everyone how much they needed to reclaim for fares and overnight accommodation. Of course, having hitched down from Hull and been staying with mates, my reclaimables for the trip were next to nothing. Not that a little matter like that was going to stand in the way of my putting in for the full rail fare and a night in a local B&B.

After rather sheepishly mentioning a combined sum of almost £50, I listened in mounting horror as two or three of my co-interviewees itemised significantly lower claims. Eventually, the interviewer reached the inquisitive-looking girl sitting opposite me. 'And how about you, Sally? Where have you come from today?'

'Ah'm from 'Ull as well,' said Sally in an accent so abrasive it could have shaped the pillars supporting the still under-construction Humber Bridge. Not skipping a beat – and doubtless knowing exactly what kind of con I was trying to pull – the interviewer kindly turned to me and said, 'And what were the expenses from Hull again, John?' While I didn't get the job, a few weeks later I did get a nice fat cheque for £48.76 that helped to temporarily quieten the wolf's relentless hammering at my front door.

Said wolf's inevitable arrival was further postponed by what I assumed was a constant, almost Warren Buffett-like rebalancing of my personal finances – to wit, one current bank account. While uni had taught me the valuable lesson that I was not nearly as clever as I thought myself to be, my bank manager, Mr. Heathcoate, was now about to impart another: Namely, that, all other evidence to the contrary, honesty sometimes really is the best policy. His understanding is the sole reason I still maintain my UK bank account in Hull to this day despite only having visited the place twice in the last 40-odd years.

Before being summoned to Mr. Heathcoate's office for that most worrisome of all topics – 'a little chat about your finances' – I had been depositing expenses from interviews to defray regular withdrawals. Despite my semi-permanent residence in an area that undeservedly neglected crime novelist Derek Raymond once called 'the crust of my uppers', I was trying to enjoy life's little pleasures as often as I could. As a result, I had precious little understanding of the term 'fiscal responsibility'. Four-and-a-bit decades later, I still don't.

Bank managers back then were still very much approachable, customer-focused figures rather than the let's-gouge-the-punters-for-all-we-can-get 'See-you-next-Tuesdays' they've now become.

Having dealt with several generations of spend-thrift former students like myself, Mr. Heathcote had seen every possible variation of my ham-hand-ed financial machinations a thousand and one times. 'John, there's only one person you're fooling with these transparently pathetic attempts to make your bank balance look more like a bijou residence than the rundown ruin it actually is, and that's you yourself. If you carry on down this road, you are going to find yourself in very serious straits indeed.'

After listening patiently to my explanations about how hard it was to break into advertising, Mr. H could not have been more understanding. Nor could he have been more generous in upping my overdraft. Happily, when combined with loans from my endlessly supportive folks, the £1,000 upper limit he gave me proved just enough for me to get a foot in the door at my first ad agency. Had he not been shrewd enough to back his faith in me, I certainly wouldn't be sitting here writing this today. It's always the bloody bankers, isn't it?

Multiple trips to see agencies in London and failed copy tests later, I eventually got a break with what was then the UK's largest and most success-ful recruitment advertising agency, 'Adam Bishop' (AB).

***

After three years spent cossetted on a student

grant heavily subsidized by my unbelievably patient parents, the £4,000 p.a. AB Manchester was offering seemed like a king's ransom. Cocooned from reality for way too long, I soon learned that my imagined riches would barely sustain a perpetually broke minor aristo from some barely remembered European dukedom.

If anyone ever tried to tell me just how steeply the cost of everything started to rise once the doors to well-feathered academia slammed shut, I wasn't listening. In no time at all, I found myself dodging the uncaring better-off pedestrians hurrying past me as I ran pell-mell for the corner of Reality Street that overlooked Shit Creek.

With music about to pour out of the city with the same relentlessness that rain fell from its skies, Manchester was fast becoming *the* place to be in the UK. Not that I noticed. On the Sunday night I arrived, I was too busy trying to find somewhere to stay.

Lacking contact details for the two people in the city I knew, I ended up booking myself into an overpriced B&B. The following morning, I learned the local bus drivers had gone on strike and I would have to walk two-plus miles to work through streets I was totally unfamiliar with.

Manchester being Manchester, it wasn't long before the skies opened and began voiding their bladders on those below. It's perhaps a cliché to point out that various parts of the world have their own unique rain fingerprint. In Bangkok, for example, it seems to start solidly bucketing down for one hour at precisely 4:00 pm each afternoon. Manchester's morale-sapping contribution to the global precipitation palette was and remains its constant mizzle.

As anyone who's ever had to walk more than a few yards in this dispiriting blend of mist and drizzle will know, the misery such downpours bring never quite goes away. Continually lashing your face, its chill, unforgiving winds carry a payload of tiny beads of moisture that squeeze through chinks in your clothes and soak into your skin. Like a dog with a bone, the torment refuses to let up until you're at risk of succumbing to terminal-stage hypothermia.

Three-quarters-drowned from my walk, I finally squelched my way into AB's office at around 10:00 am. While unfortunate and easy to explain, my tardiness proved to be the opening salvo in a two-and-a-half-year-long list of late arrivals which were anything but. For the first and only time at AB, my boss – a gruff Wolves fan with a broad Black Country accent called 'Jim Brakewell' – gave me a free pass for my lack of punctuality.

As copywriter, I was responsible for writing and then proofreading recruitment ads. Once gambolling their way across page after page of your daily paper's 'Sits Vac' section, such communications are now reduced to jostling for attention inside your 'preferred' executive search website.

Unlike more conventional forms of advertising, where creating the maximum amount of attention and action is a must, recruitment ads can be said to succeed even if only one person replies. All that really matters is that your one respondent is the perfect fit for the job being advertised.

For those of you who've never had the dubious joy of having to write a recruitment ad, there follows a beginner's guide as to how you might go about doing so.

Let's begin by waving goodbye to the 99.9% of readers/job seekers we're not interested in by including a job title (let's say, Widget Designer). Once you've got shot of *hoi polloi*, you might like to think about ladling a generous dollop of bullshit for spreading across five paras:

We are...

We want...

You will be expected to...

We will offer you...

Why Chipping Sodbury (or wherever) is a great place to live...

Let's take those paras one by one...

First up, 'We are...' All about the company

seeking staff, this para lays out a potential employer's stall.

'We are Fuckwit Universal (FU), a local/UK/European/world/galactic (delete whichever options not applicable) leader in the fascinating/demanding/highly competitive field of widgets (whatever).'

If the client has been around for a few years, you could put some lead into this sentence's pencil with words such as – 'Established in 19XX, Fuckwit is...' or 'Fuckwit has been a regional/UK/European/world/interplanetary leader in widgets since 19XX.'

By this stage, all professionally frustrated, disillusioned, or out-of-work widget designers or the terminally thick will have started planning their futures via the horoscope or TV listings pages.

Let's suppose you're an unfulfilled or unemployed widget designer whose underappreciated or undiscovered genius the hiring company so covets. As one of only a handful of readers still sticking around, you've effectively indicated your willingness to listen to FU's entreaties.

'In 'We want...' the recruiter paying for the ad will meticulously detail the sort of candidate they're looking for and why. In this para, copywriters are expected to jizz up (and should you be wondering, I do mean jizz and not jazz) the client's rather mundane vacancy as some kind of career holy grail.

A typical second para, then, might say something along the lines of: 'Recent restructuring' (i.e. most of the existing department has either left *en masse* or been made redundant/fired); or 'aggressive expansion' (well, they are hiring new staff) 'has created an outstanding opportunity'. Opportunities, like erections, are always 'outstanding' or 'challenging' – unless, of course, they're 'welcome' as is more often the case with me.

There will then follow a brief run-through of the 'stimulating' (i.e. mundane) tasks 'highly motivated self-starters' (who knows, maybe even a total numpty like you) will be expected to perform for their daily crust.

Our 'You will be expected to...' para is, of course, where it starts to get tricky. Far too up themselves to jot down four or five key bullet points, hiring companies will frequently brief in job descriptions several pages long. Although a total novice totally untutored in the vagaries of widget design, you'll then have to cherry-pick and write up candidates' 'must haves'.

Clients being clients, and therefore obtuse, they'll often scatter these essentials indiscriminately throughout their mammoth briefs. Here, again, copywriters and ad respondents are faced with potential pratfalls at every twist and turn. Be too anally retentive about the exact qualifications/number of years' experience a potential hire should possess and you're likely to scare off otherwise excellent candidates. Far better to skirt around the issue using wishy-washy qualifiers like 'around', 'some', or 'approximately'.

While it really ought to be something of a casual canter to the finish line, each ad's 'We will offer you…' para may also be filled with anti-candidate landmines at every step. This is because most employers are scared shitless of publicizing details of the salaries and benefits they offer. Instead, the copywriter must tiptoe around anodyne terms such as 'highly competitive' or 'commensurate with the appointee's age and experience'. The only other thing to remember here is that those sitting behind desks and wearing ties receive 'remuneration packages', while those risking hernias by doing the heavy lifting get paid a weekly wage.

Benefits para above looking a bit insubstantial? Not to worry. Should FU's hiring office/branch be located inside a medium- to large-sized town or city, we can just pad out our 'Why Runcorn (or wherever) is a great place to live…' para. The easiest way to do this is by bunging in a bunch of impossible to disprove waffle about how the 'successful candidate' will find himself/herself in the 'beating heart' of a 'bustling urban hub'. As we're talking about a place with presumably more than one pub, club or restaurant, the local nightlife could also quite accurately be described as being 'catnip for fun lovers from surrounding areas'.

But what if Fuckwit's office is located in a sewer like, say, Barrow-in-Furness or Workington? (Apologies if you've had the misfortune to hail from or still live in either place. As I grew up in Coventry, please rest assured that I share at least some of your pain). You can simply blether on about the 'breathtakingly green panoramic vistas' awaiting hires in the surrounding countryside when they need to escape the godawful hellhole to which their piss-poor career choices have condemned them.

Let's call a spade a spade here, those 'endless sun-dappled woodland glades' are just the job when it comes to finding a tree from which to loop a washing line and start forming a hangman's noose. That 'treasure trove of tranquil leafy lanes' is equally ideal should one prefer to succumb to a carbon-monoxide-fuelled Big Sleep by duct-taping a hose from the family car's exhaust pipe to its interior.

Large amounts of AB's billings (i.e. income) came from what were then – and following numerous expensive structurings, re-structurings and re-re-re-restructurings are now, doubtless, once again – health districts and authorities. Each new bureaucratic shake-up was a godsend for the agency whose designers would be tasked with churning out new logos/corporate identities with monotonous regularity. Whilst soul-sappingly time-consuming, the entire design process – billable as one might expect – was, however, a much-needed fillip for AB's bottom line.

With one or two exceptions, recruitment ads for nursing staff tended to follow the hypothetical five-para structure outlined above. As they have since time immemorial, nurses got the shittiest end of the stick when it came to being 'rewarded' for their efforts. For this reason, ads – particularly those aimed at nurses thanklessly labouring away in geriatric or terminal care wards – tended to be liberally larded with weasel words* such as 'incredibly satisfying' or 'uniquely fulfilling'.

First came the daunting task of tarting up the description of the hospital where anyone gullible enough to fall for our glittering prose would find themselves spending their next several years.

Those 'joining the family' at a 'historic hospital' faced becalming their career in an ancient hulk whose hopelessly outdated infrastructure and medical facilities even Florence Nightingale might have baulked at.

Dating back to the earliest days of Aneurin Bevan's then cutting-edge vision for the NHS, 'modern' hospitals were also little changed from

---

* Please refer to Appendix Three at the rear of the paperback version of this book for other useful 'Weasel Words' and examples of when and when not to use them.

the day they'd first welcomed the halt and lame.

'Purpose-built' or 'ultra-modern' care facilities sounded far more promising. Inevitably, they too were something of a pup to be sold to anyone trusting enough to believe every word of the Booker Prize-worthy ads that filled *Nursing Today*'s 'Help Wanted' section. 'Purpose-built' simply meant the hospital had been constructed expressly for medical use rather than knocked together from an earlier incarnation as, say, an abandoned Carphone Warehouse outlet. While usually less than 25 years old, 'ultra-modern' infirmaries' facilities were still likely to be far older and more infirm than those filling and emptying the pans beneath their wards' beds.

Do the tricks of the recruitment trade outlined above make me feel just the teensiest bit guilty? Not really. Like barristers in court (or indeed baristas down at your local coffee shop), copywriters must make the best possible use of what they are given and how they advocate it.

At the end of the day, an ad – no matter how well written or beautifully presented – is only as good as whatever it is it is selling. And as any marketing pro knows, nothing will kill a shithouse product or service faster than shit-hot advertising.

Once in a blue moon, us cannon fodder in AB's creative department would be tossed a juicier bone on which to snack. Early examples included major – well, major for the client concerned – non-recruitment image campaigns for South Yorkshire County Council. So delighted were the good burghers below the Humber estuary with my concept about the cost-effectiveness with which they pulled rabbits out of their magician's top hats, they quickly awarded us another campaign.

This time around, I found myself conceptualising a recruitment drive for the South Yorkshire Police, a career 'highlight' I'd not thought much about for nigh-on 40 years before starting this book. Looking back now, I hope and pray that no one involved in the cynical cover up of the 1989 Hillsborough disaster in which 96 people died became a copper after reading one of my ads.

The only memory of that campaign that has stayed with me is the agency's being given a police helmet from which to draw and photograph each ad's artwork. Said headgear subsequently went on to enjoy a long and happy life in the rear-window alcove of Jim Brakewell's Audi. It was, he hoped, an excellent deterrent to his potentially being pulled over and breathalysed should he ever indulge in a few quick post-work pints before driving home.

One of AB's most notable successes during the two-and-a-bit years I was with them came with our campaign for Preston Health District. While doubtless a lovely place to call home, Preston is probably better known for the M55 motorway out of it than as a honeytrap for diehard shoppers, winers/diners, and party animals.

Fuelled by a minuscule budget, our campaign was based on the frankly risible claim that this far-from-stellar locale's abundance of beautiful surrounding countryside somehow made it 'the high-flying nurse's choice'.

To ensure readers harboured no doubts about the heady heights involved, each ad featured a photograph of a group of nurses happily waving from a crudely drawn hot-air balloon. The all-round cheapness of the campaign can best be gauged by the fact that our balloon, nurses, and spectacular surrounding scenery had all been clumsily stripped together in AB's in-house studio. Please feel free to insert your own 'hot air' joke here before moving on to the next para.

Whenever a client greets an idea as if divine hands have passed it down to them on stone tablets carved atop Mount Sinai, you can be sure a 'but' won't be far behind. While 'delighted' by how our work might snare anyone gormless enough to want to 'build their future' in Preston, this client wanted several extra layers of gilt on his lily. Tasked with injecting our ads with a 'dash of glamour', off we went in search of the requisite pinch of pizzazz, snazz, and razamataz.

Despite my having never been trusted to actually meet the man signing the cheques, I was the mug given the responsibility of adding a bit of 'oomph' to his half-arsed campaign. Luckily, someone further up the corporate ladder who had attended the meetings told me that the client in question was something of a die-hard petrolhead.

As inspiration can strike at the most inconvenient times and in the rummest of places, the best advertising creatives are those who are totally incapable of ever fully turning off. Terry Lovelock's dashing off of the eight words that became the legendary 'Heineken Refreshes the Parts Other Beers Cannot Reach' campaign on a beermat in a Marrakesh bar is one such lightbulb moment.

Although I've never been talented enough to create anything nearly that brilliant, inspiration kindly struck me when a bus I was taking home around this time stopped at a red light. Right outside my window was a billboard on which recently retired ex-F1 champion James Hunt was shilling Castrol Motor Oil with Michael ('Ooooh, Betty!') Crawford of dubious *Some Mothers Do 'Ave 'Em* fame. Why, said I the next morning, don't we call the agency behind the posters and ask them how to get in touch with the UK's former Fangio?

AB's account director, a one-time civil servant called 'Charles', pronounced this idea to be 'capital'. As fond of acronyms as he was the sound of his own voice, Charlie-boy ordered me to track down the agency who handled the multi-million-pound

Castrol account a.s.a.p., or better still, p.d.q. The agency in question was, I knew from fruitless trawls of the vacancies pages at the back of advertising trade paper *Campaign*, called Collett Dickenson Pearce (CDP).

Before I got halfway down the corridor to get on the blower to what was probably then the biggest and best regarded ad agency in Britain, Chazza called me back. 'Whatever else you do, don't let them know what account we want James Hunt to work on.' Given CDP's reputation for turning down multi-million-pound clients, the possibility of their snatching an account whose entire budget would struggle to pay for a set lunch at Langan's seemed a tad unlikely.

***

One of the few perks myself and other younger creatives did receive while working with AB was our old friend from Coventry District Council – Luncheon Vouchers. With their then £0.30p-a-day value exhausted after three halfway decent pub snacks, they can hardly be blamed for my now Falstaffian waistline. Reduced to sarnies from the area's cheapest local sandwich shops at our desks, we juniors would all try and kill time in any way we could.

In those sepia-tinted times before colour copiers became common, Xeroxing and colouring £5 notes for dropping onto the street from our second-floor office window was a particular favourite. Our most profound hope was that our primitive forgeries would catch the eyes of especially avaricious passers-by.

Looking back, I can't help but still be amazed by just how many respectable-looking types were suckers for this absurdly childish trick. The vehemence with which they later impotently shook their frustrated fists at the four floors of blank windows from whence the dodgy fivers had issued made all the effort worthwhile.

One dreads to think of their reactions had they been soaked by the water bombs I and my classmates used to hurl out of upper-floor windows during school lunch breaks a few years earlier. The final victim of our increasingly large and elaborate water-filled ordnance was a much-derided history teacher called 'Pressure on, lads!' 'Peterson'. Having noticed how targets invariably looked up to see from whence our tiny crisp-bag-sized water bombs had originated, I and my fellow Barnes-Wallises invested in a packet of extra-large bin liners.

His trouser legs splashed by the contents of the tiny crisp packet we used as a rangefinder, poor old Mr. P couldn't help but tilt his head to the heavens. All he must have seen as he did so was a large, wobbly black orb blocking his entire field of vision. One can only imagine the look of alarm on his face as he realized our bomb was about hit him square on the bonce.

Too stunned to take any kind of evasive action, Mr. P wound up getting drenched from top to toe. My only regret is being too busy making my escape to be able to poke my head out of the fifth-form window to savour the watery carnage I and my friends had wrought. Discretion being the better part of valour, and dire messages issuing from the school's head at the following morning's pre-class assembly, Ullathorne School's 617 Squadron had flown its last mission.

***

Knowing barely a soul in Manchester, and granted only a couple of days stay in my horrendously expensive B&B by the agency's bean counters, I needed to find alternative digs fast. The one person I did know was a friend from Hull Uni called 'Janey', who was working as a researcher at the regional office of a leading TV station. It turned out that Janey had a couple of colleagues who were looking for someone to share their house.

Not for the first (or last) time in my life, I made the cardinal error of jumping feet first into the void before taking a few seconds to peer over the edge. Had I only bothered to do so, I would have soon realized just how vast a crater the rent on my new digs would end up excavating from my salary.

A couple of days in the 'real world' was all it took

to hammer home the fact that the £330 and change AB was paying me each month really wasn't going to stretch very far. To begin with, there was the £18 weekly rent on the house. After the government had helped itself to tax and national insurance, this left me with around half my salary. Then there were 'Richard' and 'Mary', the two well-heeled former Oxbridge graduates I foolishly moved in with shortly after arriving in Manchester. While Mary was OK, Dick (as Richard was by both name and nature), was a horse's arse of Grand National proportions.

Now a well-known and widely respected journalist, Biggus Dickus was an excellent example that a privileged background does not necessarily overburden its recipients with an excess of common decency. He continues to retain his now well-nigh unassailable place in the upper strata on my list of the 'Most Massive Pillocks I Have Ever Met'. And believe me, in a lifetime of working in the advertising and media industries, my available pillock pool is many miles wide and fathoms deep.

Although they welcomed the way my rent helped reduce their own outgoings, my housemates were less accommodating when it came to introducing me to their fellow media tyros. I quickly came to despise the imagined prestige that TV types arrogantly believe distinguishes them from their print media counterparts.

Years later, I couldn't help but howl with laughter when seeing Chris Morris's *Nathan Barley* skewer the pretentious, solipsistic on-air chattering classes of which Dick was an early prototype. Given his all-round knobbishness, my erstwhile housemate would probably have believed the jokes in the show to be aimed at anyone except himself.

More a case of Stuck-at-home than Stockholm syndrome, my casting as Cinderella worked in my favour due to the dizzying speed with which non-negotiable essentials were draining my salary. With so little left over for socializing, how did I go about making friends? Simple, I shamefacedly went back to the Bank of Mum and Dad, who must have rolled their eyes to the heavens in despair as they graciously bailed me out once more.

Having no ties to bind us beyond the weekly rental, my communications with the two future media magnates quickly became little more than the tersest of terse morning and evening nods.

Probably the most irritating of the Dickster's *smorgasbord* of annoying habits was the teeth-grindingly matey way he would call the few friends I ever bought round to the house 'man'. On the rare occasions I could afford to invest in a quarter-ounce of hash, D would inevitably hover round in the hope of my offering him the odd gratis toke. Sucking the life out of another jazz cigarette I could ill afford, he'd then enunciate with a stoned wheezing akin to that of Dennis Hopper in *Apocalypse Now*, 'Man, that's some seriously good shit!'

Predictably, our Richard's knowledge of combustibles was rather less encyclopaedic than he liked to make out. One of his more fanciful yarns involved his getting arrested for 'OD-ing on weed' and having his stomach pumped at A&E while still a cub reporter for his local paper. The only thing that gave this implausible anecdote any credibility was D's sheepish confession that his then editor had apparently called in favour after favour to keep other local rags from running the story. Now there's a cover-up he might care to lay bare in one of his best-selling books.

Aside from his tiresome habit of using outdated hippy terminology, Tricky Dicky's other most irksome foible was his claim to be an anarchist.

Had the Dickster kept his delusions of being some kind of late 1970s Peter Kropotkin to himself, I might have let things pass. I, however, was not best pleased that my ongoing penury and almost constant state of house arrest meant I was soon expected to field phone calls and pass along messages for his dodgy mates.

One morning early on in my unwanted (and unpaid) career moonlighting as his PA, D caught me at breakfast (in those days, a cup of weak coffee and two B&H). I should, he sombrely informed me, be very careful when answering the phone because our calls were almost certainly being monitored by Special Branch.

Seeing the incredulous 'WTF?' look on my face, he went on to confide that the reason the spooks were monitoring our calls was his apparently high standing in anarchist circles. With paranoia running rampant in the UK during the dying days of Jim Callaghan's then Labour Government, even I had to concede that this wasn't as far-fetched as it might now sound.

That said, having reluctantly spent way too much time listening to King Richard's pontifications, his claim might equally well have been a bunch of old bollocks. Either way, it wasn't very long before my being expected to man the phone with nary a thank you to show for my trouble caused the excrement to impact the aircon.

Matters finally reached a head one night when D was off to join various VIPs from Tellyland on a big night out. If the town wasn't going to end up red, it would at least be daubed in that fetching shade of pale pink so beloved by Champagne Socialists everywhere.

Knowing that the only spending I could afford was time spent slumped over a book or in front of the TV, the dickish one had issued an edict that I inform him of any calls. It turns out he had apparently been a key player in – I kid you not – organising some kind of anarchist conference in the city that weekend. As a result, it was essential that I take copious notes as to who had called and what they had said. Rather than tell the tinpot Trotsky where to stick his phone calls, I shrugged and went back to watching whatever shite was on TV at the time.

Jump cut a couple of hours and about three calls from Dick's colleagues on the (admittedly excellent) current affairs show on which he worked. The next time the phone rang, I decided it was high time I burst the bubble of self-aggrandisement with which this particular prick surrounded himself.

'Is Richard there?' said my fourth caller of the night in a cagey voice that screamed out, 'Be careful! The wet work team at the cop shop are probably listening in!'

'Who vonts to gnoh?' said I, adopting what I imagined to be a suitably exotic and enigmatic Eastern European accent.

'It's Frank from the Plymouth Anarchist Collective,' said the budding overthrower of the state at the other end of the line. 'I was just calling to double-check that all of the arrangements are in place for our arrival in Manchester on Friday afternoon.'

Never able to resist taking pot shots when barrels of fish are placed in front of me, I decided to have a little long-overdue fun at D's expense. 'Yes, indeed, Comred Fronnnnnk,' said I in a less-than-convincing attempt to channel Oskar

Homolka's Colonel Stok from 1960s film versions of Len Deighton's Harry Palmer trilogy.

'In addishun to cunveying you his froternal gritings, Comred Ritched vishes me to terl you zet ze steenk and smerk bumbs are in place and primed to ixplod at 3:00 pm sherp. Power to ze pipple and down wiz ze ronning dug emperialist leekspittles who empower ze Callaghan-Zatcherite hegemony. Long live ze glorious revolution and ze ind of capitalist tyranny,' I concluded with a rather louder shout than was perhaps necessary.

There followed an audible gasp and the hasty click of a telephone receiver clunking back into its cradle somewhere deep within deepest Devon.

Having broken the habit of my working life to date by arriving at the office early for once, I avoided seeing D the next morning. That evening, there was, however, no escape. Buttonholing me as I walked into the kitchen after work, mither rather than murder wreathed my anarchic, imminently ex-flatmate's face.

'John, man, I've just been on the phone to Frank! He and the rest of the Plymouth Anarchist Collective are very, very upset by what you said to them on the phone last night.' Confronted by a grandiose twerp whose air of wounded disappointment resembled that of a headmaster let down by his school rugby team's star prop forward, I burst into uncontrollable laughter. Not long afterwards, I moved to much more affordable lodgings. The only time I ever encountered D thereafter, he was the author of several extremely incisive and insightful features in one of Britain's better broadsheets.

Terrific journalist. Terrible housemate.

***

While the move to cheaper accommodations did make life a lot easier, my old financial sparring partner the wolf had wasted no time in clearing space for himself on my new doorstep. Having never previously worried my pretty little head with arcane concepts such as delayed gratification, I was, of course, easy prey for his lupine charms.

The blizzard of beer, fags, and new LPs on the days immediately following the arrival of each salary cheque into my poor, benighted bank account were blissful indeed. Stretching out ahead of me like winter in Anthony Beevor's *Stalingrad*, the three or so weeks before the next influx of funds arrived were somewhat more forbidding.

Someone – Mrs. Wallis-Simpson is one of several sources cited – once wrote, 'I've been rich, and I've been poor. Rich is better.' Whilst lacking similar snappiness, my then guiding principle was more a case of 'I've had enough money for a few beers, and I've had my arse hanging out of my jeans. Having enough money for a couple of pints is where it's at.'

Shoes, for example, were an unimagined luxury that could only be bought at Xmas or birthdays with my ever-generous mum and dad's seasonal cash presents. On more than one occasion, I was so broke that I had to trudge despondently home through Manchester's trademark rain-drenched streets. Try as I might, I'll never shake off memories of how filthy water from puddled pavements wheedled its way through my Swiss cheese soles and turned my crusty socks to mulch.

Whilst hardly any kind of compensatory 'silver lining' inside the personal cloud of misery hanging over you, it's true what they say – there really *is* always someone worse off than you. In my case, the worse-offs were the poorly paid labourers who shared the bedsits on one of the normally *tres chic* Chorlton-cum-Hardy's less green and pleasant byways.

Having always been a Labour voter, I naturally detested Maggie Thatcher and was determined to do whatever I could to try and stop her from getting voted into power in May 1979. Touting for votes as an unpaid canvasser, I was amongst a team of volunteers who had the misfortune to be buzzed inside a dilapidated-looking property on an otherwise picture-perfect street.

Equal parts bitterness, failure, and hopelessness garnished with unwashed socks and underwear, the stench inside was enough to overpower even my almost totally non-existent sense of smell. The general consensus of those inside was why bother voting as it would only result in yet another uncaring government. As we left, the team supervisor glumly announced – quite accurately as I later learned – 'You'd never believe this was the house where the Bee Gees grew up, would you?'

If I was to avoid sinking into the same sort of mire, a leg up was unlikely to be forthcoming from my employer. Like every agency I worked for ever after, AB seemed to be permanently cowering beneath some sharp-edged sword-of-Damocles-induced insolvency. Finances were apparently so precarious that the awarding of some – any – kind of raise to juniors like myself would send it careering over the edge and spiralling into the endless abyss below.

Hammering out a template that my employers all over the world subsequently followed, AB also parroted relentlessly about how it was one big happy 'family'. Members fortunate enough to reach the sun-soaked Elysian Fields on the upper levels of the corporate pyramid would, of course, never, ever lack for contentment.

Doomed to gaze heavenwards for all eternity, we poorly paid peons busily scrabbling away at the creative coalfaces far below could at least console ourselves with how well our masters had done.

One colleague who made a great show of his

own dissatisfaction with the agency was my art director, 'Ken'. Determined to try and escape the dead end that was recruitment advertising, I was phoning and firing off CVs to every agency executive creative director (ECD) in the north of England. When my blanket bombing of agencies eventually paid off with a couple of copy tests, I suggested Ken and I tackle them as a team. If our subsequent work hit a brick wall, we would at least have the bare bones of a portfolio we could then use to showcase our creative capabilities for other potential employers.

Had I suspected how quickly Ken's initially endearing attempts to make himself seem interesting by exaggerating meaningless issues would become terminally infuriating, I wouldn't have bothered. For all his undoubted talents as an art director, Ken, it soon turned out, was something of a pathological liar.

Having met several serial fantasists over the years, I've grown depressingly familiar with the compulsive behavioural patterns of *pseudologia fantastica* (a.k.a. mythomania) sufferers, as identified by the condition's discoverer, Anton Delbrueck, in 1891.

On typical Monday mornings early on during our stillborn collaboration, Ken would arrive at work swearing he'd met and set up meetings with some hugely promising contact over the weekend.

When asked to commit to a time we could start producing work to show to these 'contacts', Ken would mumble tortuous excuses as to why the meetings had been put on hold.

Not having thought about him much since I left Manchester all those years before, I decided to do what everyone else does nowadays and hit the internet. When I Googled Ken while writing this chapter, I discovered he was still working for AB's latest incarnation almost four decades after I myself had tunnelled my way to freedom under the agency wall.

Still struggling futilely to make ends meet, I ended up moving to a series of ever-cheaper and less 'des res' accommodations. Eventually, I found myself sharing a house in a rather rundown part of southern Manchester called Levenshulme. Social life in the area revolved around the Pack Horse, one of the UK's oldest pubs, if Bill the landlord was to be believed.

While Bill may have been absent from school on the day history was taught , he was the soul of discretion when it came to customers. Many of them were, I quickly learned, members of a thriving cabal of the city's busiest small-time crooks. It also turned out that Levenshulme also possessed the dubious distinction of being the heroin capital if not of Europe, then at least North West England.

Oft-times in the Pack, you were literally never

more than 15 feet away from someone who had fresh tracks on their arm, or had been newly decanted from Strangeways nick. The good news from my point of view was that most between-jobs crooks handled concert security at key music venues such as the Apollo, the local poly, and uni. In the year or so that I lived in the area, I must have got into to something like a hundred gigs by various big name artists and musical heroes for free.

In Neil Young's sleeve notes for his triple-album 1970s retrospective *Decade,* he talks about heading off to the ditch, where you get to meet an awful lot of more interesting people. My time in Levenshulme was, I guess, my personal ditch year.

The cast of characters I met while there – now, one would imagine, mostly dead – included a lovely man called Jed and his slightly unhinged wife, Marian, plus a once-talented artist I knew only as 'Dash'. After discovering smack at art college, Dash now spent more time feeding his habit by selling his dwindling stock of pre-addiction paintings than he did creating new canvases. A quick look into his drug-deadened eyes was all that was needed to convince you that not too many masterpieces lay in his future.

The old adage that misery shared is misery halved is never truer than when it comes to those caught in the awful trap of heavy drug use. And like all hardcore junkies, Dash was keen to suck you into his habit by offering you a free ride on his spike. Happily, that one look into his eyes also served as a warning you'd soon be following him into the ground should you be foolish enough to accept his offer.

When US First Lady Nancy Reagan first advised potential drug users to 'Just Say No!' in 1982, many members of my generation laughed at her for being hopelessly out of touch. The story of Jed and Marian is a salutary reminder that, like the stopped clock which is accurate twice a day, even someone as dunderheaded as Nancy might sometimes have a point.

When I first met them, J and M welcomed me into a beautifully decorated ground-floor flat in a leafy, stolidly middle-class Manchester suburb. Packed to the rafters with fascinating artefacts J had picked up on his travels with the merchant navy, every room of their home was a trip of a non-druggy kind.

As Keith Richards would undoubtedly tell you at great length, heroin in its purest, most un-adulterated form almost certainly won't kill you. Various research experiments in which drug de-pendents (let's not call them addicts) given strictly quality controlled doses of H have led productive and perfectly normal lives bear this out. What often does prove fatal is the shit – baby powder if you're lucky, scouring powder or rat poison if you're not –

with which dealers step down their supplies when striving to maximise their profits.

The trouble was that while fairly disciplined when keeping their heroin habits in check, J and M were incapable of displaying any kind of self-control when it came to amphetamine sulphate. While snorting a couple of lines of speed before heading out is a great way to enjoy a night on the town, the comedown the next morning is gut-wrenchingly bad. The secret to not getting hooked is to resist the considerable temptation to dive back in and sprinkle some sulphate on your Shredded Wheat.

In the end, a single prolonged heroin drought was all it took for J and M to move lock, stock and barrel into that netherworld the UK Sunday redtops invariably refer to as 'Drugs Hell'. Touched by the unearned kindness they had offered me, I had a lot of time for the pair. Unfortunately, it wasn't too long before the speed and the various adulterants it had been poisoned with began to kick in. Soon, every time I visited their home, I'd find another charming curio from halfway around the world had vanished to be replaced by yet another sleazy druggie from just across town.

Eventually, Jed, Marian, and their newfound 'friends'' drug-fuelled paranoia meant even the simple act of casually dropping in for a chat had mutated into something far darker and less pleasant. After I moved to nearby Didsbury in late

1980, I learned that J and M had relocated to Moss Side – the fire to Levenshulme's frying pan when it came to drugs and crime.

By the time I got the call to go to Saudi six months later, I'd lost all touch with them. For all my failings as a person, I've always done my best to be a loyal friend so my inability to catch up with J and M wasn't for lack of trying on my part. Despite travelling up to Manchester whenever I returned to the UK during my first couple of years away, everyone seemed clueless about their whereabouts.

I was to never see or hear from either of them again.

Like most people who become expats, I quickly realized that the more places I got the chance to visit, the more places I wanted to see. After a couple of years, my trips back to the UK became shorter and shorter, and the gaps between them grew longer and longer.

Before I knew it, my opportunities – and inclination – to chase up old friends started vanishing faster than the gewgaws that used to disappear out of Jed's front door. In no time at all, mates who were once bosom buddies had dwindled into ever-tinier specks in life's rear-view mirror. While they were far from the only people l lost touch with when Manchester dropped off my list of must-visits, I'd have loved my final image of J and M to be a healthy and happy one.

For chronic drug abusers, 'healthy' usually means being dosed up to the eyeballs with a fresh armful of skag or speed. To paraphrase Jane Austen, there is one universal truth about those who can never shake off their addictions. They are always, but always, going to give up the gear tomorrow. Just one last armful to get them focused, and they'll be good to re-enter and start conquering the straight nine-to-five world first thing in the morning.

The big problem here is that since many heavy users wind up taking a kick-ass goodbye shot their weakened systems can't handle, tomorrow is a destination they are doomed never to reach.

The other desperately sad truth about drug dependents is that long-term friendships matter far less than finding cash to pay for their next short-term fix. Been stupid enough to invite a strung-out friend into your home? Better count your Ry Cooder albums before they come and after they've left! Worst of all, when not promising to detox or blatantly attempting to swipe your stuff, they're hell-bent on recruiting you into the same endlessly miserable cycle they themselves inhabit.

Drugs, well some of them, were – and I would imagine still are – great fun, but only if you can control what you take and where (and with whom) you take them. Luckily, I was fortunate enough to have been gifted with sufficient common sense and strength to know when to stop. Not that I didn't make a few Grand Guignol-style fuck ups before I did call it quits after my regular lost weekends. If only poor Jed and Marian had also been able to 'Just Say No!' every once in a while.

***

As trite as it sounds – and let's not forget that the reason clichés are clichés is that they usually contain some truth – there really *are* moments when one's life reaches a defining crossroads.

Mine – and that of my then flatmate, 'Jack' – came in the winter of 1980 in the darkened surroundings of Manchester's legendary Factory Club in Moss Side. Unrepentant dope smokers, the pair of us had gone to see some then hot band whose drum kit logo time's mists have now fully shrouded.

To maintain our collective high and fortify ourselves for the entertainments ahead, Jack had insisted on rolling and bringing along a couple of spliffs. Just before the main act took to the stage, he produced one from his pocket and proceeded to light up. After taking a couple of tokes, he passed the joint to me, and I then took a sociable drag or two before returning it.

Just as Jack was about to take another lungful of hash, he was tapped on the shoulder by someone immediately behind him in the crowd. The tapper was the obvious leader of a scary-looking gang of skinhead types who wanted a bit of Bob Hope for themselves. Just as I – and pretty much everyone I then knew – would have done in similar circumstances, Jack handed the joint back to the skin. Before he knew what had happened, Jack found himself face down on the club's beer-infused carpet of discarded cigarette-butts. My poor friend's laboured attempts at drawing breath were not helped by the painful presence of the man's knee in the small of his back.

While not a great way to start a night out, things seemed to be pretty salvageable. 'Just give the guy whatever stuff we've got left and him and his mates'll fuck off and leave us alone,' said I. Horrifyingly, all the well-intentioned words in the world were never going to be sufficient to save poor Jack from the Job-like misfortunes he was about to suffer.

'You're nicked, mate,' said the skinhead-in-chief. If all this wasn't bad enough, the man barely paused for breath before telling Jack that he wasn't just having his collar felt for 'possession'. No, this was Manchester in the early 1980s, and policing was overseen by zero-tolerance Chief Constable James Anderton (a.k.a. 'God's Copper').

As Jack had handed drugs over to an officer of the law, he was being busted on the far more serious charge of 'possession with intent to supply'. Moments later, Jack was being roughly frogmarched out the door, and I was being physically restrained from trying to accompany him to the cop shop by our tormentor's various sidekicks. Small wonder why I and so many other people of my age and background hold the British police in such contempt.

Eventually, I managed to find out the station to which Jack had been taken and was able to get down and offer him what little help I could. Unfortunately, the duty solicitor appointed to work on Jack's case was no Perry Mason when it came to fighting his corner.

Had Jack been caught and charged in a better-off suburb where fewer black people lived, his 'crime' would almost certainly have been punished with a slap on the wrist such as a small fine. Instead, the poor guy found himself bailed out and given a trial date several months hence.

Long before he got his day in court, Jack was fired from his job and was ordered to return home to the bosom of his fairly well-heeled family or face being forever ostracised. Today, the plod would have simply relieved Jack of his stash, given him a metaphorical clip around the ear, and told him to piss off home.

When he finally appeared before the magistrate several months later, Jack was lucky to 'get off' with a sizeable fine rather than the custodial sentence the arresting officers were pushing for. Had he been black, he almost certainly would have been hit with a lengthy spell inside for breaking a stupid and unfairly administered law.

A couple of years later, towards the end of my time in Saudi, I managed to track down and meet up with Jack in London. Luckily, his run-in with Anderton's goons didn't seem to have done him any lasting harm, and he'd wrenched his career back on track. Finally back in solvency's black after repaying my folks the thousands of pounds I owed them, I'd not done too badly myself.

As I headed back to where I was staying, I couldn't help but wonder how differently things might have panned out if it had been me and not Jack who'd been pulled in.

To begin with, I'd never have stood an earthly chance of getting a work permit to go to Saudi. I'd then never have got to pay off my debts, escape the awfulness of a druggy future in Levenshulme, or got given and seize my chance to see the world.

But then, looking on the bright side, you'd never have had to pay to pick up and then waste hours reading these memoirs either.

Chapter Three

Just arrived! The great Saudi Arabian Advertising boom!

'One of the most extraordinary facts about Saudi Arabia is that it only abolished slavery in 1962,' said the head-hunter. 'Of course, they quickly got around the problem of how they were going to cope without unpaid labour by introducing the two-year contract; a copy of which you are about to sign.'

And, deeper in debt to the Bank of Mum and Dad than I could ever begin to comprehend, sign the contract for a Saudi Riyals (SR) 7,500 a month (about UK1,000-tax free*) copywriting job with 'Crown Advertising', I duly did. Kudos to Jim Brakewell at Adam Bishop for telling me to clear my desk and quit the office the day I handed in my notice. Rather than the unthinking brush-off I first thought, AB's payment of my full months' notice proved far more decent than the treatment I received from far bigger multinational agencies later on in my career.

There were two main reasons why 'experts' (I know, I know, I had problems believing that one

---

* To avoid repetition and mistakes caused by my appalling maths, an exchange rate of Saudi Riyal 7.5 = £1 has been used throughout chapters three and four.

myself) like me were being hired as 'boots on the ground' in the Saudi of the early 1980s. The first was the obscene sea of petrodollars sloshing around in the royal family's coffers. The second was to try and eradicate culturally insensitive translations of ads intended for overseas markets that were of little or no consequence for the head offices of agencies or clients. With places like Saudi Arabia marooned at the bottom of everyone's to-do list, the quality of work foisted on what advertising folk now call emerging (i.e. cash cow) economies frequently beggared belief.

In Saudi Arabia's case, this was largely due to there being no TV ads or other high-profile media channels where art directors and writers like me could showcase our creative chops. With bugger all else to do come sundown, almost every male in the kingdom in possession of a pulse fired up his big gas-guzzling American car and began cruising the streets. A friend neatly summed their behaviour up as 'going mad and going nowhere'.

The resultant huge captive audience meant you didn't need to be Einstein to work out that Brobdingnagian outdoor billboards were agencies' and advertisers' preferred media of choice. As the market was still fairly new to advertising, and posters need to be seen and understood in split seconds, simplicity was key. And as the late Steve Jobs once famously said, 'there's nothing more complex than simplicity.'

With most clients in Saudi content to run bland messages saying nothing more attention-grabbing than 'Just arrived!' the field was wide open for ballsy, more adventurous ads. Fortuitously for me and my bank balance, they weren't coming from the world centre of advertising excellence in London.

Desperate to hit the pub or head to Dingwalls to catch next week's next big thing, creatives there would knock off any old rubbish in their rush to be first out of the agency door. As a result, locally run ads originating in the UK tended to be hilariously inept.

One classic of the immaculate misconception genre was a three-panel billboard touting one of the UK's biggest-selling washing powders.

Frame one showed a hardworking Arab housewife inserting a grubby *thobe* (the standard long white garment all Arab males wear from the age they can walk) in a gleaming white washing machine. In the middle of this triptych was a frame showing our leading lady leaning on her Hotpoint and reading a magazine while she meekly waited for her menfolk's clothes to wash. The third and final frame showed our now deliriously happy heroine holding up her husband and son's freshly pristine washing with a look of quasi-post-coital contentment on her face.

All very solid – if a little unspectacular – when it came to pushing products in places like the UK, where everyone reads from left to right. Unfortunately, the ad was rather less effective in Arab markets, where readers' eyes travel in the opposite direction. Reluctant to stump up for a soap powder that boasted how it transformed spotless clothes into grime-encrusted rags, Saudi's rather literal consumers killed the brand overnight.

Don't feel too badly for the client. Years later, I'd be in a meeting with the same maker of best-selling household cleaning products. Expecting to be given a 'brand bible' an inch-and-a-half thick to study, I was surprised when I was asked to think up a name and pick two or three claims. I was then totally taken aback when I learned that the client would then formulate a detergent to match their chosen name.

Another wonderful example of overseas agencies' couldn't-give-a-fuck-attitude was a roadside poster for Jaguar. In the UK, the marque was using top motoring mags to run double-page ads showing a seductively lit glamour shot of their oh-so sexy top-of-the-range car. The headline for this petrolhead wankfest? 'Unstoppable Power'.

Unfortunately, Arabic-speaking ad translators were nothing if not slavishly literal. By the time it had been written up, printed, and plastered on roadside posters the length and breadth of Saudi,

Jaguar's ad read: 'This is a very fast car with no brakes.'

Perhaps the hardest lesson a Western marketer learned due to such habitual 'Will this do?' arrogance was the fate that befell the makers of Zube throat lozenges. Too intent studying UK sales figures to properly research their trademark's suitability in other languages, Zube's makers were blissfully unaware their product's name was a syllable-by-syllable duplication of the Arabic slang for penis. Suffice it to say, sore throats kingdom-wide remained unsoothed long after the brand's local rubber-stamping of the 'Suck on a Zube' campaign that had proven so effective elsewhere.

***

With Chaz and Di's royal nuptials, the Brixton Riots, and Botham's Ashes all just a kick in the pants away, the early summer of 1981 was a fascinating time to be in Britain. With ITV's recently broadcast *Death of a Princess* documentary still causing diplomatic ructions, it was not perhaps the optimal time to be upping sticks and heading for Saudi Arabia.

Any doubts I might have had about making the step were quickly dispelled when my new employers furnished me with a BA Club class ticket from Heathrow to Jeddah. A then still bold mash-up of the airline's first and economy classes, Club promised unimagined luxuries such as extra-wide seats with more legroom. Best of all, it offered passengers a chance to lord it over the proles at the back of the plane by quaffing an unlimited flow of free beer, wine, and spirits.

In those far-off days, I was totally unfamiliar with the niceties of international air travel, I didn't bother to check my ticket that carefully. Only after my arrival in Jeddah did I discover that, in the aviation equivalent of providing a hearty breakfast for the condemned man, the agency had only paid for a one-way fare.

Once airborne, I predictably indulged in wave after wave of complimentary top-ups from BA's drinks trolley. Luckily for me, my hammering of my vital organs was considerably less severe than that of the two Scottish gentlemen I'd encountered in the bar at Heathrow just before take-off.

Already pissed as parrots, 'Riff' and 'Raff' boarded the plane and fell into their seats in an uncoordinated heap of flesh and foul language. Though several rows ahead of me, the paralytic pair's endless supply of coarse epithets were uttered at a volume that probably even the mufti of Makkah's Grand Mosque could have heard.

Legend had it that several months before my departure, a Jeddah-bound passenger had asked a BA cabin attendant how far his watch needed to be turned back. The reply – 'About fifteen hundred years, sir' – had apparently led to the cabin attendant's instant dismissal upon his return to London.

Whilst less cataclysmic for his cabin crew, our pilot's cheery pre-landing announcement was not great news for anyone who'd spent the previous six hours trying to empty his plane's in-flight bar.

'We are now approaching King Abdulaziz International Airport in Jeddah. Please be advised that anyone found to have over-indulged in alcohol whilst onboard this flight faces the possibility of immediate deportation or even imprisonment,' Captain Sensible smugly intoned. 'Thank you all for flying with BA tonight. We look forward to treating you to our in-flight hospitality again soon,' he added with a degree of drollery unshared by those of us who'd liberally soaked up his airline's onboard munificence.

Alas, the message had arrived far too late to be understood – or acted upon – by Jimmy One and Jimmy Two up towards the front of the Club class compartment. Wobbling unsteadily down the stairs to the arrivals terminal shuttle bus, the two seemed almost certain to fall foul of the combined effects of gravity and alcohol.

Several over the eight ourselves, I and my fellow Club classmates watched, horror-struck, as one of our paralytic pals subsequently did indeed fall – headlong onto the baggage carousel.

The tartan terror's spectacular return to earth and temporary disappearance through the baggage retrieval belt's rubber curtains was met with loud guffaws from his still more or less upstanding travelling companion. Briefly reunited after his mate's reappearance, both of our blethered buddies were subsequently led away by heavily armed guards.

I later learned that – very fortunately for them – rather than being forced to listen to their cell door key being flung far, far away, the pair were sent straight back to Heathrow. One can only imagine their confusion when discovering they'd arrived back in Blighty on the same aircraft on which they'd only hours before flown out.

Equally astounding – well, it was for me as a first-time visitor – was the barrage of heat and humidity that started boxing my ears moment I emerged from the plane. Jeddah's average summer temperature often exceeds 40 degres Celsius, and the gods of climate were doing their damnedest to provide me with their very warmest welcome this particular June 1981 evening.

Aside from the head-hunter's all-too-prophetic insights about latter-day slavery, almost everything I knew about Saudi in those pre-Wikipedia days had been gleaned from ancient copies of *The Encyclopaedia Britannica*.

The dusty old tomes' authoritative (if rather dated) section on Jeddah stated that the city's name meant 'Grandmother' due to its apparently being the resting place of an Adam-free Eve. Had she gone searching for apples in the modern-day city, Eve might have found former UK *popmeister* Leapy 'Little Arrows' Lee selling them from a market stall. Or so one UK tabloid of the time would have had its readers believe.

Other sources quoted called the city 'the Bride of the Red Sea'. More cynical Jeddah expats generally claimed that this was the result of its being liberally impregnated by seamen each time a ship entered and docked in its port.

While a nationwide figure of six or seven million was usually given, Saudi Arabia has always been cagey about the exact size of its population. The reason for this is often darkly hinted as Saudis' paranoia about their near neighbours (i.e. Israel) learning how many people they'll need to subdue should they ever decide to invade.

Darker still were the mutterings that the Israelis were just a couple of semi-automatic Uzi bursts away from doing just that. While I lived there, rumours were rife that Israeli air force pilots had free rein to keep their Saudi brothers up at night by flying low and buzzing their military bases.

A more insightful source of info for this particular first-time visitor to the kingdom was former MI5 spy and arch-traitor Kim Philby's autobiography, *My Secret Life*. Interestingly, Philby's father was noted Arabist Harry St. John Philby; together with T.E. Lawrence and Ernest Thesiger, one of only a handful of Brits to have ever 'got' the Saudis.

Early on in his autobiog, Philby senior's treasonous son had described the kingdom as being 'a country whose landscape has majesty but no charm; and whose people are conclusive proof that ignorance and affluence do not mix.'

Having only ever left the British Isles once before, I was naturally curious to see what hints – if any – the journey between the airport and the city might reveal about the Arab world. Frustratingly, pitch blackness ensured the accuracy of Philby's opinions about the country and its people would just have to remain a Churchillian riddle wrapped inside an enigma for just a little longer.

When we eventually arrived, my new 'home' turned out to be an anonymous three-storey block – two three-bedroomed flats to a floor – opposite a mosque just off Makaronah Road. The street's name apparently resulted from its formerly being the site of Jeddah's only macaroni factory. Years later, I read in Lawrence Wright's insightful book about the rise of Al Qaeda, *The Looming Towers*, that other area residents at that time included a young whippersnapper named Osama bin Laden.

Was the future terrorist tyro pushed over the edge by his family compound's close proximity to the bunch of oafish *ajnabis* (Westerners) who lived in Crown's apartment block? That's a fascinating avenue of possible cause and effect that remains unexplored by either Wright or any of the dozens of experts who've agonized over 911. What I do know for sure is that the agency occasionally created ads for the Bin Laden family's local VW dealership, Samaco. So, who knows, maybe young Osama was dragged around our office on some misguided 'Bring a Potential Terrorist to Work' day and became unhinged after one too many sniffs of Spray Mount adhesive.

***

My arrival in Jeddah marked what I later learned was a remarkably alcohol-free night – one of very few I would ever endure in this supposedly 'driest' of 'dry' countries. After being introduced to my new workmates – the European and Aussie ones anyway – I headed to bed. After what seemed like just a few minutes' shuteye, I was roused from my jetlagged slumbers by the *muezzin*'s pre-dawn call to prayer. Futilely trying to get back to sleep, I began to wonder just how large and vindictive a pup Crown's London recruiters had added to my growing litter.

That evening, I was to learn that there was just one TV and video player to entertain the constantly shifting cast of 12 Westerners who shared the building's four lower-floor flats. Worse still, the agency hadn't even bothered to provide even one of the apartments with a phone. Anyone wanting to make or take an urgent call from home had to wait until they went to the office, or waste an afternoon or evening queueing up at Jeddah's Central Post Office.

All in all, the extravagant expat package I'd been promised in my letter of appointment was starting to look very spartan indeed. While simple, the moral of the story – always get everything in writing before you catch your flight out – was one that took me many years to grasp.

My new flatmates, I soon learned, were the agency's charming but hopelessly ineffectual company comptroller, 'Dick Jones', and raving-alcoholic creative director (CD), 'Joe Clay'. As I was to discover time and time again over the next two years, Jeddah was not the place to be if you were running away from any kind of problem. This was especially true if the monkey on your back's thrashings could only be temporarily stilled by swilling industrial quantities of alcohol – as was tragically the case with poor old Joe.

Our nextdoor neighbours on the ground floor were a three-man sales team led by a blunt Yorkshireman called 'Seth Davis'. Sharing with Seth were 'Chris Varick' (a.k.a. 'Charley' after a similarly named movie of that time) and 'Greg Weinstein' (a.k.a. 'Greg F' – the 'F' standing for the 'fucks', 'fuckers', and 'fuckings' with which he liberally peppered each sentence).

Upstairs were located two further floors of flats.

The first of these housed two of my creative department colleagues, John Livings and Mike Hawkins,
and an account executive (AE) called Graham
Ead. Directly opposite them lived two other AEs
called 'Jeremy Hindley' and 'Robin Davidson'.
The third and uppermost floor was reserved for
the company's account director, 'Gewad Ghaben',
and his large Glaswegian wife, 'Val' (sadistically
nicknamed 'Valumnia' by a former employee who'd
obviously read Dickens' *Bleak House*). Making up
the numbers was the agency's clueless Egyptian
CD, 'Suleiman Shabila' (unkindly, if accurately,
dismissed by one and all as 'Slowman Shabbily').

If our digs were more messy than 'des ressy',
they were unimaginably luxurious compared to
those Crown's large contingent of Filipino, Indian,
and Pakistani finished artists and salesmen had to
endure. Cruelly dismissed as 'TWNs' (Third World
nationals) by many other expats, the Asian guys
could not have been friendlier or more welcoming.
Nor could they have been more generous when
it came to sharing what little they had with their
ajnabi colleagues when they occasionally invited
us over to feast on their superlative curries.

***

Not having had a TV for most of my time in
Manchester, I was curious about getting my first
taste of foreign-language telly. To say that the tube
in Saudi Arabia has had something of a chequered

history would be a colossal understatement. King Faisal bin Abdulaziz Al Saud, the country's third monarch between 1964 and 1975, viewed the medium as being a vital tool in bringing his subjects kicking and screaming into the modern world.

If he was to succeed in his aims, he would have to overcome considerable opposition from hardliners whose reading of the Quran left considerably less wriggle room for interpretation than his own. Like everyone's then still idealized image of John F Kennedy, Faisal seems to have been that rarest of rulers: a genuine progressive who was looked up to by most of his people. Nor did the similarities didn't end there; for just like JFK, Faisal wound up getting cut down by an assassin's bullets.

While this is not meant to be a formal history book or travelogue, there are one or two things the casual reader does need to know about Saudi. The most crucial of them being the fact that the only thing that can be said to unite the country's royal family is its members' infinite hatred of one another.

Generally considered as a wastrel, Faisal's spendthrift predecessor, Saud, ruled from 1953 to 1964 before being overthrown and exiled, first to Egypt and finally Greece. There, he spent the remaining four or five years of his life watching his hated brother wield the power he was too ineffectual to hang onto and exercise himself.

The ending of slavery, the improvement of education, bureaucracy, and religious inclusiveness, plus a total overhaul of Saudi finances all ranked high on Faisal's wish- list before he assumed the throne. Of all the modernising steps the new king embarked upon, the introduction of TV in 1965 proved the most contentious.

At the front of the queue of those incensed by Faisal's rush to drag his country into the 20th century was his half-brother's son Prince Khalid bin Musaid. Effectively the country's first television critic, Khalid was fatally shot following a failed raid on Saudi TV's central broadcast facility in 1966. Never mind, another of the kingdom's most fervent anti-reformers, Khalid's sibling Prince Faisal bin Musaid was waiting for his own moment in the glare of the klieg lights.

Perhaps the most admirable (and happily enduring) of all Saudi traditions are the regular Friday morning *Majli*s that allow citizens of all ages and backgrounds* to petition the king with their grievances.

Those attending the *Majlis* on March 25, 1975 included our old friend Prince Faisal bin Musaid. When, as is the Arabic custom, the king leant over to kiss his nephew on the cheek, the younger man pulled a pistol from his *thobe* and shot him twice

---

* Well the men anyway. Women were not allowed to attend the *Majlis* until 1999.

in the face at point-blank range. Amazingly, the then 69-year-old monarch managed to make it to hospital, where he underwent a blood transfusion and various life-saving massages of his heart before eventually succumbing to his wounds.

Initially declared insane, Faisal the younger eventually got his comeuppance when they publicly beheaded him outside of Riyadh's Al Hukm Palace of Justice in June that same year. Given the younger Faisal's antipathy to all things televisual, it seems unlikely that any cameras were in attendance. That said, anyone with the stomach for such unpleasantness might find it well worth visiting YouTube in search of grainy action replays.

Despite the late king's noble intentions, TV in the Saudi Arabia of the early 1980s was easily the worst I had – and still have – ever had the misfortune of trying to watch. Whilst it would be plainly unreasonable to expect any Arabic-speaking country to do more than pay lip service to foreigners, English-language broadcasting in the kingdom really was the pits.

The highlight of the week came with the airing of 15-year-old episodes of *Lost in Space* at 10:30 pm on a Friday night. While I myself never found the show's bacofoil-clad female stars to be particularly comely, Saudi males had developed quite a soft spot (well, perhaps not exactly soft) for the pair. Jumbo-sized boxes of Kleenex close to hand, single male fans of Marta Kristen and Veronica Cartwright would doubtless 'oooh', 'aaah', and 'urgh' their way through each starlet's less-than-stellar weekly antics.

Saudi TV's other main English-language show was the nightly news. These broadcasts were anchored by an elderly toff-type whose clipped moustache and pronunciation made him look and sound like a refugee from the BBC during Lord Reith's heyday in the 1930s.

Each nightly bulletin usually consisted of incisive updates about whatever larks the late King Faisal's half-brother and successor, King Khalid, had been getting up to earlier that particular day. Typical top-of-the-hour stories would cover Khalid's conveying of cordial greetings to some inconsequential overseas dignitary who'd fleetingly zipped through Saudi airspace at top speed while flying somewhere else.

On days when some worthless nonentity's plane did actually land in Jeddah – more often than not for a rapid, F1-style refuelling – Saudi TV pulled out all the outside broadcast stops. Anyone still *compos mentis* was subsequently rewarded with endless footage of the country's bored-looking ruler and his assorted hangers-on watching their latest 'VIP' mucker as he struggled to drink their treacly coffee.

Aside from the king, the man – and this being

Saudi, it was never, ever a woman – who most often made the news was former Palestinian Liberation Organization (PLO) leader Yasser Arafat. Although vociferous in their condemnation of the Israelis' despicable treatment of their Palestinian brothers, the Saudis were – and probably still are – an unfeasibly cowardly bunch. As a result, any direct action they ever took rarely extended beyond railing impotently at the heavens.

On those days when Yasser's plane did make a flying visit, he and the king would share some quality time bonding over a refreshing hot beverage and a basket of juicy dates. Backslapping over and a nice, fat cheque or money order surreptitiously slipped into the chest pocket of his fatigues, Yasser would then depart until PLO coffers needed their next topping up.

For viewers who could receive it outside the petrochemical giant's vast city complex in Saudi Arabia's Eastern Province, ARAMCO's in-house channel was far more palatable. Set up in the 1930s, ARAMCO employed tens of thousands of mostly US citizens, none of whom had a hope of surviving without being spoon-fed regular doses of their favourite home comforts. Not even the fact that every programme had been cut to ribbons by the Saudi censors could tarnish the channel's appeal.

When initially chancing upon ARAMCO's TV

listings in the daily paper, those unversed in the ways of the kingdom would be slightly flummoxed to find shows started at the oddest times. *Columbo* at 7:12 pm, for example, would be followed by *Hill Street Blues* at 8:57 pm, etc. The reason for this was that, as with all other aspects of Saudi life, literally everything – and I use the word 'literally' in its truest sense – stopped for prayers.

Such divine interventions were especially discombobulating when cop shows' exciting climactic shootouts were paused mid trigger pull for a few words from Him on High. More vexing still were the Saudi censors' ham-handed attempts at excising potentially contentious words from each show's soundtrack. Thus, sentences that probably ran something along the lines of 'We'll ship the heroin in via New Jersey' or 'Wowzah! Look at the rack on that babe!' would become unintelligible gibberish such as 'We'll ship *SILENCE* New Jersey!' or 'Wowzah! Look at the *SILENCE* on that *SILENCE*!'

Typically shit-scared of exposing its members to corrupting Western influences, the local censorship board had obviously binned their invites to refresher courses designed to update their knowledge of modern slang. As a result, phrases like 'Just another fucking junkie who OD'd while mainlining H' or 'Jeez! Look at the top bollocks on that bitch!' sailed through the censors' office without the slightest alteration.

The one passion the Saudis shared with many of the booze-soaked barbarians who'd once lurked safely outside their borders and were now flooding into their country with impunity? A love affair with all things football.

The end of my first 12 months in Jeddah – a period most expats referred to as their 'year for need' – was to culminate with the 1982 World Cup in Spain. With all bar 10 days of the tourney to take place during the Holy Month of Ramadan, there was a real chance of everyone's being able to catch all 52 games.

Even in those pre-red-button days of instantaneous access to multiple matches and translated commentaries, the prospect of three or four weeks of wall-to-wall footie action was proving irresistible for one and all. As the big day of the June 13 opening match approached, even the agency's Egyptians, Indians, Filipinos, Pakistanis, and Sri Lankans had begun to succumb to the World Cup bug.

In readiness, everyone in our apartment block had chipped in for sizeable supplies of illegally distilled alcohol called *siddiqi* (friend) or sid. In what must have been a first, fermenting home-brewed wine that would normally have been consumed well before its yeasty depths had cleared was also being left untouched until maturity.

Who cared if every World Cup since the Brazilian triumph in the unbearable heat of Mexico 1970 had been forgettable tosh. Several weeks of mindless enjoyment stretched ahead of us like the oases I was so fond of referring to when stuck for a hoary old phrase to pad out an ad.

The date *Shaban 21,* 1402 (or June 13, 1982, to us heathens) will go down in history as the day the first game in the 1982 World Cup got underway. Unfortunately for anyone living in Saudi at the time, it was also the day that, instead of kicking the ball, 68-year-old King Khalid was announced as having kicked the bucket.

While Islam prohibits personal aggrandisements such as statues and the country's hot climate means elaborate state funerals are out of the question, the Saudis were firm believers in prolonged periods of national mourning. The fact that Khalid's death would result in a blanket ban on TV football was, however, only half the reason for any personal sense of sorrow I experienced at his passing.

With the Quran decreeing fasting during daylight hours as one of the five pillars of Islam, the holy month of Ramadan is a sacred observance for devout Moslems the whole world over*. A hard-earned reward for those who've spent the previous 30 days refraining from food, drink, and cigarettes between sunrise and sunset, the resultant *Eid Al Fitr* holiday is every bit as cherished.

Together with the King's Birthday and Saudi National Day on September 23, the *Eid Al Fitr* and post-*Hajj*-pilgrimage *Eid Al Adha* holidays were hugely profitable periods for Crown. The reason for this is that whilst not legally required to do so, almost every company in the kingdom made the sound business move of issuing fawning congratulatory ads for the reigning king.

As kings in feudal monarchies such as Saudi do not stay kings forever, it is also wise for enterprises conveying their greetings to stay on the right side of those jostling for succession. As a result, companies took pains to salute the various brothers and half-brothers who'd have cheerfully stabbed the king in the back, front, or sides in their rush to depose him.

In my rarer, more dutiful moments, I had taken

---

* In case you ever find yourself on a quiz show, the remaining pillars are: accepting that Allah is the One True God and that Mohammed is His Prophet, praying five times a day, and giving alms to the poor. Those who can afford it should also do their best to make the pilgrimage, or *Hajj*, to Makkah in the lead-up to the Islamic world's other key holiday of *Eid Al Adha*. Should you take home a cash prize as a result of reading this book, I think a small donation to yours truly would be only fair. Crossed cheques can be made out to John Fuery (no animals or gifts in kind, please). Money can be deposited via the PayPal address towards the back of this book.

to dashing off the odd congratulatory message to replenish the stock of ads I kept handy for just such occasions. Faced with a distressingly high pile of now useless congratulations and felicitations messages,

One by one, the trite clichés of grief flowed out of my pen before being furiously pounded out on my typewriter. Within a couple of hours, what had once been a humble chorus line of inspiring-sounding greetings had been rebuilt into what I hoped was a Busby Berkley extravaganza of gut-wrenching woe.

In his own 68-year life – deep breath – King Abdulaziz bin Abdul Rahman bin Faisal bin Turki bin Abdullah bin Muhammad bin Saud (or ibn Saud to his mates), founder of the 'modern' Kingdom of Saudi Arabia, had taken some 22 wives. When not attempting to dodge neglected spouses, the priapic potentate had found time to sire around a hundred sprogs, 45 of them sons. With each new fruit of ibn Saud's loins detesting and mistrusting his brothers or half-brothers with a vengeance, in-fighting between the lengthy line to be the country's One True King was inevitable.

Small wonder, then, that rumours quickly began spreading about delays in the announcement of Khalid's death. Eventually, the deceased monarch's half-brother Fahd became the fourth (of six) of ibn Saud's sons to rule the kingdom. A few years later, he also assumed the title of Guardian of the Two Holy Mosques. Not bad accomplishments for someone whose youthful attempt at breaking the bank at Monte Carlo (he ended up losing £6,000,000) had resulted in his being denounced as feckless.

Trifles such as becoming collateral damage in a coup aside, the biggest immediate impact Khalid's death had on local expats was a 21-day period of officially sanctioned sadness. As everyone's long faces would be expected to extend right through the World Cup's initial group and quarter-final stages, the eagerly anticipated 'Feast of Football' began looking like very meagre fare indeed. In the end, I caught about half of one semi-final before flying back to the UK for some well-deserved (and much-needed) R & R.

Saudi TV left me with two other impressions I've never quite managed to shake off.

The first was the country's coverage of the Sabra and Shatila massacres of September 1982. Watched over by uncaring Israeli Defence Force members, right-wing Lebanese Christian phalangists had casually murdered between 750 and 3,500 civilians – many of them refugees from nearby camps. The music the Saudi TV channel's overseers had chosen to accompany the rather distressing footage of the slaughter? What more fittingly sombre soundtrack than Edward DeSouza's rather perky *Liberty Bell*

March – better known to successive generations of Western viewers as the theme from *Monty Python's Flying Circus.*

My second coffin-bound memory of Saudi TV is tied up with the country's love of a good beheading or stoning.

In Saudi and across the Arab world, Friday is generally the only full day each week most people don't have to work. What made the weekends here so singular – perhaps singularly unpleasant might be a better phrase – were the public executions.

One Thursday evening early on during my stay, the guys at the Makaronah Road flats insisted I watched an extended pre-weekend news bulletin. Compassionate to the last, the Saudi authorities had granted the show's makers creative *carte blanche* to film whatever wretches were to be separated from their heads the following day. The alleged perpetrator of this particular week's heinous crime spent the subsequent 45 minutes re-enacting his terrible deeds for the ghoulish hordes – of which I was now a reluctant temporary member.

As Saudis were a God-fearing bunch who never, ever broke the law, drank, gambled, or fornicated for purposes other than procreation, locals only ever featured in these shows as victims. The true 'star' of each week's mini-movie was usually some unfortunate Filipino, Korean, or Yemeni whose only misdeed was to be found in close proximity to a rape or murder victim. It didn't require the combined forensic acumen of Scooby and Scrappy Doo to deduce that, more often than not, the real perpetrator turned out to be a family member of the accused's Saudi employer.

Barely investigated by the police, the cases covered each week would reach their sad denouement with the alleged wrongdoer's beheading in one of Saudi's many 'chop squares' the following lunchtime. With 156 public executions in Saudi in 2016 alone, things don't seem to have moved much further forward than they had when I was there 30-plus years ago. Indeed, with some 47 apparent 'terrorists' – three of them minors – put to the sword on one January day in 2016 alone, things seem to keep moving backwards.

Sickeningly, there existed a tiny hardcore of *ajnabis* who made a point of never missing these 'What's My Crime?' Thursday night jamborees. Their sole reason for doing so was to secure a bird's-eye view of whatever bodily extremities were to be disarticulated or detached in their local chop square the next day.

Not that there was any real need to arrive especially early. Expats who did pitch up for each week's public executions by either accident or design were usually shunted to the front by the baying mob. At the end of the day, the Saudis weren't just fiercely proud of their justice system's heavy-handed punishment. They were determined to let morally bankrupt foreign devils stupid enough to think about violating their laws witness the brutal penalties awaiting them from the best seats in the house.

It disgusted and horrified me then and still appals me now that I had several clients who moved heaven and earth to attend these ghastly spectacles. One of them took great pride in telling everyone he was a prefect at a famous public school whose fags* included a leading member of Britain's royal family. To hear this oleaginous slime ball gleefully recite the atrocities he'd seen the previous weekend was just too nauseating for words.

Barely able to sit in the same room as him for the duration of a meeting, it was easy to ignore his reassurances that 'it isn't as bad as you think; you really should come down one weekend and see for yourself.' It was, our public-school-educated toffpot chuckled, 'one of the few things the Saudis have got right and a lot more fun than it probably sounds.'

Early on during my stay, I'd resolved that if I was ever unfortunate enough to unsuspectingly end up somewhere an execution was taking place, I'd realistically have to consider staying. Happily, this never happened, as the rather optimistically named

---

* In the UK rather than the US sense of the word.

'29 Palms' where Crown's expats usually spent Fridays was 30 miles in the opposite direction from Jeddah's own chop square.

**

With shit TV, a limited supply of restaurants, and no cinemas, illegal video clubs distributing grainy Betamax tapes of recent British and US TV shows and films were windfalls from on high. And what better way to prepare for a night slumped in front of the tube than by first making like Fred Astaire and putting on the Ritz at the local shopping centre?

When visiting supermarkets in Jeddah's growing number of 'gleaming' modern shopping malls, most expats would kill time by strip-mining the shelves of the latest bootleg cassette tapes.

Their sonic quality might have been shite, but at 10 riyals per tape, or 15 titles for just 90 riyals more, who was complaining? Well, maybe my sister, who still has suitcases full of unplayed, and probably now unplayable, 747-branded pirate tapes in her attic.

With convivial Golden Cross- (or Crescent-) style boozers conspicuous by their absence, Saudi males idled away their evenings slouched around the tables of each emporium's numerous *al fresco* coffee bars.

Buckling under the multiple burdens of too

much time, money, and impacted semen coupled with too little empathy and intelligence, the next generation of this once-dignified nomadic race was not a pretty picture. Ramped up to the nines on endless cups of thick Turkish coffee, the sex-starved young bucks would drool at any non-Saudi female foolish enough to try and walk past. Those not wearing the traditional black *abayah* (cloak) Saudi menfolk happily forced their own mothers, sisters, daughters, and wives to hide beneath were, of course, the recipients of the vilest catcalling.

The undisputed biggest seller in any Jeddah 'shoppers' paradise' worth its salt was grape juice. The reason for the drink's popularity was that it was an essential ingredient for fermenting wines whose potency reduced entire apartment blocks of bored *ajnabis* into a paralytic mess.

As briefly mentioned a few pages back, the main type of hard drink in the kingdom was sid. Broadly speaking, sid fell into three categories.

The most desirable (and therefore pricey) of these was crystal-clear sid, which had apparently been 'triple-distilled' for smoothness and safety – or so its sellers would have you believe.

A little more affordable were less-well distilled variants that still had worrying bits of black carbon left over from the distillation process floating inside.

Last but not least came indeterminate sids,

which carried a premium price but were probably just cheaper sids with the worrisome black bits removed.

On the frequent occasions no sid of any kind was to be had, everyone was reliant on home-brewed wine or beer to get wasted.

In the early 1980s – and, I daresay, today – the largest area of any supermarket in the kingdom was given over to jumbo-sized cartons containing a dozen one-litre bottles of grape juice. All would-be oenophiles then needed to stop whining and start wining were several kilos of sugar and a pinch of yeast.

While understandably unavailable in Saudi shops, the latter was easily smuggled past customs. Everyone venturing overseas was ordered to bring fresh supplies of the catalyst by secreting it deep within their pants and just behind their scrotal sacks.

Once laid down in a sanitized (well, sani-tized-ish) dustbin in an apartment's darkened broom closet, vino was meant to be left to ferment for 10 days. The homemade *aqua vitae* was then supposed to be decanted and left to clear for a further 96 hours before being declared 'fit to drink'.

In reality, so severe was everyone's despera-tion to escape the grinding monotony of Saudi life that wine rarely ever made it more than one or two days past decanting. The end result was a murky, yeasty, residue-accentuated red slurry whose toxic morning-afters would have caused even hardened connoisseurs of the grape like Hugh Johnson to take the pledge.

Given the ubiquity of booze in their flats and compounds, crippling hangovers were very much the norm for many Jeddah-based expats. It practically goes without saying that Crown's compliment of *ajnabis* was no exception. Arriving at work to find their so-called superiors stinking as if they'd showered in the previous night's illicit rotgut had long since become a daily norm for the agency's many non-Western staffers.

There were various ways of attempting to combat the unfortunate after effects of one's over-indulgence. The two most effective involved the suicidal step of having a drink before work the next morning, or the wolfing down of several powerful painkilling tablets.

While on a trip home, a colleague had discovered and brought back several packages of a painkiller called Veganin whose miraculous hangover-eradicating efficacy had quickly become the toast of the Makaronah Road flats. Anyone bound for the UK subsequently received strict instructions to return with as many king-size packs of this remarkable restorative as they could carry.

Late one night, Graeme decided to read the in-pack leaflet. Detailing how the tablets had been specially formulated to ease women's monthly period pains, the many female-oriented disclaimers buried deep therein effectively deep-sixed the pick-me-up's popularity there and then.

The big question you are now doubtless asking yourself (I know I certainly was) is how such levels of inebriation were possible in a country where booze was expressly prohibited? 'Surely,' I hear you say, 'the Saudis could easily call a halt to such shenanigans at any time.'

After all, all the local fuzz had to do to put the fear of Allah up every expat was raid a couple of compounds and bust open a few throbbing heads. Simpler still, officers could just hang around outside a supermarket and trail any of the literally hundreds of expats emerging with trolleys piled high with grape juice.

The answer is that the Saudi authorities had no desire whatsoever to start getting tough on the expats who used illicit alcohol to blow off steam. They knew only too well that their doing so would cause huge numbers of Europeans, Americans, and Aussies to quit their jobs. The country's economy would then have hit a brick wall faster than a car in the hands of a moroculous motorist.

Of course this doesn't mean to say the 'blind eye' the Saudi government turned to drinking was totally devoid of vision. Quite the contrary. To be pulled over pissed in a public place or in possession of alcohol and in control – or even travelling – in a car meant landing in serious shtook. Your chances of subsequently wriggling your way out of jail were largely dependent on three factors: who your sponsor was, how well he was connected, and last but not least, whether or not he liked or valued you enough to bust you out of the big house.

When not three sheets to the wind, Seth, the agency's sales chief, was sailing perilously close to it – as evinced by his two arrests for drinking and driving. The first time Seth found himself spending the night at King Fahd's pleasure, agency grand poohbah Assam Ibn Himar had made some calls and sprung him within a few hours.

Whether Assam's fondness for his head salesman was personal or extended beyond the lengthy lines of noughts on the revenue cheques he and his team were bringing in remained a moot point. As Seth eventually found out to his cost, even Assam had his limits. The second time the agency's sales supremo wound up incarcerated on the wrong side of the wrong kind of bars, Assam's patience snapped. Before poor Seth knew it, he found himself packing his bags for a one-way flight back to Heathrow, and Assam had earned himself the nickname 'Asshat'.

***

Whilst our social circle expanded slightly, it never grew to the point where we became mainstays of Jeddah's glitterati. Not that the city's expat social swirl was all sweetness and light. Some two years before my arrival, a British nurse called Helen Smith had 'fallen from' (or very possibly been pushed or thrown off) a balcony at a party in downtown Jeddah. Her retired policeman father, Ron, had been fighting for an inquest/forensic enquiry ever since her death. Despite finally getting his day in court in 1982 (the jury at the inquest returned an open verdict), it would not be until 2009 that Helen Smith's body was cremated and her ashes scattered on Ilkley Moor.

Although we remained permanently rooted in the murky dregs at the bottom of the city's party fish pond, the guys and I did occasionally get invited to other expats' compounds. That the cops rarely ever busted such enclaves was a big plus for their residents, who routinely self-medicated away their boredom with gargantuan helpings of intoxicants and tumescent tomfoolery. *Ice Storm*-style swingers' sessions where partygoers' wives picked their sexual partners for the evening by taking a lucky dip of car keys from a big bag were apparently a particular favourite. Given the prodigious amounts of Sid'n'7 Up (Sid'n'7) I put away at such events, it was probably just as well I didn't drive.

The downside was that, waited on hand and foot by houseboys and free to imbibe and fornicate as recklessly as they liked, many compound residents quickly lost their grounding in reality. Repeated to me *ad nauseum* by almost everyone I met upon arrival, there was no getting away from the 'one year for need, one year for greed' mantra.

Unwilling to abandon unimaginably luxurious lifestyles they'd never have enjoyed in a million years 'back home', many long-term compound dwellers were doomed to become more ossified with each new two-year contract they signed. To meet people who had been living in Saudi for a decade or more was fairly common. To engage them in any kind of intelligent conversation was as likely as non-driving me having someone jump my bones at that weekend's car key party.

A far more interesting – if slightly less upwardly mobile – class of expat was to be found on the weekly Thursday afternoon Hash. Established by a bunch of hungover and bored Brit executive and officer types in Selangor, Malaysia, in 1938, the Hash House Harriers had begun life as a Monday evening hare and hounds run. By the early 1980s, the Hash's runners had begun flexing their especially energetic legs the whole world over.

Still sharing the paper-chase stylings of its original incarnation, the Jeddah event was a genuine one-of-a-kind opportunity to take in the desert around the city. With nowt else to do on Thursday evenings before uncorking the first bottle of wine or sid, the Jeddah Hash had established itself as a highlight of many expats' social calendars – my own included.

While the desert vistas just outside Jeddah were nowhere near as awesome as the Moroccan and Jordanian stand-ins featured in David Lean's *Lawrence of Arabia*, the sunsets were utterly magical. What with the Hash, regular games of squash, and Friday snorkelling sessions at the beach, I was probably fitter than I'd ever been before – and regretfully ever since.

If only Joe Clay, the agency CD when I arrived, had spent a little more time getting fit and less time fucking up his liver on dodgy firewater. By the time I met him, poor Joe was on his third and, poignantly, final go-round with Crown. He'd also acquired his very own stool at the main bar of life's Last Chance Saloon.

As talented as he was – he'd had once radio plays performed on the BBC Home Service – Joe was the most hopeless alkie I've ever met, and believe me, I've chinked glasses with more than my fair share.

The Joe-shaped room in my memory palace is dominated by the day Gewad made a rare trip upstairs to the creative department. In search of some urgently needed ads that Joe had promised to bang out, Gewad had been fruitlessly searching high and low for the one-time creative *wunderkind*.

Naturally, it never dawned on Gewad to peek inside the cupboard in the errant CD's office. Had he done so, he would have discovered the old boy fast asleep with the last remaining dribbles of a bottle of high-alcohol-content Hai Karate aftershave staining the chest of his shirt.

Years later, I ran into Joe again when he briefly became CD with a rival ad agency to the one I ended up working for in Bahrain. My heart over-ruling sensible advice from my head, kidneys and liver, I accepted his invitation to join him for 'catch-up drinks' in his hotel suite one Thursday night.

We subsequently wound up boozing until way past the point where I was in any kind of fit state to hail a taxi. I crashed out on the sofa and left Joe to it. Anticipating another Promethean day and night on the piss when I awoke to find Joe polishing off his first 'cleansing ale' of the morning, I made my excuses and headed home.

I can only assume Joe, who was already several stops beyond paralytically pissed when I left, carried on getting tanked up. Renewed by the recuperative embrace of my bed, I made it to the office in reasonably chipper condition on Saturday morning. Despite my gentle urgings to take his own foot off the pedal, Joe, unfortunately, did not. When I phoned his office to check if he was OK the next day, I was told he'd left the island the previous evening. I never saw or heard from him again.

Another Crown vet I was considerably happier about never seeing or hearing from – or indeed of – again was Joe's odious replacement, 'Dan Dinkins' (a.k.a. 'Dapper' or more often 'Desperate Dan'). As if his absurd name wasn't enough of a cross to bear, DD bore an uncanny resemblance to popular 1970s TV detective *Jason King*.

By the time he slid onto Joe's suspiciously brown-stained CD seat, Dan must have been well into his mid 1960s. As one of the guys put it, this was quite apt as his idea of advertising seemed to have remained landlocked back in the same era. With his outdated creative chops, inability to handle his booze, and quickness to turn nasty when losing at poker, DD did not endear himself to his expat colleagues.

Never having been much of a gambler, I tended to steer well clear of the Makaronah Road card school. As a result, I was happily spared the Dapster's inevitable explosion and fusillade of baseless accusations of cheating after fingers of sid had been served and hands of cards dealt.

What I did, however, witness on a regular basis was the nasty and condescending way he abused the agency's Indian and Filipino finished artists. Far from fluent in English, most of the studio guys were terrified of losing their jobs should 'Mr. Dan' decide to make their lives even more miserable than they already were. 'Is this what you call artwork,

Sayed? Why, a trained monkey could produce a layout neater than this shambles.'

And woe betide any poor dupe foolhardy enough to point out any of the frequent incidences of Dan talking out of his bony backside.

'Are you trying to tell me these lines are, in fact, straight and true, Kante?', the dapper/desperate one would bellow at his latest uncomprehending and probably perfectly blameless victim. 'Well, listen here. I'll bet my monthly salary against your monthly salary that they're not!'

With a 'ya boo sucks' wave of a gnarly hand gripping the latest in an endless procession of foul-smelling ladies' More cigarettes, DD would begin resurrecting yet another ad from advertising's golden age.

But all of the above hijinks still lay somewhere in the future. During my first few days at Crown, I couldn't help but notice how my new colleagues – well, the Western ones, anyway – kept banging on about something called 'the IBM syndrome'.

Unsure whether this meant the computer manufacturer or if it was a variant on the centuries-old 'get me a round tuit' prank played on wet-behind-the-ear apprentices in Coventry, I simply nodded sagely. I subsequently learned that the IBM that gave the syndrome its name was actually an acronym aimed at anyone sufficiently brave or cretinous to try to do business in Saudi.

What IBM meant in this case was *Inshallah* (God willing), *Bokra* (Tomorrow), and *Malesh* (It doesn't really matter anyway). Remember and stick slavishly to those three guidelines while working in Jeddah, I was advised, and I would never go far wrong.

The IBM syndrome was, of course, just the tip of the skew-whiff inverted-logic iceberg facing anyone trying to cram their pockets full of their Saudi masters' petrodollars.

Take Crown (or 'Clown' as it inevitably got tagged by its savvier Western staffers and clients) itself. It was not only an ad agency, but also an in-house studio for *The Saudi Telegraph* – a.k.a. the less credible and widely read of the country's two largely fact-, opinion- and insight-free English-language dailies.

This meant that the entire creative department was expected to drop everything and create and get ads approved and printed for the paper at ludicrously short notice. The workload became even worse when the paper pioneered a bullshit 'business bible' (called with brain-deadening predictability *'The Saudi Tradeopedia'*) as well as an anorexically thin 'What's on?' guide called *'Jeddah Now'*.

With Saudi occupying the same paranoid universe as North Korea and Enver Hoxha-era Albania, *JN*'s listings pages were unsullied by meaningful listings or reviews of any kind. The ruling House of Saud was ultimately extremely anti any activity that might allow its citizens to gather together and begin plotting their overthrow. Consequently, those enthusiastically scouring *JN*'s pages for ideas for big nights out found only anodyne ads and glowing reviews for shopping malls and restaurants they'd visited dozens of times before.

Despite any non-Moslems attempting to enter being turned back by armed guards, the two places every curious expat did want to experience were the holy cities of Makkah and Medina. The only 'non-believers' to have effectively ever set foot inside the former were apparently the French paratroopers the Saudis had quickly converted to Islam to end the late 1979 occupation of the Grand Mosque.

Less militarily inclined souls could take advantage of the generous cash incentives then on offer for those converting to Islam. Robin from the second floor at Makaronah Road actually did the deed and eventually banked around £10,000. Luckily, he didn't even need to be circumcised, and ended up collecting his nice tax-free earner for doing little more than attending a few lessons and changing his name to Dawud.

As my potential landlord in Nairobi, Mr. Powell, was to discover two decades later, the only drawback of becoming a Moslem came if you later decided to renounce Islam. With the penalty for such apostasy usually involving death by stoning, whatever cash benefits were on offer quickly lost their lustre.

***

Apart from Seth D, Charley V and Greg F, the bulk of the sales for the newspaper, book, and guide were generated by a large team of Indian and Pakistani sales executives. As most of the sales guys worked hard and did their best not to overload the studio, they got on extremely well with the expat creatives.

There were, of course, one or two exceptions. The most unprofessional, and therefore unpopular, of these was a gentleman called 'Mr. Alex'. Few sounds in the top-floor creative department produced more groans than the iconic clump, clump, clump of Mr. A's platform shoes as he barnstormed up the stairs brandishing another absurdly unrealistic workload.

Unwelcome as the sight of Mr. Alex's enormous gut and mile-wide kipper tie hoving into view around the office door was in the agency's creative department, he remained, hugely popular with clients. Ultimately, the man's Gollum-like desire for commissions was so insatiable he would promise any company with a few riyals to spare an endless stream of low-cost or no-cost ads, mailers, and brochures. With Mr. A having personally guaranteed their delivery within impossibly tight timeframes, the creative team would then have to labour far into the night to try and finish everything.

On more than one occasion, so impatient was Mr. Alex to line his pockets that he actually began writing ads on his own. His headline for a distributor of educational aids for toddlers, 'Toy is Joy!' being more than enough to earn him his immortality in these memoirs.

Mr. Alex's low standing in the creative department plummeted to previously uncharted depths the afternoon he met the Jeddah distributor of a famous US car manufacturer. Sensing some wavering on the part of the client, Clown's least popular salesman recklessly promised he would be back to present a hugely ambitious multi-model ad campaign the very next day.

About 15 hours later, Mr. Alex was up in the creative department demanding that someone come along and help him present his hastily thrown-together series of ads. With my partners having repaired to their beds for a well-earned rest, Mike Hunt here was left with the never very pleasant task of meeting and talking to the client.

The car company's local agent was an impossibly ancient man called 'Shaikh Ibrahim'. Dressed like an unused extra from Bryan Forbes's *Ice Cold in Alex* who'd never bothered changing in the quarter-century or so since the film's release, the Shaikh was, it turns out, almost totally blind. Gracelessly snatching the layouts Mr. Alex passed over to him, the old boy would adjust his Coke-bottle glasses and peer intently at the contents of each proposed ad.

Routinely used to stand in for yet-to-be-approved body copy by time-poor art directors, the gibberish Latin type he found there seemed to vex him greatly. 'Whet is thees "*lorem ipsum dolor*" you kip wreeting, and whet hes it do with our kerrs?' the wizened one would ask, poking the offending copy with a callused finger.

Pained by our ads' inexplicable inability to magically restore his sight, the Shaikh summoned what I assumed was his marketing manager to provide a second, perhaps more specialized appraisal of each ad. The 'expert' who eventually arrived was one of those antediluvian 'tea boys' that seem to be a regulatory mandatory for those running offices across the Arab world.

As nonplussed by the latter half of the 20th century as his master, Mohammed would scornfully dump our layouts onto the floor as fast as Mr. Alex could hand them over. Fuck! Everything would now have to be done again.

'Well, I think that went quite well,' Mr. Alex beamed as we drove back to the office. 'A couple more rounds between now and the weekend, and

I think Shaikh Ibrahim will sign off on the ads,' he breezily announced.

I don't know whether it was John and Mike's burying of the words 'Mr. Alex is a fuckwit' deep within each ad's body copy, but the second presentation worked like the proverbial charm.

Chapter Four

'We are talking international here!'

On the rare occasions a larger or more ambitious (i.e. rasher) client tasked Clown with creating multimedia (TV, press, brochures, etc) campaigns, leadership from Suleiman or Gewad came there none. The agency's participation in the great Saudia Airlines pitch of 1982 was a classic example.

Despite its only just having splashed out millions of US dollars on a stylish new corporate ID, the client had become a global laughing stock. Freshly revamped at great cost and more wanky than swanky, the airline's latest logo had featured a gap between its 'i' and 'a'. All perfectly innocuous until someone pointed out that the resultant white space had formed a *verboten* Christian cross.

Like Saudia's planes, the error had soared far over the heads of the corporate high-fliers who'd approved the work. Desperate to claw back some semblance of dignity, the airline was now asking leading local and international agencies to pitch for a second hugely expensive worldwide image relaunch.

For some bizarre reason – probably the country's pervasive nepotism – Saudia's senior managers had ignored their 'leading' prerequisite and invited Clown to take part. Despite having no overseas experience and an international 'network' comprising just two domestic offices, Gewad and Suleiman were entrusted with leading the bid.

Early on during the pitch, Suleiman's most trusted deputy trekked the 750-odd miles across country to the agency's only other office in the delightfully, if deceptively, named east coast city of Al Khobar. And what a trek it proved to be. Exhausted by the gruelling 125-minute flights there and back plus an onerous two-night stay in a five-star hotel, Suleiman's envoy took fully three days off work to recover from his jet lag.

Shortly thereafter, Suleiman himself apparently contracted sunstroke somewhere between our apartment building's front door and the pavement outside while washing his car. He then remained predictably *incommunicado* for almost the whole of the remaining period when work for the airline's relaunch was being prepared.

Fifteen or so perfectly serviceable international ads duly created for a pitch we had no chance of winning, I joined Graeme and Gewad in Asshat's office for the presentation. Still apparently hovering perilously in the twilight zone between sense and sensibility, life and death, Suleiman was, of course, nowhere to be seen.

Faced with one of the most flint-faced clients I've ever seen in a 40-year-career positively filled with the fuckers, Graeme and I began running through our work.

The next three quarters of an hour was one long awkward silence broken only by the clinking of coffee cups and the chink of my Zippo lighter firing up an uninterrupted chain of cigarettes. The only sign of sentient life in the room came midway through the meeting, when Graeme presented a concept ad for the Middle Eastern edition of *Time* magazine. 'We are talking international here,' Gewad sagely intoned with his trademark cutting insight.

The last layout we presented inevitably fell dead on the same stony ground as had claimed its many brave brothers before it. Keen to fill the terrible quiet with something, anything, I brightly enquired, 'Anyone got any questions?' Seconds later, Graeme and I were quickly and quietly dismissed from Assam's presence and cast back into the outer darkness. If Saudia ever got back in touch, neither Graeme or myself ever heard a dicky bird about it.

***

Having got this far, you'll probably have noticed that there's one big question that's lounging elephant-like in the corner of the room: how many Saudis did I really get to know during my two years advancing the cause of advertising in the country?

Aside from the various clients we bearded in

their offices (rule of thumb: the more garish the decor, the more dim-witted the dickwad behind the desk), the answer was a big fat zero. The whole time I was in Jeddah, I only really had any kind of meaningful contact with three or four Saudi nationals. And one of those was an oceanic onanist whose vigorous beating of the meat you'll read about a few pages hence.

The reasons for this were many and varied. Firstly, there was the country's unyielding racial hierarchy. While the westerners who came second only to Saudis at the top, might chat happily to the Yemenis who subsisted at the very, very bottom, the locals would never countenance doing so. Even supposing more interaction between the various groups had been encouraged, the Royal family's fear of overthrow meant there was no sufficiently level playing field where it might take place. Last but not least was the fact that no members of any non-Saudi group had ever been given sufficient reason to respect or trust their local lords and masters.

The first local (even if he did claim to have been born to a British mother) I got to know was a soon-to-be-former agency designer called 'Zeb'. The sole reason he has stuck in my mind all these years is that he performed the well-nigh impossible task of being fired from the agency for incompetence.

Given the paranoia that afflicted Westerners

the length and breadth of Saudi, it was unsurprising the guys had been leery of Z since he'd parachuted into their ranks. What made his arrival appear even more suspicious was that it had come at a time when no other staff were being hired. Z's story about where he'd lived in the UK (Brighton) set still more alarm bells ringing. Should you snap shut this book, sally out into the street, and start talking to a Saudi, he'll almost certainly tell you he studied English at a language school in 'Brighton by the Sea'.

Jesus, even the all-conquering Asshat, had been to the city. It was while in Brighton that he apparently met and – unlikely as it sounded – tripped the light fantastic with his future wife at the local Tiffany's Disco. My only meeting with the fragrant and surprisingly airs-and-graces-free 'Tracy' came at a party during my second year. 'Hello, my name's Trey-suh,' said the solitary woman in a roomful of partially pissed men.

'Before you get carried away by the sight of a single female who isn't' a Saudia stewardess, I think you should know that I'm married to your boss, Ass-ham!' And with a bright laugh, she shot off to talk to someone more interesting on the other side of the room. It all goes to show that while you can take the girl out of Tiffany's Brighton, you'll never take Tiffany's Brighton out of the girl.

With the benefit of almost four decades of

hindsight, everyone's mistrust of Zeb sounds horribly irrational and racist. Having grown up in Coventry as the child of immigrant parents myself, I certainly initially thought so. With everyone in early 1980s Jeddah desperate to avoid being gaoled for serving booze to a Moslem, I came to learn that such qualms were firmly grounded in reality.

After making a few awkward attempts to casually 'drop by' the house in Makaronah Road after his firing, Zeb slowly vanished off everyone's collective radar. Predictably, he never furnished any details of the 'friends' he was apparently staying with or the other company who'd hired him before becoming yesterday's news. Regardless of the suspicions everyone else seemed to harbour towards Z, I couldn't help but feel a smidgeon of sympathy for the guy. Labouring the double burden of expats' caginess and Saudis' contempt for those whose noble Arab lineage had been be-smirched by corrupt influences, his life couldn't have been a barrel of laughs.

**

Saudi society was ultimately built on a very fragile balance. On one side of the scale was well-heeled local employers' disdain for the various Western 'experts' and unskilled TWNs without whose hard work their businesses would simply have ground to a halt. On the other was the country's ruling class's genuine dread of the horrors that might befall them should their poorer brethren ever tire of themselves and their whims.

The House of Saud was ultimately so fearful of its subjects that, whilst it was OK for commoners to collectively cheer on their teams in sunny football stadia, cinemas were strictly not on. Perhaps the king, his brothers, and the country's thousands of pampered and useless princes didn't want local film buffs quietly criticising the merits or demerits of Ingmar Bergman's latest *meisterwork*. Then again, maybe they simply didn't want to countenance how the movie of their lives might end should dozens of their disaffected countrymen ever start swapping notes in a darkened room.

Stonings...floggings...forced amputations...beheadings...were all toppermost of the choppermost on the Saudi statute books. Long-term prospects for any Moslem who decided that perhaps this God business was not all it was cracked up to be and embraced apostasy were even briefer and less bright.

Reluctantly jostling for position at the front of the lengthy line marked 'Death Penalty' were those held to be insulting Allah or his Prophet. A few places behind them in the queue for agonising humiliation was anyone caught plotting against the House of Saud. Rumour had it that locals found guilty of treason were taken out in a plane and then callously dumped out over the country's vast, unforgiving Empty Quarter. While never satisfactorily proven, the lack of alleged transgressors who'd fallen (no pun intended) foul of the king and the various other freeloaders clinging to the royal teat gave these speculations some credence.

Legend had it that our beloved leader Asshat was supposedly one of the very few real journalistic iconoclasts to have ruffled the House of Saud's feathers and lived to tell the tale. Not that he ever did. Apparently once known for writing hard-hitting column after column exposing assorted princes' profligacy, the youthful Assam had mellowed with age. Either that or he'd been effectively declawed after being treated to a much closer view of the Empty Quarter than he might have cared for.

The running joke in Clown was that Asshat had been born to a hugely wealthy family as the youngest of male triplets. When all three sons came of age, their father asked each of them to name a gift they believed would enable them to live a future life full of contentment.

When the eldest of the three brothers asked to be given an airline, the elderly shaikh went out and bought him Saudia, the country's national carrier. The middle son was keen on hospitality and was rewarded with the country's franchise for the Hyatt hotel chain. When it finally came to Asshat's turn, he told his dad the thing he wanted most in the world was a cowboy outfit – at which point, the old man summoned one of his minions and told him to go forth and snap up Crown.

Asshat was ultimately something of a mystery man whom new hires such as me were lucky to see within their first two or three months with the agency. My initial close encounter of the turd kind came when a bunch of us returned from lunch one day to find an Arab gentleman in full *thobe* and *goutrah* (headgear) in the agency's studio. Pre-empting the trend for photoshopping selfies by fully 30-plus years, Asshat was ordering a terrified Indian finished artist to straighten his elderly mother's crossed eyes in a family portrait. Vain? Possibly. But a lot less bothersome – and expensive – than flying old Ma Ibn Himar to London for an appointment with a Harley Street specialist.

Another notable Asshat encounter came one morning during a (thankfully) very rare booze drought (or 'Dramadan' as one wag in the office called it). It was then that a carload of us arrived bang on time for work – a practically unheard of occurrence.

Aware that his expats were turning up the worse for wear pretty much whenever they liked, Asshat positioned himself behind the agency's reception desk from whence he would personally berate any late arrivals. With his atypically punctual workforce serenading him with a cheery morning chorus as they ambled up the agency stairs, the be-*thobe*d one could only sit silently and seethe.

The only other real exchange of note I ever had with Asshat came one Thursday morning when I was summoned to his office just as everyone was preparing to leave for the weekend. Once in the great man's presence, I was announced to the man sitting opposite him with the tersest of introductions: 'This is Fuery, our English writer. He may be able to help you.'

Pleasantries all squared away, Assam busied himself with shuffling various papers and left us both to 'get on with it'. It turned out the man was a senior marketing officer from the country's biggest financial institution, the 'Saudi First Commercial Bank' (SFCB).

The 'it' Assam spoke of was a striking photograph of Mahmoud Bandar's stunning white marble sculpture, *The Supplication*, on Jeddah Corniche. The pair of hands raised in prayer in Bandar's work are those of the late King Faisal. Carved into the work's base is a quote from the Quran which says, 'O my Lord! Expand me my breast; Ease my task for me.' Had he only witnessed the jiggery-pokery members of Jeddah's gay community were getting up to in the nearby bushes, Faisal's hands would have been raised in dismay rather than devotion.

Was there any way, the client sweetly enquired, for me to help turn the picture into a nice house ad for his bank? A quick trip back to my office and three cigarettes was all it took for me to hammer out an ad called 'Faith'. The client's genuine delight with the words I had written aside, it remains the only ad from that era of my life I am remotely proud of. It remained a permanent feature in my portfolio until the point at which employers stopped asking to see my work before offering me jobs some 18 years later.

In case you're interested, I subsequently learned the man I'd been left to talk to was the SFCB's chairman and one of probably the two dozen most powerful non-royals in Saudi Arabia. While the financial wizard was very happy with the work I had done, Asshat was his usual stone-faced self. Although far more than I expected, his indifferent 'That will be all, Fuery' was all the thanks I was ever offered or was likely to get.

***

As we've seen and will continue to see, the Saudi Arabia of the early to mid 1980s was one of the most rigidly controlled and sexually repressed places on earth. Despite the arrival of satellite TV and the internet, one would imagine nothing much has changed. The only people who seemed to enjoy any kind of active sex life were expats who had company cars in which to swan around with Saudia flight attendants.

Then there was the city's gay contingent.

While homosexuality was usually punishable by fines, floggings, or lengthy prison sentences, sex acts between expat males and Saudi men were more common than you might think. Those foolish enough to get caught doing so twice risked facing the death penalty. Hardly surprising that most expat gays sensibly kept their sexual inclinations to themselves. The only person at Crown who'd kicked down the closet door and was out, loud, and proud of his gayness was a finished artist called David Parker, or 'Madge'.

I use Madge's real name here freely because his liver was so fucked when we became friends he's almost certainly long since booked into the great 1970s' New York bathhouse in the sky. In the unlikely event you're still out there, Madge, mate, do please get in touch.

Madge, as he was never shy of telling us, was 'camper than one of those closing-down sales Milletts always seemed to be having'. An accomplished paste-up artist, he would spend his time turning messy concepts into flawless artworks for printing in the next morning's paper. Business all done for the day, Madge's nights were devoted to cruising the endless nooks and crannies of Jeddah's corniche in search of what he smilingly called 'trade, darling.'

Once in *situ*, Madge would be quickly end up performing the beast with two backs with the latest in a succession of gagging-for-it Arabs of all ages and income groups. Say what you like about David, you couldn't call him snobby or prejudiced. In his worldview, 'A cock was a cock, darling no matter how rich or poor its owner'.

He was equally broadminded when it came to how he bestowed his sexual favours. The most graphic of methods usually involved the gear sticks of cars or open-back trucks driven by members of his rapidly swelling fan club. Each morning after his latest bacchanalian night before, Madge would enliven everyone's drive to work with blow-by-blow retellings of his capital-punishment-worthy antics.

The only person less than amused by Madge's yarns was the rather straitlaced and prematurely balding AE, Jeremy Hindley, or 'Bone Dome' as he was not so affectionately nicknamed. His thin lips pinched into a sour *moue* of disgust, Jeremy would listen with horror as Madge meticulously detailed the ins and outs of his latest night of depravity.

Please don't take the above as implying that Madge was totally devoid of discrimination when choosing his sexual partners. Frustrated by Jeddah's desperate shortage of unattached women, an Egyptian salesman called 'Bedi Niknak' decided to hedge his bets and begin exploring life as a man's rather than a purely ladies' man.

Having almost certainly heard of Madge's

nocturnal couplings, Bedi seemed dead set on indulging in a bit of illicit, although fairly wide-spread, 'homosexy' fun himself. Clad in his trademark absurdly inappropriate heavy tweed jacket, Bedi peacocked his way up the length of the creative department and plonked himself down on Madge's desk. 'Daveeed,' he cooed across the mess of set squares, cow gum, and partially completed artworks, 'I wann to fark jew like nowan has ever farked jew in your intire layfe!'

'Darling,' said Madge, not bothering to look up from what he was doing, 'I suggest you take your place at the back of what is already a very lengthy queue. While you wait, I recommend you pass the time by giving your teeth and body a thorough and, dare I say it, long overdue scrubbing. In the unlikely event I still have breath in my body when you near the front of the line, I'd still never allow your pathetic excuse for a penis within five miles of my backside.'

***

Weekends in Saudi – and indeed across most of the Middle East – consisted of a half-day off on Thursday and one whole day's R&R on Friday. When returning to the UK, friends often used to disappointedly remark that I wasn't 'really that brown' – as if my entire life in Jeddah had been spent idling on the beach.

Their crestfallen mood invariably started to

brighten when I told them that the country did, in fact, suffer the occasional downpour a couple of times a year. Short and brief, these rainstorms were inevitably presaged by the king's announcing a nationwide drought and calling for a round of full-on prayer from all faithful Moslems.

Once Allah's ears had been prised open, the skies would follow suit, and within a few days, everyone would be splashing away down the drain-free streets like Arabic Gene Kellys. There's ultimately nothing quite like being able to conjure up computerized weather forecasts from a man-made satellite to prove the existence of a Divine Power.

Roughly 52 of the 360-odd days on which the rain didn't fall were Fridays. As this was the holy day for Moslems, the *muezzin*'s five rounds of prayers meant the mosque directly opposite our house was mobbed from dawn to dusk. After five-and-a-half days of going stir crazy, not even the most ruinously hungover of us really wanted to waste their one full day off lying around the house. Those sufficiently hale and hearty subsequently piled into the agency's fleet of crappy Hyundai Pony cars and headed for the beach.

Rather glamorously called '29 Palms', the area we used to frequent actually consisted of 17 rather listless-looking giant ferns. Not much further beyond this forlorn clump of greenery lay the Red Sea and one of the world's most spectacular coral reefs. To see someone strolling the couple of hundred yards out to the start of the reef was to watch them perform the biblical feat of miraculously walking upon water. My badly sunburnt first day at the beach aside, it was a trip I took every chance I got.

One's sense of being dwarfed by something infinitely vaster than yourself became even more vivid while diving into unimaginably blue waters from what was effectively a hundreds-of-feet-high cliff. Many are the happy Friday hours I spent snorkelling off the reef here. Conscious of the need to 'take away nothing but photos and leave behind nothing but footprints', the only pieces of coral I removed were things that had already died and been washed up on the shore. Several of the shells still reside in my sister's bathroom in Reading to this day.

Underestimating the strength of the sun's relentless beating down and getting seriously sunburnt on one's first trip to the beach was effectively a rite of passage for new arrivals. Despite having packed and applied maximum-strength sunblock and limited my first exposure to the sun to short bursts totalling around 30 minutes, I was no exception. I subsequently spent most of the next two days in a cold bath futilely attempting to soothe the body-sized blister that had magically encased my back, my arms, my neck, my everywhere.

On very rare occasions, drivers like Graeme or Mike would succeed in corralling several delightful (if less than discerning) Saudia hostesses to join us for a frolic on the sand. Starved of female company for weeks, it was only natural that various loins began stirring each time the girls massaged factor-50 sunblock into each other's lithe, brown bikini-clad bodies.

Speeding past in a bottom-of-the-range Subaru truck, one local wasn't quite so backwards in coming forwards. Swerving off the rudimentary sand path, the man drove into the shallow beachfront waters and parked about 10 yards in front of us. After a few minutes, it became apparent our new bessie had no intention of going away any time soon.

When a couple of the guys went up to remonstrate, they found a portly, middle-aged Saudi still frantically – if fruitlessly – spanking the plank in his lap. Seeing the looks on Mike and Graeme's faces, the man dropped what he was doing and started frantically trying to get his truck into first gear and away. Leaving him and his engine to its futile, asthmatic wheezing, we all climbed in our own cars and drove a couple of miles up the beach.

Several months later, the agency 'won' the Movenpick Hotel account and my flatmate, Mike Gordon (he of the save-my-drunken-ass-from-arrest fame detailed later on), was appointed AE. Granted free passes to the hotel pool every weekend, Mike was generous in sharing his privilege with his colleagues.

Three particular standouts of the enjoyable Thursday afternoons I spent doing length after length of the pool (i.e. lying by its side, clutching my *siddiqui*-fuelled-throbbing temples) have stayed with me.

The first is of Mike quoting from an article about the rapid rise of sexually transmitted diseases (STDs) in the US. These, let's not forget, were the early days of what was then thankfully wrongly described as the 'AIDS epidemic' (often callously dismissed as a 'gay plague' – much to the amusement of Madge). My memories of this particular day are tinged by the sad thought that by now, Madge, his liver shot through drinking and apparently endless casual sex, may well have had the disease himself. One of the most alarming statistics Mike read out was that some 50 per cent of New Yorkers under 30 were now herpes sufferers. 'Bloody hell, these yanks don't do things by halves,' he said, a visibly appalled look on his face.

Also in my Movenpick top ten is Madge and his apparently bottomless (pun intended, he'd have appreciated the wordplay) treasure trove of rough trade tales. The merest mention of sex, and Madge would begin gleefully filling in any gaps in our knowledge about what the UK's tabloid press then still laughably referred to as 'London's seedy gay underbelly'.

The climax to his story about an acquaintance he claimed liked to place live budgerigars into wellington boots he would wear during vigorous sex sessions was especially gruesome. At *la moment critique*, Madge's mate would apparently stamp the wellies hard against the bedstead with presumably fatal consequences for both blameless birds.

Madge's bittersweet *piece de resistance* from around the Movenpick pool concerned an 'ageing queen', two royal guardsmen and a saucepan of eggs benedict. More than half a lifetime since Madge, lips positively smacking with relish, first span me the yarn, the mere mention of his 'stately homo' homey's favourite dish continues to leave a bad taste in my mouth.

It seems Madge's lonely friend Victor used to conduct regular nocturnal trawlings of Hampstead Heath in search of potential playmates. Most nights, the pensionable one would strike up a conversation with like-minded young squaddies from the Mounted Regiment of the Household Cavalry. His ultimate hope was to bring whatever new friends he made back to what Madge mischievously described as his 'poky little bedsit' for a little mounting of his own.

One night, the old letch struck gold in the

'bouncy bounty stakes', returning home with not one but two of what Madge unforgettably described as 'incredibly buff although sadly not bear-skinned young buckos'.

Alas, it seems that despite his penchant for sexually ambivalent members of Her Majesty's armed forces, Victor's regimental flagpole rarely ever stood up straight and true. This rather limited his attempts at heavy petting to a couple of clumsy minutes on the sofa. His sexual urges apparently sated for the night, the old queen usually repaired to his flat's tiny kitchenette to whip up a snack for his latest paramours.

Left to their own devices as their host busied himself elsewhere, this particular evening's two young stud muffins spent the next God knows how long admiring knick-knacks and exchanging small talk. Every doodad and back issue of the *Spartacus Gay Guide* sandpapered bare of possible topics of conversation, the first of the soldiers remarked upon the unusually long time Victor had been gone. It was quickly agreed that he would enter the kitchenette to make sure the old roué hadn't fallen over and knocked himself out or spontaneously combusted.

Kitchen door delicately opened, the soldier was horrified by the sight of the elderly cottaging king enthusiastically – if fruitlessly – masturbating into a steaming saucepan of hollandaise sauce garnish. Pausing only to give Victor a good kicking (something Madge invariably referred to as the 'cost of doing business in gay circles, darling'), the pair fled into the night.

My last – and least happy – recollection of our poolside afternoons came the day the calm of our post-lunch siestas was shattered by the anguished wailing of a large Egyptian lady. Gesticulating wildly at the centre of the pool, the increasingly hysterical woman eventually succeeded in attracting the attention of a lifeguard, who promptly began urging everyone out of the water.

I say everyone, but there was one tiny bather who seemed deaf to the lifeguard's instructions and remained worryingly motionless in the pool after his fellow swimmers had hauled themselves out. As the woman's keening grew more piercing, it became horrifyingly apparent the boy wouldn't be swimming to its edge anytime soon.

It's often said that losing one's child is the most unimaginable pain any of us can suffer. The look on the poor mother's face as the newly arrived paramedics frantically tried to breathe life into a shell from which it had departed was one of the most heart-breaking sights I think I've ever seen. Eventually, the two men shook their heads in defeat.

Tenderly placing and covering the dead boy's body on a hospital gurney, they incredibly gently ushered their formerly vibrant cargo and his distraught mother away.

***

In closed environments such as public schools and army barracks, it's inevitable that someone – usually the person least equipped to defend themselves – draws the short straw and becomes everyone else's whipping boy. The four-apartment space in which Crown regularly squeezed as many as a dozen young and, for the most part, extremely sexually frustrated males was no exception. With his permanent 'Why me?' expression of suffering and thinning hair, poor Jeremy Hindley was a shoo-in as the agency's designated punchbag for the year or so our stays in Jeddah overlapped.

As unsavoury as he found Madge's endless litany of explicit anecdotes (later replenished with regular replies from a 'Pen pals wanted' ad in *Gay News*), Bone Dome wasn't without – ahem – 'manly needs' of his own. He eventually brought still more opprobrium crashing down around his ears after returning home from the fleshpots of Thailand pledging his undying love for a bar girl called 'Po'.

Barely had the single-syllable name of his new soulmate escaped Jeremy's mouth than she had been cruelly nicknamed 'Gazunda' (as in 'goes under the bed') by Mike and John. JH had apparently met the love of his life while visiting Bangkok's 'notorious' (there seems to be some law that red light areas are always described thus) *Soi Cowboy* district. Having paid Po's *mama-san* (female pimp) a hefty bar fine, he'd then taken his conquest back to his hotel and foolishly fallen hairless-head-over-heels in love with her.

Oscar Wilde once remarked, 'Sex is the price that women pay for marriage and marriage is the price that men pay for sex.' Substitute the word 'money' for 'marriage', and you get some idea of the dynamic at work in Thailand's sleaziest girly bars.

Typically sold into prostitution by unimaginably impoverished families, the girls here simply dream of snaring a hopefully wealthy *farang* (Westerner) who'll take them away from their abject lives. Far from abandoning those who so cruelly exploited them, they usually continue to support their families by leeching off their new partners. Ultimately, life in Thailand's backwoods and boondocks is so backwards that even the most dirt-poor white-trash European, American, or Aussie soon starts looking like the International Monetary Fund on legs.

Her relationship with Jeremy having survived the few nights of Singha-beer-fuelled 'Let's get jiggy!' fumblings and fuckings, Po had begun laying the groundwork for a lifelong payday. Hardly had JH's return flight from Bangkok taken off for Jeddah than his new inamorata began penning urgent appeals for Thai baht on an almost daily basis. Soon, even Jeremy's cruellest tormentors had begun advising him that Po's vagina was effectively a yawning maw that would eat up every last riyal of his hard-earned Saudi savings.

Deaf to everyone's perfectly sensible urgings, Jeremy took his new sweetheart's mainly Thai-language missives to the country's embassy for translation. With a sigh and seen-it-all-before shrug, the Thai official there told him that he was wasting both his time and his money. Undeterred, Jeremy continued to despatch funds to Bangkok, and eventually, he and Po got married. After leaving Saudi, he cut all ties with his former colleagues and few remaining Jeddah friends.

Despite my never having been especially unpleasant to him, and his living quite near my sister, JH never answered my suggestions we meet for catch-up drinks the first few times I was home. While I've seen many similar relationships flounder, I always felt a bit sorry for JH, and I hope he and Po managed to achieve some kind of happiness wherever their lives took them.

***

Although nowhere near as full of between-the-sheets horizontal fun as JH's, my own first getaway was equally noteworthy. Frustratingly, the kingdom's major *Eid Al Fitr* break fell at the end of Ramadan just a month or so after I'd arrived.

Despite my not having had a proper holiday since 1975, this was way too early for me to have made any appreciable dent in the sizeable debt I owed my folks. Stuck in the apartment, my kidneys, liver, and I hunkered down for a teetotal and hopefully efficacious week of reading and watching videos instead.

Happily, it was only a few months before the kingdom began readying its glad rags for its second big holiday of *Eid Al Adha* at the end of the annual *Hajj* pilgrimage. It's around this time every year that Jeddah's King Abdulaziz International Airport (KAIA) is swamped with millions of devout Muslims bound for Makkah.

The only one of the five pillars of Islam dependent on one's financial well-being, the pilgrimage is a spiritual high that forever burns brightly in the hearts of all who can afford it. For the hundreds of *Hajji* pilgrims who die in the fires that regularly sweep through the airport's magnificent tented city before they even reach Makkah, 'burning brightly' has an altogether more sinister meaning.

Although only 54 miles from Jeddah, Makkah was totally off limits to infidels such as those whose bouts of frenzied boozing were inconsiderately interrupted by stints at Clown. Whilst Graeme, John, Mike, Madge, and I did once drive up to and around the city, the heavily armed guards who policed its gates represented a convincing argument against trying to gain admission. Too attached to our heads and other extremities, none of us wanted to risk chancing our arms and aping the pilgrims who threw stones at the devil.

The only apparent instance of unbelievers entering the holy city came during November 1979 after firebrand preacher Juhayman al-Otaibi and a mob of armed militant Islamists seized and occupied its holiest buildings. Angered by their belief that the House of Saud no longer represented Islam and had corrupted the *Masjid al-Haram* (Sacred Mosque) and *Kaaba*, the hardliners held tens of thousands of pilgrims hostage.

Predictably too shit-scared to try and tackle the problem themselves, the country's ruling family dithered about what to do for the best part of two weeks. Eventually, the authorities gave a bunch of elite French GIGN commandos a special dispensation to assist various Pakistani forces in storming into the city and doing their dirty work for them. The sacred sites duly liberated, back down slammed the shutters.

After four months of squirreling away every penny I could to repay my parents, I had resolved to go somewhere spectacular the moment I was out of the red. Having always wanted to see the pyramids and the great museums of Cairo, deciding to visit nearby Egypt was something of a no-brain-er. Happily, by the time *Eid Al Adha* rolled around in autumn 1981, I'd finally repaid sufficient money to be confident that I could soon be debt-free. I am proud to say I have avoided veering off that particular stretch of straight and narrow ever since.

While it seems almost impossible to believe in a world where Wi-Fi and web pages are the norm, booking a holiday in the early 1980s was a real nightmare. Of course, living in a near-dictatorship where the twin curses of paranoia and censorship ran rampant didn't help when trying to obtain telexes confirming one's flights and hotels. Saudi Arabia was then (altogether now, probably still is) one of the very few countries that not only required a visa to enter but also a stamp in one's passport to leave. The latter was usually done by paying Mohammed, the office fixer, to visit various official offices and make incomprehensible and seemingly immovable bureaucratic mountains disappear on your behalf.

Bribes (sorry 'facilitation charges') paid and paperwork all present and correct, I headed off for the airport late in the afternoon of Tuesday, October 6, 1981 (or *Dhu al-Hijjah* 8, 1401 if you lived in Saudi and followed the *Hijri* calendar).

With no bars, few restaurants, and – amazingly for a travel hub frequented by bargain-mad labourers journeying home to Third World countries – precious few shops, KAIA was then international aviation's least passenger-friendly airport. Still, not to worry! After waiting over six years to go on holiday, what were a couple more hours in a departure lounge – even one that offered so little to occupy the bored traveller's mind.

There are few more exasperating aspects of flying than the news that one's flight has been pushed back for the nth time when 'n' is a very large number indeed. What makes such irritations infinitely worse is airlines' annoying habit of endlessly postponing take-offs in increments of between 30 and 120 minutes until the point at which everybody's patience is about to snap.

Each new stated delay almost ended, the formerly moribund airport departure board creepily reanimates, and – hey presto – another two hours has been magically added to your journey.

Even more annoying when you are champing at the bit to escape countries like Saudi are those nagging worries that aren't quite so easily allayed. Are my papers really in order? Will I get stopped at passport control and turned back for some minor or imagined infraction? Worse still, will I get shoved in jail and left to rot there for no other reason than I'm a shameless 'ho' the Saudis can do with as they choose?

In no time at all, the book I'd taken to read was finished, and I'd grown heartily sick of the sight and taste of inedible food washed down with cans of lukewarm 7 Up. Annoyingly, it would wind up being nearly six hours before we were finally ushered onboard our two-hour and 10-minute flight. Once safely out of Saudi airspace, I sparked up a fag and indulged in my first hygienically distilled and properly brewed drinks since leaving Manchester at the start of the summer. Come hell or high water, I was determined to enjoy every last minute of my holiday.

Like the man says, 'if you want to make God laugh, just tell him your plans.'

Despite our arrival being scheduled for 8:00 pm, the unexplained on-the-ground delays meant it was past 4:00 am before we were decanted into Cairo's Matār El Qāhira El Dawly Airport's cheerlessly shabby arrivals hall. It was around about now that the old adage that 'if things can get worse, they almost certainly will' really started to kick in with a vengeance.

To live outside the UK is to enter a world filled with whingeing Brits who travel loaded down with the unreasonable expectation that everything should be just like it is at 'home'. While I've never been big on rending my garments and gnashing my teeth, it's surely not unrealistic to expect that taxi drivers serving international airports have some grasp of their home cities' geographies.

Not in Cairo they don't. After waiting almost 90

minutes for a ride, I found myself sharing a taxi driven by probably the only cabbie in Northern Africa whose English was worse than my Arabic. Understandably resistant to driver Ali's promises of 'nice, clean girls', my non-English-speaking fellow traveller got out at a hotel about halfway into town. 'The President Hotel, Zamalak!' – I then instructed Ali with more confidence than I felt.

Rattling through Cairo's eerily deserted streets, our Egyptian Robin *'Confessions of a Cab Driver'* Asquith merely nodded his head sagely and said, 'Shiratun! Yes, we go Shiratun! Viry good hotel! Mehny, mehny Wisterrn jeernalists thir!'

'No, no, not the Sheraton, the President, the President Hotel, Zamalek!' I said to little effect. At that moment, realisation slowly dawned. 'President Sadat, President Hotel!' I beamed, satisfied that at last, my message must have achieved some easily understandable local context.

No sooner had it lit up than my lightbulb pinged back into darkness. Having briefly skimmed through coverage of Sadat's rather heavy-handed dealings with the country's sizeable Coptic population only days before, a rather unpleasant truth slowly began to dawn on me. Perhaps the good president wasn't as popular with his people as those of us in the West had been led to believe.

Ali's next foray into the worryingly deep and fast-running waters of the conversation I'd just initiated was even more baffling. 'President Sadat, he mad! Mad! Bangabangabanga! Mad!' Ali jabbered excitedly. Taking one hand off the steering wheel, he then mutated into full Travis Bickle mode as he mimed a gun being shot. Perhaps my new friend knew more English than he was letting on and was trying to share his insider's take on Cairo's always rather fervid local political scene.

It was just as dawn began to illuminate the city that – more by luck than judgement – I caught a glimpse of a street sign reading 'Zamalek'. Within minutes, I was at the President Hotel's reception and – fuck the expense and eye-watering hotel mark-up - ordering a bottle of Johnnie Walker Black.

'Has something perhaps happened in relation to President Sadat recently?' I enquired, bleary-eyed, of the hotel's night manager.

'President Sadat was assassinated yesterday afternoon,' I was told.

Incredibly, despite my late arrival and their having been inundated with last-minute reservation requests from overseas hacks, the hotel had honoured my booking. Up to my room, I went. Unscrewing the top of the bottle, I took an unhealthily large glug of Mr. Walker's finest and silently cursed the country's recently deceased supreme leader.

With the day – as presumably all days in Cairo do – dawning bright and sunny as I finally prepared to hit the sack, I poured myself a second generous slug of Scotch and drifted off to sleep.

With no CNN and endlessly looped highlights from Sadat's life on every TV station, all Egypt seemed to have succumbed to the Princess Di-like grief that would sweep the UK 16 years later. Outside the hotel, anyone miraculously unaware of the previous day's massacre of not only Sadat but also 11 other people would not have noticed anything amiss.

The prospect of a lip-smacking eight full days of fun ahead of me, I decided to use what remained of my first morning in Cairo to get acquainted with the city. Once I had my bearings and knew my way around, I'd spend the afternoon exploring Egypt's apparently magnificent main museum. The next two days were then earmarked for discovering the ancient excavations at Memphis and Saqqara followed by the Giza pyramid complex. If I could manage to swing myself a ticket and hotel, I planned on spending my remaining four full days on a cruise down to the Valley of the Kings at Luxor.

First, though, I would score some hash. While the years have taught me that buying dope in Third World countries is rarely ever a sensible thing to do, my folks were still alive, and I was still full of piss and vinegar back then. Eventually, I found a taxi driver who would sell me a half an ounce of what proved to be very, very potent oily black cannabis resin.

As skins proved almost impossible to come by, I would chow down on chunks of the foul-tasting dope before I left the hotel each day. Although eating hash is never pleasant, its high is far more intense and sustained than that delivered by smoking. Best not think too hard about the unspeakable bodily nooks and crannies your stash might have visited on its journey from its growing region to your gullet, though.

Largely spent in Cairo's Museum of Egyptian Antiquities, day one of my long-overdue holiday was a blast. As were my subsequent trips around the thousands-of-years-old burial grounds at Memphis and Saqqara on day two. Filled with pleasant dope highs and delicious Arab *mezzes* washed down by bottle after bottle of Egyptian Stella (no relation to Artois) beer, everything about my break was going gangbusters.

But (and no matter how fulsome the praise that has gone before, a but there will always be), nothing nice ever lasts forever. In my case, the warm, fuzzy feeling didn't even manage to saunter into the second half of my holiday.

The real trouble started when I hired a taxi driver called Mahmood and visited the Giza Pyramids on the third afternoon of my trip. In those days, it was still possible to take a guided tour that involved a visit to a burial chamber deep inside the giant Khufu (Cheops) Pyramid.

Although then goggle-eyed with fascination at the prospect of being able to experience something so strangely timeless, I now wonder why any sane person would want to do such a thing. My only mitigation is that my younger self was full of more derring-do than the less-trusting ancient who totters the earth all these years later. Given the large chunk of hash I had ingested with my breakfast, I was also by this point laid back to the point of almost being horizontal. The end result was I was putty in Mahmood's piastre-magnetic hands when asked to cough up the several large denomination notes needed to join the next tour group.

There followed what seemed like an eternity of crawling up and down a never-ending warren of tunnels so cramped only a two-thousand-year-old midget could have stood up inside them. Eventually, we came upon a chamber that measured about 15 feet wide by 15 feet long and a further 15 feet tall. Flaming torch in hand like a guide in a mummy movie from Hammer Horror's 1960s heyday, our tour guide flung his arms wide with a flourish. Standing back, he ushered me and my three or four fellow tourists to enter the attraction we had taken such great pains to visit.

However flip I might sound in the paragraph above, entering the abandoned burial chamber remains amongst the most extraordinary things

I've ever done. Words simply can't begin to describe to just how crushing the weight of the thousands of years of history accumulated in the stones all around us felt as it pressed down. Still overawed as my tour group eventually blinked its way back into the brightness of the 'modern world', I wanted nothing more than to go and sit down for a half an hour.

It still being fairly early, I sensibly declined the offer of the latest in what was fast becoming a conveyer belt of bottles of Stella and ordered up a lemonade. Expecting a bottle of fizzy pop, I was rather surprised to be given an enticingly moisture-beaded glass of cloudy-looking lemon juice with ice and a straw peeking jauntily over its rim.

Too busy congratulating myself on my abstemiousness, I foolishly forgot everyone's advice to only drink liquids that had been a) boiled or b) poured from bottles/cans I myself had opened. Greedily gulping down the entire glass with relish, I ordered a second helping. The hideous yawing and rolling of my gut in the taxi back to town soon convinced me that – like so many allegedly 'wholesome' practices – temperance ain't all it's cracked up to be.

Once safely back inside my room, I made a run for the toilet that would not have disgraced multiple Gold medal-winning Olympic athlete, Carl Lewis. Effectively welded to the seat of the loo, I promptly voided what looked and felt like the entire contents of the Blue Nile from my beleaguered bowels.

Ordeal finally over, I weakly teetered to and fell onto my bed only for the distressing pitching and plunging business to start afresh. Back to the toilet, I heaved my aching body for a fresh round of anal gushing. Once back in bed, everything kept on repeating like some spin cycle from hell's busiest laundromat.

Unable to concentrate enough to read, I turned on the in-room TV. An irritating precursor of today's endless 24/7 news cycle, the highlights from the career of the newly deceased President Sadat began parading past my eyes in an endless loop. The next several days were a blur of frequently thankless trips to the toilet accompanied by highlights from Sadat's life, with consistently distressing outcomes for both myself and the late president.

By the time I was strong enough to stand on my own two feet and actually venture any further than the hotel lobby, I was something of an expert in President Sadat's life and times. Had I entered TV's *Mastermind*, I'd have been a shoo-in for whatever grand prize was on offer that year. Pity that my hard-won knowledge was unlikely to impress the locals as it was by now far too late for anything bar my flight back to Jeddah.

Sunk back in the back of the taxi on the way to the airport, I declined my latest taxi driver's well-meaning offers of still more potent hash and nice, clean girls. My brain still befuddled by my bout of chronic diarrhoea cum dysentery, the piastre finally dropped. My trouser pocket still housed the considerable remains of the sizeable chunk of dope I'd bought upon my arrival and that my sickness had stopped me from scarfing.

At this point, I was faced with three choices...

Option A: I could revisit the colonial past and patronizingly give the hash to the cabbie as a tip. Given the tight security blanket that had belatedly descended over the city and its airport after Sadat's shooting, this idea was quickly dismissed.

Option B: I could roll down the window and chuck the still rather largish lump of combustible material in the street. Bit of a waste, really, so a no-go.

Option C: I could neck the dope and salvage at least something of my holiday by spending the flight back to Jeddah stoned out of my gourd. Not surprisingly, this far more attractive and enjoyable prospect ended up the winner on the night.

The hash kicked in just as my plane was giving that worrying pre-death rattle that aircraft invariably emit as they hurtle down the runway towards take-off.

Expecting a gentle plateauing-off similar to that produced by the hash I'd sometimes chomped in the UK, I was in for a nasty shock. The intoxicating effects of the Egyptian variant were growing even more intense with every mile our plane moved closer to Jeddah. Rushing to the toilet, I was horrified to discover just how red the whites of my eyes had become and how reluctant my sickness-ravaged body was to expel the recently swallowed contraband.

There comes a point when almost everyone who has ever smoked or eaten dope experiences 'The Fear' and one's worst anxieties start running rampant. After briefly weighing up my increasingly unappealing options, I returned to my seat to try and spend the remainder of the flight sleeping things off. With visions of my being manhandled while bending over to reach the soap in some hellhole Third World prison washroom filling my head, any Zs I tried to catch proved worryingly elusive. Resistant to the indulgent doting of their mums and dads, the screaming army of pampered brats dotted around cattle class did little to help.

A sleepless, paranoia-packed couple of hours later, I finally arrived in Jeddah Airport's arrival hall just before midnight. While the waves of arriving *Hajji* pilgrims had long since ebbed away, the hall was thronged with returning expat holidaymakers. For once, the fact that the queue for the immigration desk was moving with molasses-like slowness came as very good news. For perhaps only time in my life, I thanked the gods of travel for making the line of arriving passengers so lengthy.

I, it practically goes without saying, was the only person of the hundreds – thousands? – in the whole of the vast arrivals area wearing sunglasses.

Slowly but surely, the queue to which I had gruffly been directed by an armed guard continued to inch slothfully forwards. As we approached the immigration desk, I was horrified to see just how keenly the surly looking official was scrutinising the faces of those handing over their passports for stamping. To try and offset my fears, I was silently rehearsing the cheery hail-fellow, well-met *'kaif halak'* (peace be with you) with which I would greet this Satan of the arrivals stamp.

Each time a new passenger reached the front, my hopes of cursory document processing followed by a dismissive wave through to the luggage retrieval area were dashed. What if this Pound Shop Saddam Hussein did his duty and ordered me to remove my shades? From thence, it was but a small hop, step, and jump to the alarmingly vivid vision of his summoning a phalanx of armed guards to arrest and take me away.

Praise the Lord, the minor Bond villain at the head of my queue was replaced just as the clock clicked over to midnight. The terminally bored jobsworth who took his place simply stamped my passport and waved me through without a second glance. A huge septic tank, Jeddah airport might well have been, but I can honestly say I've rarely if ever been happier to collect my bags and head home.

***

Knowing it represented an inexhaustible fountain of tourist dollars, the Egyptians were at least hanging on tightly to their heritage. Their country awash with petrobucks, the Saudi authorities had no such qualms. I once heard it said that 'to forget who we once were is to lose sight of who we are and might yet become.'

Arrogance and ignorance having been hardwired into their psyches, the Saudis had – as they always did – foolishly chosen to pay no heed to these wise words. In their rush to build themselves a gleaming but ultimately bland and soulless 'urban hub', the country's planners had set about eradicating all traces of the past.

The above development did not bode well for the cheerfully chaotic mess of stalls selling spices, silks, gold, and perfumes, and the beautiful old coral houses that surrounded them in Jeddah's *souk* (bazaar). What made the steady march of progress here even sadder was that the *souk* remained one of the very few areas in Jeddah where it was still possible to feel as though you were stepping into the pages of the tales from *One Thousand and One Arabian Nights*.

But as fascinating as they were, the little alleys and byways jampacked with traders selling impossibly exotic treasures weren't all the *souk* had to offer. One night, the guys from work took me to the area's rear where we saw the humble dwelling T.E. Lawrence had stayed while visiting Jeddah some 60-something years before. 'Take care and drink it all in now while you can, John Boy,' said Graeme. 'It almost certainly won't be here in 10 or 20 years' time.'*

Planners aside, the only threatening cloud in the starlight night skies over the *souk* were routine visits by officers of the country's feared *Mutaween* (religious police).

A muscle-bound arm of the government's wonderfully named Committee for the Promotion of Virtue and Prevention of Vice, dim, unquestioning *Mutaween* officers had been making people's lives a misery since *Hijri* 1359. Now, there's a slogan I wish I'd gotten to write.

As all dictators eventually find out to their cost, there's a gaping chasm between being feared and

---

* Happily, Lawrence House, the last remaining building of Jeddah's former British delegation was still standing at the time of writing. The house where Lawrence actually lived in Yanbu roughly 200 miles up the country's west coast is apparently 'barren' and deserted because of the 'bad feelings' it has engendered in the few who have dared to visit.

being respected. To repeat the well-worn Saudi expat joke: Why do *Mutaween* officers always travel around in threes? The first officer can read, the second one can write, and the third? Well, he's just there to report back to head office on his two intellectual workmates.

When the *muezzin*'s calls to prayer began echoing out of the *souk*'s many surrounding minarets, the only competing sound was the crashing shut of literally hundreds of shop shutters. And woe betide any merchant whose shutters were a split-second late in coming down, or whose 'closed for prayers' sign was slightest bit sluggish in going up.

Equally at risk of the *Mutaween's* unwelcome attentions were any Western females caught braving the cool evening air with an insufficiently covered arm or leg. Especially unlucky girls or women found themselves being daubed with paint in front of a jeering mob of visibly delighted locals before being ordered home in shame.

Aside from one very drunken evening when I was snoozing off my overindulgences in my flatmate Mike's car (of which more later), I managed to steer well clear of the Jeddah constabulary. One of the rare occasions when our paths did cross came one day outside a local supermarket. Having gone there for lunch with Seth, Chris, and I, Greg F decided he wanted to buy a football for kick-arounds at the beach. Ball successfully purchased, he proceeded to attempt a game of keepy-uppy in the mall's carpark. 'Greg, mate, for Christ's sake, give it a rest,' said Seth.

'Why the fuck should I? It's a fucking fr...' replied Greg. Before the erroneous words 'free country' had finished emerging from the mouth of Makaronah Road's Maradona, a jeep loaded with *Mutaween* officers swept magisterially into the car park. Luckily for us, the zealots onboard were too intent on resolving more pressing matters inside the mall than chucking this particular bunch of godless *ajnabis* in the clink. Pausing only to retrieve his ball, our foul-mouthed friend silently jumped into the car, and we all sped back to the office.

Having succeeded in totalling one company car while I was in Saudi, Greg F didn't have a great deal of luck with motors. No surprises then that, his were invariably the last passenger seats waiting to be filled at the start and end of each working day. His perceived lack of skill behind the wheel was not helped by his dreadful taste in music.

One morning, nursing predictably colossal sid-and-unfermented-red-wine refluxes, a gaggle of us reluctantly squeezed into the passenger compartment of the Gregster's Hyundai Pony. Right hand on the wheel to help him career in and out of the city's godawful traffic, Greg fumbled for a tape.

Soon, a tinny recreation of the unmistakable wak-ka-wakka-wakka intro to Kool and the Gang's 'Celebration Time' began dribbling out of the Pony's tiny speakers.

'Sel-uh-bray-shun tahm! Kurm-on!' Greg tunelessly bellowed, pounding time on the roof of the car with the hand the end of his exertions with the tape deck had suddenly freed up.

'Sel-uh-bray...' our driver's tin-eared first-degree murdering of the early 1980s disco classic continued unabated until Graeme's hand snaked out to the tape deck. Before Greg could object, Graeme had ejected the cassette. Barely missing a beat, he'd opened the window and thrown the tape beneath the wheels of an oncoming articulated-lorry. Stunned by what was an astonishingly fluid movement for one so obviously still crocked from the night before, even Greg was stymied from his usual effing and jeffing.

**

When I arrived in Jeddah, I was full of good intentions such as staying off the booze, getting fit, and finishing all the classic books everyone says they'll start but somehow never does. Who knows, maybe I'd even discover the get-up-and-go needed to write one of my own – even if it did eventually take me the best part of 35 years before Mr. Pen began impregnating Ms. Paper.

One of the most ambitious targets I'd set

myself was learning to drive. In common with many failed novices, my initial behind-the-wheel fumblings and bumblings had been with my dad. And in common with many failed novices, my early attempts at mastering the tricky art of clutch control and moving off were – like the family car's gearbox – doomed to be ground into submission.

While obviously less life-wrecking than incest, murder, or country dancing, asking a loved one to teach you to drive is one of the worst decisions it's possible to make. Ultimately, everything but everything in the car that goes wrong (or gently hints it might be about to go wrong at some indeterminate future date) becomes your fault.

Soon, money became tighter, and my reasons for learning to drive became less pressing. When studying at Hull University, for example, a much younger and fitter me had cycled pretty much everywhere. After my move to Manchester, the bus service was so frequent and dependable, I soon had less and less need to get behind the wheel.

Jeddah, I determined, would be different.

Needless to say, it wasn't. The traffic in the city was an absolute nightmare, with no one seeming to pay the slightest attention to even the most basic rule of the road – stopping at red lights.

There was one story – possibly apocryphal, but there were invariably kernels of truth in most tales about Saudi – regarding said lights' introduction to the country's streets a decade or so before. Not too long after the kingdom's first light blinked into life came the inevitable first accident. It seemed an experienced expat driver had complied with the red light at a crossroads by only moving off after it had changed to green.

As the expat pulled away, a local's unnecessarily ostentatious American glitzmobile had smashed into and demolished the side of his bog-standard company-issue Japanese saloon. Come the expat's day in court, it was inevitably he, and not the local, who ended up getting fined. As the beak apparently ruled in no uncertain terms: 'The lights are there for you foreigners to obey and not us Saudis.'

The other classic tale about driving, Saudi-style, was told to me by an expat who worked in the marketing department of the local BMW concession. It seemed that one of the hundreds of Saudi princes with too much money and too little sense had taken his *habbibi* (special 'friend') out of town for a spin in his spanking-new state-of-the-art BMW. Assuming that the car's cruise control was an auto-pilot, our sex-starved Saudi prince and his main squeeze had clambered in the back for a bit of cuddling and canoodling.

But as long and straight as they were, even the broadest highways in Saudi sometimes encountered the occasional curve. And so it was that BMW, prince, and pal ended up impacted in a tangled mess at the bottom of a dried-up *wadi* (river).

By the early 1980s, Saudi's road safety casualty levels had soared so alarmingly high that Jeddah's municipal government had started running campaigns urging everyone to drive more safely. Booker Prize-winning author Hilary Mantel was one of those around to witness the early results. In her wonderfully evocative 1988 novel, *Eight Months on Ghazzah Street*, HM rather waspishly recounts one of the major gimmicks used to attract attention. Unfortunately, despite visually screaming, 'Avoid Distractions! Keep Your Eyes on the Road!' the billboards the municipality erected around the city wound up causing more crashes than they prevented.

Totally unfazed by the failure of their first strategy, the authorities, in their infinite wisdom, next decided to do away with words altogether. By the time I moved to Saudi, they'd hit upon on a can't-miss plan in which eye-catching displays of wrecked cars were placed at major intersections. Amusingly – well, perhaps not if you were rear-ended in one of the resultant pile-ups – accident levels once again rose rather than fell.

A few juddering stops and starts along the beach aside, the reason I skipped learning to drive in Saudi was whatever misfortune might befall me should I cause a minor fender bender. Or even more worryingly, what calamities lay in store if I ran someone over and seriously injured or killed them.

Were you ever to find yourself behind the wheel of a car in which you had just knocked someone down, the advice of old Jeddah hands was un-equivocal. Reverse back over your victim to make sure they were dead before accelerating the fuck away from the scene as fast as humanly possible. Drivers 'stupid' (the old-timers' words, not mine) enough to stick around after hitting someone were faced with just two choices: take out a standing order to pay 'blood money' to their victim and his family, or start making arrangements for a lengthy stretch at King Fahd's pleasure.

At the end of the day, money didn't just talk, walk, and dance in Saudi Arabia – it also drove. That was certainly true of the locals – every man jack of whom seemed to have their own car, or – if especially poor – an open-back Toyota Hilux truck. Prohibited from driving until 2017, women weren't nearly so lucky.

The Filipinos, Indians, Koreans, Pakistanis, and Yemenis who made up the underpaid underbelly without which the kingdom would have ground to a halt had drawn even shorter straws. With the average 'blood money' payable for seriously harming or killing a 'TWN' labourer then roughly R35,000 (about £4,500), their lives were worth less than many Westerners' average monthly salaries. While I never did meet anyone who admitted to committing vehicular manslaughter, conventional wisdom had it that paying cash was infinitely preferable to prison.

Mercifully, the only time I did come close to adding several days, weeks, months, or even years to my stay in Jeddah occurred after a party across town. Several stations past plastered on the sid-fuelled Oblivion Express, I was sawing logs in the back seat of a car belonging to my flatmate, Mike.

For whatever reason, Mike got pulled over by the traffic police, who, catching their first sight of my prone body, somehow got it into their heads that I'd 'had drink taken'. Luckily, my quick-thinking flatmate managed to persuade the senior of the two officers that I was 'tired and emotional' after a long trip back from Europe. Thanks to Mike, the two cops gave me the benefit of the doubt, and we got home safe, if not quite dry.

A good friend and boozing buddy called 'Connor' wound up being not nearly so lucky.

One Friday during my second year in Jeddah (the one for greed), our Moslem-convert colleague, Dawud, threw a party to celebrate his upcoming marriage to a lovely Filipina woman called 'Belinda'. With mucho – for once crystal clear – red wine and Sid'n'7 having been consumed by all, the soiree was all sweetness and light.

Although there were still ample supplies left, Connor decided that more sid was needed urgently and that he was the man to get it. Foolishly disregarding everyone else's advice to stay put, he slid behind the wheel of an American car the size of a football pitch and promptly roared off into the late afternoon.

Had this been one of those films where the passage of time is symbolised by a clock on the wall, its hands would have started spinning at disorientingly dizzying speed. This being Jeddah on the weekend, the only clocklike items present were the various round bottles, cans, and glasses on the table that had spent the afternoon being steadily emptied.

An hour passed, and then two, with neither hide nor hair of our bosom boozing buddy. By now, we were all starting to get seriously worried. With almost everyone having attained the fourth (invulnerable) stage of drunkenness[*], none of us voiced any fears that Connor might have been hauled in by the cops. No, our biggest concern was that he had gone MIA as a result of some sort of problem at home. Only much later that evening did Connor's colleague 'Smithy' (a.k.a. 'Smudger', what else?) learn that his flatmate would not be coming home that night. Nor, it turned out, was he likely to be

---

[*] I am reliably informed the five stages are: intelligent, irresistible, infallible, invulnerable and invisible.

coming home any other night for the foreseeable future.

The next day, Smudger rang around to share the grim news that Connor had been pulled over for some minor traffic violation. In the great scheme of things, this would have been no biggie. Unfortunately, the attending officers had found a four-gallon plastic container full of uncut sid in the boot of his car.

A proudly forthright Northern Irishman whose uncompromising nature meant he had not enjoyed the best of relationships with his slapdash Saudi sponsor, our mate had landed himself eyebrow-deep in effluent.

To describe poor Connor's imprisonment in Jeddah's central jail as being a serious spot of bother is to trivialize his plight. The only positive aspect of his awaiting trial was that he was allowed far more visits than if he had been sentenced to a lengthy spell

of incarceration. But surely the British embassy couldn't and wouldn't allow such a thing to happen to one of the subjects in its care?

It not only could – it would and it did.

Then very probably the only British embassy in the world to be located outside a capital city, Britain's Jeddah diplomatic mission responded with uncharacteristic speed. Early on during

Connor's incarceration, a low-ranking Foreign Office dogsbody sat him down in the prison governor's office and given him a harsh lesson in the facts of life, Jeddah-style.

Given the booze-related nature of Connor's 'crime', it seemed Britain could not be seen to intervene with any offer of meaningful assistance. To do so would be to further damage bilateral trading ties already seriously harmed by the Helen Smith and *Death of a Princess* scandals.

Between busily and ineffectually wringing hands he assured our friend were bound tightly 'at the highest level', the junior diplomat did, however, have a favour to ask...

Back then, the swingeing sentences doled out to expats found guilty of alcohol-related offences were often greatly reduced or totally waived if the offender accepted a public flogging outside the prison gates. While a welcome combined 'get out of jail' card and one-way ticket home for those who accepted, such lashings inevitably whipped the UK tabloid press into a frenzy of self-righteousness. Hence the government's need of a favour.

Given that such publicity was terrible for both Britain and Saudi, would Connor perhaps 'do the decent thing' and respectfully decline the authorities' offer of corporal punishment and early release? Immune from Mrs. Thatcher's eagerness to sell the Saudis more military aircraft, tanks and missiles, Connor despatched the flunky with a choice array of Empty Quarter-sized obscenities ringing in his ears.

Shortly before his formal sentencing, Graeme and I joined Smudger on a visit to see Connor in chokey. Accustomed to meeting our friend in the reasonably civilized setting of the governor's office, our hackles began rising when we were herded instead to a decrepit-looking cement cell block. The building measured about 30 feet wide by 80 feet long and had two elderly looking wall-mounted aircon units on each side to cool its four dozen or so Western occupants.

Inside was a small 'reception area' housing a cage measuring roughly eight feet high by 10 feet wide and six feet deep. Gouged out of its rear wall was a roughly hewn hole of about three feet by four feet at which were pressed the haggard, haunted faces of dozens of prisoners.

Occupying every available inch of space to the hole's front and side could be heard a baying mob whose members were desperately trying to attract the attention of a bored-looking Pakistani guard. In Saudi Arabia, virtually every menial job was and is doubtless still done by a foreigner – the locals being way too precious to perform any kind of demeaning task themselves[*].

Randomly snatching parcels from visitors' outstretched hands, the guard would tear off wrappings and contemptuously drop the bulk of the food, books, and toiletries inside on the filthy floor at his feet. The scant remains of each package would then be disdainfully tossed into the melee of those desperately trying to see and be seen through their sole remaining window on the world.

An unspoken 'There but for the grace of God...' hanging heavy in the air, we walked disconsolately back to our car. 'You think that's bad,' said Smudger, 'have a quick *shufti* (look) at the next cellblock!'

Twenty or so yards to the left was another building of roughly the same size and dimensions as the one in which Connor now languished. It took a few seconds of double takes to realize that this hut housed two or three times as many prisoners and had no aircons at all.

With the relentless midday heat of Jeddah seldom dropping below 35 degrees Celsius, one cannot begin to imagine just how dire life inside this awful structure must have been. Even more in-

---

[*] In 2018, reports started leaking out from the Kingdom that the economy had become so bad, poorer Saudis had started taking menial jobs such as working behind the counter of fast-food restaurants. McDonalds' outlets in the Kingdom remain the only ones in the world to sell giant-sized portions of humble pie.

excusable was the fact the hundred or so Indians, Filipinos, Pakistanis, Yemenis, and Koreans interned inside had all been left to rot by their employers and governments.

Outside the prison, we were shouted at by an orange-haired Pakistani labourer who began taunting us about the might of the Islamic world's Sharia justice system in broken English. So distressed was Smudger by what he had just seen that he thrust the gloating man against a nearby wall in order to start pounding the shit out of him. Had the rest of us not managed to intervene, the three of us might soon have found ourselves adding to the overcrowding in Connor's cell.

Fortunately, our car had been swallowed up by a plume of dust before Mr. Orange managed to pull himself together and summon Sheriff Sharia and his not-so-merry men to form a posse.

While it very rarely happens, life is sometimes generous enough to give you an unmistakable sign that it's time to cut and run. My experience with Jeff Kirkham in Outside Collection in Coventry seven years before had been one such portent. Here, halfway around the world, was another. With my need-and-greed years almost over and one very narrow escape from incarceration still fresh in my mind, it was time to get the hell outta Saudi.

Chapter Five

Shit or get off the pot

If my own recent brush with the law hadn't been enough of a wake-up call, Connor's gaoling symbolised my groggily awakening to find a dozen *Mutaween* officers standing over my bed. Needless to say, the prospect of Ahmed Law's shouting '*Ahlan! Ahlan! Ahlan!*' *(Hallo! Hallo! Hallo!)* What's this big dustbin filled with scummy red liquid doing in your airing cupboard, then?' in my face was not at all attractive.

Despite my initial intention to return to the UK at the end of my needy and greedy years, my desire to do so was diminishing with every passing day. The big question now was 'Where to next?' Luckily, to paraphrase the late, great Marty Feldman, 'The pen isn't only mightier than the sword, it's considerably easier to pack into a suitcase.'

God knows how or where I got hold of overseas agency addresses in Saudi. The incurable romantic in me pictures them in the back of an abandoned copy of Asshat's absurd *Saudi Tradeopedia*, where they'd been secreted by Crown's equivalent of the man in the iron mask. In truth, I almost certainly found them in beer-and-fag-ash-stained copies of ad industry trade paper *Campaign* that a colleague had bought back from the UK. Either way, source the addresses, I did, and letters to the most likely employers were despatched about six months before my contract's end. To ensure no one at the agency got wind, I used Jeddah Central Post office at one end and my sister's address in Reading as a sort of clearing house at the other.

The 20-something letters I optimistically cast upon the waters produced just two replies – one of them from an agency in Bahrain called 'ADept'. Whilst the agency currently had no vacancies for a copywriter, they'd be interested in meeting me should I ever find myself on the island (actually an archipelago of 33 smallish islets).

With a holiday due imminently, I scheduled a Bahrain stopover during my upcoming trip to the UK in February 1983. Aside from catching a glimpse of dolphins cavorting in the waters beneath the plane, I remember little of my initial visit save for the fact that I got offered and accepted a job.

When my two years in Jeddah finally ended, I took off for a few days of hard-earned R&R in Cyprus before flying down to Bahrain to start the second stage of my expat career. The fact that the ADept office where I was to spend the next three-and-a-half years resembled – albeit slightly – the ad agencies I'd visited in London seemed promising. But then, even the converted dining room where I'm laboriously pecking out these words looks more like an ad agency than the ramshackle hovel my previous employers had called home.

Despite its recent and, one suspects, terminal descent into the toilet when it comes to human rights, the Bahrain of the early 1980s was a surprisingly pleasant place. Not only were there bars; women were free to work and even drive. Best of all, there was – as yet – no causeway that would admit the drunken Saudi hordes who have long since turned Manama into Basra on a bad night.

The man who ran ADept was, however, very much in line with his Saudi brothers when it came to treating people atrociously. Small wonder long-term staffers had taken to calling the agency 'Inept' when out of his hearting. As he is – at time of writing – still very much alive and has always had a Robert Maxwell-like list of libel lawyers on his speed dial, let's call my new boss 'Manuke Khara'.

Fresh off the plane and with nowhere to hang my hat, Manuke put me up in the agency-owned 'Juffair Hotel' for my first few weeks in Bahrain. While I've never taken advantage of agencies' largesse when visiting unfamiliar places on business, there are certain expenses employers really do have a moral obligation to meet. When you can't cook or clean for yourself, claiming back all (or at least some) of the grotesquely overinflated prices hotels charge for meals and laundry hardly constitutes grand larceny.

Viewing me as modern equivalent of 1960s pools

winner Viv 'Spend! Spend! Spend!' Nicholson, Khara took a dimmer view of the expenses I'd 'run up' during my three-week stay at the Juffair. As a result, I was miffed to discover that in-hotel meals and washing had cost me around a third of my first salary cheque of 550 Bahraini Dinars (BD550 – then about £1,110[*]). As partial owner of both the agency and hotel, my new boss would, of course, collect a sizeable chunk of my bill for the over-priced bed and board.

Any inclination I might have had to chalk Mr. K's avarice up to experience and move on instantly evaporated when I opened my next month's salary. This time around, my wages had been lightened by BD50 in 'caution money' to defray the cost of any fixtures, fittings or equipment I might damage or destroy while at work. Adding another few yards of insults onto Khara's impressively high pile of injuries was the BD2 monthly levy he charged staff for 'perks' such as coffee, toilet paper and office cleaning.

When I visited the company accountant, 'Javid', (apparently later gaoled for embezzlement) to complain, he simply sighed with the exasperation of one who has heard it all before. Everyone, but everyone – including Manuke himself – apparently paid for the privileges of wetting their whistles and wiping their arses.

---

[*] An exchange rate of BD2 = £1 has been used throughout this chapter.

'You don't believe me?' said the accountant. 'Well, here's Mr. Khara's salary statement!' And there, nestled at the bottom of Manuke's four-figure monthly stipend, was the 'deducted BD2 for coffee and toilet paper' message.

Khara's brazenness in screwing trifling sums of money out of his staff was only surpassed by his ability to soft soap big multinational agencies desperate for representation in the Middle East. Any conglomerate falling hook, line, and sinker for Mr. K's promises of partnership happily coughed up a sizeable monthly retainer to secure ADept's undying loyalty.

Like many men who have 'built business empires', Manuke was not only in thrall to the sound of his own voice but also felt everyone else should be, too. The story – greatly embellished a colleague later claimed – of how he had started life selling cold drinks to well-heeled holidaymakers on the beaches of Beirut was amongst his 'Greatest Hits'.

Having been bored rigid by this particular yarn more times than he cared to count, my art director, 'Jack Elliott', took every opportunity to take the piss. After one too many retellings of how our formerly sweat-stained supremo had single-handedly hauled a super-sized esky of cold tinnies up an endless expanse of sun-parched sand, I soon joined in.

One of my favourite Manuke stories occurred the morning that, having endured one yelling match with his boss too many, Jack finally snapped and walked out, vowing never to return. Skipping work for the rest of the day, my partner went home and promptly arranged an interview with a rival agency.

While changing employment visas in Bahrain was a bureaucratic nightmare, Jack's wife, 'Diane', worked for the well-connected local who owned the 51 per cent of ADept that Manuke legally couldn't. As a result, moving companies would not pose the problems it might create for less well-connected salary slaves such as myself.

Having almost certainly worked out Jack's cunning escape plan, Khara was all over our shared office like flies on shit. 'Any sign of Jack?' he enquired breezily just after lunch on the day of the errant art director's dramatic exit. 'Jack still not back yet, then?' he'd quiz me as the afternoon wore on. Come evening, the Soft Drink Sultan of the beaches of Beirut was beginning to get seriously worried.

The next morning, Jack was back at work, and we were discussing some new campaign we'd been asked to develop. Magically popping up out of a previously unseen trapdoor in the office floor, pantomime villain-style, there was Manuke. 'Jack, my son, how lovely to see you. I was looking for you all afternoon yesterday. Where on earth have you been?'

The slightest gleam of purpose in his eye, my want-away mate looked up from what he was doing and said, 'I was seeing a man about a dog, Manuke.'

Pausing only to remove the ever-present Zeppelin-sized cigar from his mouth, Jack's soon-to-be-former boss replied, 'You're buying a dog?'

The 'wall of fame' Manuke lovingly tended in his upstairs office was another source of merriment. It was here that Khara proudly displayed pictures of himself and assorted wannabe slebs in a variety of matey poses and situations. Initially, pride of place in this shrine to the second-rate went to a picture of a sharkskin-suited Khara practically prostrating himself before the Philippines 'Commander in Thief', Ferdinand Marcos.

That the image was a slap in the face for the agency's two Filipino finished artists, whose families' futures Marcos had effectively stolen, did not concern Manuke in the slightest. All that mattered to him was that his VIP happy snap struck the right chord with visiting representatives of 'Philippine Island Express Airways' (PIE). Or at least, it did until the morning of Tuesday, February 25, 1986. Opening the windows of Manila's Malacañang Palace to find a sea of angry Filipinos demanding the return of the billions they'd stolen, the despot and his shoe-addict wife, Imelda, promptly fled.

The next morning, the picture – rather like Ferdy and 'Melda themselves – was nowhere to be seen. While the duplicitous duo eventually resurfaced in Hawaii, the fate of Khara's snap remains as mystifying as the whereabouts of Shergar, or Ed Milliband's famous 'Ed Stone' from the 2015 UK election. Not that this deterred Jack or me from loudly discussing what was missing from the wall the next time Manuke summoned us upstairs for a PIE in the sky meeting.

***

With boozing in Saudi – by necessity – restricted to swigging sid in various jerry-built apartment blocks, Bahrain's comparative abundance of bars promised a much richer social life. Frustratingly, the main watering holes in those pre-King Fahd Causeway days were either bland hotel lounges or godawful cod-themed pubs. The biggest of these, The Sherlock Holmes, was first port of call for sex-starved expat business travellers desperate to hook up with bored Gulf Air cabin attendants (a.k.a. Gulfies).

Often unfairly derided for being as thick as past its sell-by date mince, the Gulfies were a fountain of amusing anecdotes, many of them involving various nationalities' foibles when speaking English. The funniest one I heard was from a girl who'd had to endure the nonstop attentions of a far-from-frequent flier during a flight to Delhi.

Wearying of the snail-paced in-flight service in economy class, our increasingly irate passenger began gesticulating wildly at my friend. 'Missie! Missie!' he began first hissing and then shouting so everyone could hear. Eventually forced to go and try and calm the man, my friend was amazed to hear him say, 'Missie, I've been fingering you for 15 minutes, and still, you have not come!'

Cordially detested by anyone possessing a nodding acquaintance with the concept of excess, theme pubs have always been avoided like the plague by hardened boozers such as myself. The Sherlock Holmes was no exception. Boobtube-deep in Victorian-style swirling pea-souper fog each night (just joking), its bar areas were totally devoid of the sort of lifelong topers I was itching to hang out with. Armed with an Arabian Gulf-sized thirst, it wasn't too long before I fell in with a bunch of likeminded journos from the local *Gulf Daily News (GDN)* English-language daily newspaper.

The hacks' favoured drinking hole was the rather cheerless *shebeen* that was the windowless bar in the Omar Khayam (sic) Hotel A dive, it may well have been, but just a hundred yards away from my flat's front door, the OK quickly became my home-away-from-home for most of my first year in Bahrain.

Despite its close proximity to *chez Fuery*, I was once so incapacitated after a night there that I awoke the next morning in one of the hotel's rooms. While the accommodations at the OK were, like the bar, rather less than lavish, the bill I was presented upon leaving most certainly was not. Including set breakfasts customized by each nationality's apparently favourite beverage – coffee for Americans, tea for Brits and Foster's lager for Aussies – the room service menu did, however, raise a rueful smile.

Regular OK habitués included *GDN* journos such as Peter Welton, David Makinson, and David Fox. Despite his insistence on reducing my credit on articles I later wrote for his paper to first eight- and later six-point type, Peter has remained my closest friend for more than 35 years. Seriously, how can you not be mates with someone who cheerfully sacrificed the bonnet of his car to prove that phew-what-a-scorcher-type stories about frying eggs on unbearably hot sunny days were a bunch of bollocks?

Another intrepid propper-up of the OK bar was 'Jed McTeague', a Scots photographer who always claimed he kept a charred teddy and passport in his camera bag 'just in case'. Shortly after Jed returned to Scotland, teddy proved surplus to requirements when Libyan terrorists provided plenty of alternatives after blowing up Pan Am Flight 103 near his family home in Lockerbie.

Jostling for elbow space at the OK as the nights wore on were several local Arabs. Prominent members of the latter group included a man called 'Asa Al Yagrout', whose cousin 'Shaikh Samir' – another OK regular – was a high-ranking officer in Bahrain's police force. Perhaps the most notable thing about Asa was his not-inconsiderable BD33,000 (then an eye-watering £66,000) bar tab. Probably the most impressive thing about this gargantuan drinks bill was the fact that its owner never once stood me, or indeed, anyone else at the OK, a beer.

Understandably terrified of being gaoled or repatriated to their then unimaginably impoverished homeland, Indian head barman Krishna and his team's only reaction to Asa's barked orders to jump was to ask, 'How high?' On quieter evenings, I sometimes used to amuse myself by surreptitiously watching Krishna's reactions to his regulars. Although concealed by the reflections in his oversized Coke-bottle-thick glasses, K's hatred of his regulars blazed as brightly as the sun that would never penetrate the OK's windowless walls.

Midway through my stay in Bahrain, a chap who would eventually become a good friend, Tony McIver, opened up a pub called The Londoner at Manama's Bristol Hotel. A far-brighter environment than the OK, The Londoner soon started overturning our former watering hole's previously unassailable ranking as Bahrain's hardiest winos' drinks dispenser of choice. As soon as Krishna took the foolish step of barring one of the island's thirstier and more boisterous journos, every other Westerner downed their pints and left the bar for the last time. But tempting as it is to hit another pub for a further round or three, let's call a halt on our mid-afternoon on the piss and reluctantly head back to the office.

***

Having had one argument with Manuke too many, Jack eventually quit, never to darken the agency's door again. Mr. K's short-sightedness in losing Jack was one of the most stupid things he did while I worked for him. I was just one of the many Bahrain newbies that Jack and his wife, Di, took under their wing and into their home for meals and movies until we found our feet. The amount of money their kindness must have saved Khara's agency in return airfares for homesick new arrivals wanting to turn tail and head back to the UK must have been huge.

The salary review I'd been promised when signing my contract – a BD50 (£100) increase after three months – was anything but. With my perfectly reasonable requests for payment falling on deaf ears (Number One of Fuery's Ten Expat Commandments: 'Always get it in writing before you get on the plane!'), I was developing itchy feet myself.

Former OK regular Alan Carcary (now ascended – descended more like – to a realm far, far away from phone lines with libel lawyers' numbers programmed in) couldn't help but note my frustration. About to start a PR/advertising consultancy called 'Sceptre International', Alan dangled the carrot of doubling the unpaid raise Manuke had promised me.

A serial offender in the failing-to-think-things-through stakes and with my reasoning muddied by the contents of a free liquid lunch, I, of course, was easy prey for his spiel.

One minor detail I should have paid more attention to when Alan was exhorting me to 'shit or get off the pot' was Asa Al Yagrout's role as Sceptre's silent partner and co-owner. I also failed to pay sufficient heed to Peter W's caveats about Carcary himself. 'The moment his left eye starts twitching, take whatever he says next with a gigantic sackful of salt,' said Welts in a friendly warning that inevitably soared high over my unheeding head.

Come the first Saturday in February 1984, there I was, seated at a new (well, newish) desk in a brand-spanking-new office. If a fledgeling company's choice of address tells potential clients precisely what kind of people they're dealing with, Sceptre's home some 50 yards from the front door of the Omar Khayam did not augur well.

As we've already discovered, Manuke's view of his perceived eminence differed radically from that held by his staff and industry peers. My short-term departure from ADept shows just how pronounced that variance could be. Having corralled in-house snapper Gregor into photographing myself and several other new arrivals outside the office, Manuke was too tight-fisted to recommission a replacement shoot after I left.

Despite knowing full well that I was mates with most of the island's English-language journos, my former boss simply captioned me with the name of my short-term replacement, 'Phil Spicer'. When the incorrectly captioned press release pix finally arrived at the offices of the *Gulf Mirror* (*GM*) just two stories above the ADept office, much merriment ensued. Indeed, so pronounced was the hilarity caused by my apparent major reconstructive surgery, the paper ran a light-hearted story about it the following week. Rubbing further salt in Manuke's increasingly raw wounds, the rag gleefully concluded by remarking that I was alive, well, and now working for a rival agency.

Incensed by what he saw as being an unwarranted personal attack on his dignity, Khara took to his Dictaphone and fired off a hysterical diatribe to the *GM*'s editor. The angry rant about reporters dying for the truth while battles raged around them duly appeared in the paper's next issue. How a deliberately mis-identified picture of an ex-staffer in a meaningless press release relates to journalistic ethics in wartime is a topic best left for Manuke to explain in his own memoirs.

Even in a life as littered with catastrophically poor decisions as my own, there are inevitably going to be two or three real doozies. My short-lived and extremely ill-fated move to Sceptre (let's do as everyone else who worked there did and call it Septic) was an especially subterranean low in a career positively crammed with suicidal dips.

The extent of the colossal mistake I'd made began to become apparent the moment I joined two of my new colleagues, both of them former *GDN* staffers, on my first day. The first of these was Nick Bevens, a thirsty Scot who remains a good friend to this day, if no longer quite so thirsty. The second was a Bahraini called Younis, who passed away in the late 1980s after apparently indulging in one too many bare-backed rides in Bangkok.

Joining us was in-house photographer Jed McTeague (of charred teddy fame). Usually off in the arse-end-of-nowhere herding senior local salary slaves into groups at various unimaginatively named state-owned enterprises, Jed normally only hit the office at pub o'clock each evening. Of Asa and Alan, there was rarely if ever any sign until just before Krishna whipped the towels off the pumps in the OK bar at around noon. Such chronic timekeeping proved to be especially galling for Nick and Younis – very probably because neither one of them had been paid for about six weeks.

These early days were as close to the good times as it got with Alan and Asa's all-conquering new enterprise, alas. Our main task – filling the in-room guest magazine of Bahrain's pre-eminent five-star hotel – was not made any easier when Alan hired a man called 'Terry Desmond' to sell ad space.

In life, you can either sell or you can't. As Arthur Miller grasped when writing *Death of a Salesman*, the only commodity a salesman or woman can legitimately be said to be selling is him or herself. Unfortunately for all who sailed aboard HMS Septic, Despond Desmond's arrogant, little Englander demeanour was never going to earn the trust of the clients on which his – and our – success depended.

As Jed joked at the time, if Dirty Des had been an iceberg floating in the Atlantic in April 1912, the Titanic would have turned tail and made great haste to sink itself. Looking back now, it beggars belief just how unsuited he was not only to a sales career but also to any kind of expat posting where cultural sensitivity was a pre-requisite.

After first meeting the objectionable little shite, I began to wonder if Carcary hadn't hired him as the result of some kind of booze-fuelled bet that had gone horribly wrong. You think I'm settling scores here? When selling the 'coveted' high-profile back cover of the one issue of the five-star hotel's house mag I got to edit, the only client Despond could find was a pest control company. Not exactly the sort of image or association Bahrain's then premier hotel was trying to create amongst its jet-set clientele of high-spending Arabs and frequent business travellers.

Aside from his *tres* punchable fizzog, the thing I personally found most objectionable about Terry was how he'd been dumped on me as a flatmate. For the three months or I was at Septic, there was to be no escaping his vile smug mug, morning, noon, nor night. Worse still, nor was there any hiding place from his mortifying taste in music.

Crippled by a particularly crushing Friday morning hangover, I once awoke to hear the unmistakably icky parp, parp, parping rhythm of Herb Alpert and his Tijuana Brass. Had Despond stopped filling my flat and, worse still, my head with one run through of the Herbmeister's maddeningly chirpy 'Spanish Flea', I might have let the matter drop. But no. No sooner had one jarring

Ba-dap-da-da-duh-duh-*duuuuur*,

Ba-dap-da-da-duh-duh-*duuuuur*,

Ba-dap-da-da-duh-duh-*duuuuur*,

Daaaah-dap-duuuuur-duuuur-duuuur,

Duuuuuuuuuuur-duuuuuuuuuur-duuuuh-duuuuh,

Duuuuuuuuuuur-duuuuuuuuuur-*DUUUUUUH!*

hook ended for the first time than up it all started again. If my unwanted flatmate was doing his damnedest to try and antagonize me, he was having considerably more success than he was in selling ad space.

Worst of all, too parsimonious to buy a stereo of his own, the wanker was befouling my ears with the expensive and lovingly tended high-end hi-fi I had placed in the living room. Rousing myself from my pit, I wrapped a towel around my then still surprisingly svelte waist and stomped into the living room.

There, standing in front of the hi-fi and energetically air-conducting the massed ranks of the Herbster's mighty horn section, was the Tijuana Asshole himself. The horrified 'O' Dirty Des's mouth formed as I ripped the offending tape from the machine and painstakingly unreeled, stretched, and shredded its brown entrails proved to be a wonderfully efficacious hangover cure. If I could have started bottling, labelling, and selling the rush of endorphins I got that morning, I'd be a millionaire today.

My mind having been blissfully unblemished

by thoughts of Despond and his self-satisfied gurning mug for the best part of three decades before I started to write these memoirs, I turned to my mate Google.

Rather than end up in chokey as the sexual plaything of some musclebound psychopath as I thought – hoped and prayed – he might, Terry went one better. He ended up as a Tory councillor deep in the blue rinse belt south of London.

Still, given Tory politicians' tendency to find themselves in jail after becoming embroiled in various scandals, I don't think his potential cellmates should throw away those well-past-their-use-by-date lubricants just yet.

***

With salaries usually paid weeks rather than days late, staff morale at Septic was perilously close to flatlining. Matters were not helped by Alan's continually flying up and down to Thailand and the Philippines (on business class, natch). Oddly, the lucrative publishing opportunities he was working so hard to cultivate never seemed to materialise. Further accelerating his putative publishing empire's Gibbons-style *Decline and Fall* was Carc's habit of finding 'positions' for every halfway attractive jobless woman he met in the pub each weekend.

With the 1984 Summer Olympics in Los Angeles fast approaching, local sprinter Ahmed Hamada was being hailed across the Middle East as giving Bahrain a real shot at its first-ever medal. Cynically spying the spark of excitement that had begun to rouse the islands from their apathetic slumbers, Carcary hit upon the seemingly genius idea of mounting a Bahrain Olympics Appeal. Nick, Younis and I subsequently spent the following week struggling to raise any enthusiasm for producing cack publicity materials for the latest in Alan's endless line of dodgy endeavours.

Bored of an initiative even the stray cats in the street outside could see was doomed, I pushed back my chair one lunchtime and did a creditable imitation of Titus Oates at the South Pole. 'That's it. I've had enough, and I'm off. If anybody wants me, I'll be in the bar at The Londoner,' were my parting words, Nick B informed me a few years later.

Luckily, seeing the awfulness of the writer with whom me old china Manuke had replaced me, and knowing of my abrupt departure from Septic, my former colleagues had been agitating for my return. For the first, and perhaps only, time in my life, I was in the right place at the right time. In the end, a short sit-down with Manuke was sufficient to secure me the salary hike that had been rightly mine three months before and get me back behind my typewriter.

All of which doesn't mean to say that I lost touch

with my former colleagues at Septic. As Bahrain is ultimately a tiny place with a population then akin to that of my hometown of Coventry, staying in touch wasn't too problematic.

The biggest story on the Carcary and Co. front was – cue trumpet fanfare – an Olympic Appeal Charity Auction with a brand new Porsche as the blue-ribbon attraction. Having been contributing video reviews to the local radio station every Friday, I was asked if I wanted to be part of the team covering the event. Still struggling to throw up the remainder of the several servings of bullshit I'd been fed by Carcary, I declined.

With BD22,000 in the bank for the Bahrain Olympic Committee (BOC) by day's end, the auction was pronounced to be a qualified success by the local press. Eager to start spending the auction's proceeds, the various high-ups at the BOC wasted no time in getting on the blower to touch bases with the event's prime mover and shaker.

Frustratingly, young Alan seemed to have gone into full-nervous-twitch mode and was not answering calls at either his office or his flat. Enervated by his sterling work, he'd apparently grabbed the first available flight to Manila to talk column inches and multiple insertions with the pubic relations over-achievers at the Firehouse girly bar.

Nostrils flaring with the unmistakably acrid whiff of scandal, Alan's ex-*compadres* on the *GDN* and *GM* quickly began bombarding Septic's office with queries of their own.

In less time than it would have taken Bahrain's Olympic medal hopeful to circle a cinder track, there were grave mutterings about the whereabouts of not only Carcary but also the auction proceeds. Just a few days after the moment of his greatest triumph, Carcs was in disgrace, his name all over the front pages of the papers he'd once helped to write.

A few years later, Alan pitched up in Hong Kong to work for the *South China Morning Post (SCMP)*. Early on during his stay, he agreed to meet Pete Welton and me for drinks at the Foreign Correspondents' Club (FCC). He told us – and for once, his eyes weren't twitching, so I had no reason to doubt or disbelieve him – that he and Asa had hightailed it to the Philippines immediately after the auction.

Once cocooned in the Firehouse, Asa had announced that rather than fund Bahrain's Olympics efforts, all auction proceeds would be used to settle the considerable debts Alan had run up at Septic. Before leaving, Asa had made it clear that his soon-to-be-ex-media-magnate pal would be wise to give the Middle East a wide berth from that day forth.

I'm not sure if Carcary later made any attempts to launch an Xmas savings club for *SCMP* staffers after arriving in Hong Kong. If he did, I'm sure his efforts were pitilessly smothered in the crib by Pete in full-on King Herod mode.

***

As mentioned briefly earlier, something I did get to do in Bahrain I'd have struggled to break into in the UK was work as a movie critic for the local radio and press. My 'employer' on the former (if you could call him that – he never paid me anything) was a boorish DJ called 'Richie Hayward' or Vinyl Richie as he styled himself. It could have been worse, I suppose. A rival expat DJ called Richard had branded himself as Rick O'Shea (cue annoyingly unconvincing **tuhzzzzing!** bullet-pinging-off-concrete-canyon sound effect).

Every once in a while, you meet someone whose adoration of themselves is so intense that their hot air levels swell to Hindenburgian proportions. Self-appointed 1970s TV detective Shoestring lookalike – as he insisted on describing himself in his nails-down-the-blackboard West Country burr – Vinyl was one such person.

I fell into the 'job' when a journo mate called Phil Moore (RIP) became *GM* editor and could no longer be arsed to review the latest pirated videos for Vinyl's show. One joint session together with Phil later and I was on my own behind the microphone. Could a future spent sinking cocktails with Jack Nicholson and Clint Eastwood as the Concorde whisked us to lavish premieres in LA be far away?

Alas, yes.

When it became obvious that the only form of remuneration heading my way was free videos, the scales fell from my eyes about why Phil had left me clutching Richie's unbecoming baby. Still, as I've always had an insatiable appetite for books, records, and films, the job was not without its compensations.

Each week, I'd drop into 'Adliya Video', see a man called 'Jabar', and pick up a pile of new releases he was eager to foist on his members. While there, I'd also help myself to several more obscure titles I wanted to watch for my own pleasure. All that remained was to view the videos, structure some kind of review for recording, and listen to my dulcet tones flowing through the ether on Vinyl's weekend show.

The fact that virtually every review was written in and on Inept and Manuke's time and dime on Thursday mornings was another added attraction. Work done for the week, I would promptly scoot down to The Londoner and quaff several pints with Welts, Makes, Foxie and various other journalistic ne'er-do-wells. Before my eyes became too glazed and my gait too unsteady, I would then head over to Radio Bahrain to pre-record my segment for each week's Friday morning broadcast.

That I was generally half-cut before I set foot in the studio didn't seem to make a jot of difference to Vinyl or his listeners. Reviews in the can, it was off home for something to eat, a quick side trip up the wooden stairs to Bedfordshire, and back to the pub. Sometimes – probably more often than was probably sensible, really – I even used to skip the food and sleep elements of this meticulously balanced calculation altogether.

On one Thursday afternoon, I and the lads from the *GDN* embarked on a mammoth bender that took us from The Londoner to Tony McIver's other pub, The Joyce. Friday, it practically goes without saying, was a total car crash. When I eventually shuffled sheepishly up to The Londoner bar for a post-work pint of hair of the dog that Saturday evening, Tony was there to greet me. 'Well, if it isn't Manama's very own wild colonial boy!' he chortled, much to my fellow old soaks' merriment. 'God, John, I've seen you pissed in the past, but Thursday in The Londoner was something else.'

'What do you mean Thursday in The Londoner was something else?' I said defensively. 'I was sober – well, in the same postal code as sobriety's city limits – when I left that afternoon!'

'Oh, I'm not talking about Thursday lunchtime!' said Tony triumphantly. 'I'm talking about when you came back at about 11 pm that night.'

I immediately began apologising profusely for any chaos that might have ensued with myself at its epicentre. Tony was having none of it. 'John, you're never any bother, even when you're pissed out of your skull. Now, shut up and have a pint on me!' It was (and remains) one of the nicest things anyone has ever said to or about me.

***

Although it had succeeded in evolving into a fairly successful financial and media centre by the mid 1980s, Bahrain has long been probably the poorest of the Gulf states. Bypassed by the God of Oil's generous sprinkling of black gold and the arrogance such arbitrarily distributed riches bestowed, most 'ordinary' locals were far friendlier and welcoming than their Saudi cousins.

The one failing many better-off Bahrainis did share with their neighbours a hop, skip, and a jump across the water was resentment of the outsiders who ran their businesses and kept them rich. How the knowledge that their newest Ferrari had been paid for with foreigners' hard work and managerial flair must have galled them every time they stuck a key in the ignition.

Aside from one – insanely brave – gay colleague called 'Halam' in the ADept office, I barely made one Arab friend the whole five and a half years I lived in the Middle East. This isn't due to any sense of racism on my part; aside from Halam, no local ever really bothered to make any effort to mingle with the hired help.

Carcary's discredited Olympic Appeal aside, the biggest development during my time in Bahrain was the ongoing construction of a 16-mile-long US$800,000,000 causeway linking Manama's Al Jasra area, to Saudi Arabia's Eastern Province. Happily, this insanely poorly thought-through project remained unfinished until after I was safely in Hong Kong.

Although barely 14 yards wide, the resultant King Fahd Causeway ended up spewing forth a tidal wave of untold misery every Thursday through Sunday. Before you could say *'marhaba'* (welcome), the hotels of Manama were packed to the rafters with Saudis with too much money, too little sense and a virtually negative-level tolerance for alcohol.

Had the visiting riff-raff restricted themselves to simply getting legless, life would have been bad enough. Depressingly, the darker side of their libidos fuelled by too much drink, the thirsty invaders had not the slightest concept of self-control. In no time at all, incidences of sexual assault began what friends who remained behind described as being 'an unstoppably dizzying upwards climb'. Having long viewed Bahrain as a vent for those driven doolally by their unyielding anti-this, anti-that, and anti-everything-in-between laws, the Saudi authorities couldn't believe their luck.

In common with its nextdoor neighbour, Bahrain's population was largely split between the Sunnis (a smaller but richer and, therefore, more powerful group) and the larger but poorer (and so, ultimately powerless) Shiites. Doing a sterling job of maintaining a delicate balance between the two the whole time I was there was Bahrain's Emir, Shaikh Isa bin Salman Al Khalifa.

Once Shaikh Isa died in March 1999, no replacement was able to replicate his uncanny ability of keeping each faction from ripping out the other's throats. By the early years of the 21st century, the whole rotten edifice had begun to crumble and decay into the appalling mess Bahrain finds itself in today.

With expats such as myself allowed to come and go pretty much as we pleased, life in the Bahrain of the early to mid 1980s was if not one hundred per cent happy, then at least largely peaceful. The one main exception was *Ashura*, during which hard-line Shiites take to the streets and attempt to atone for their apparent culpability in the martyrdom of the Prophet Muhammad's grandson, Hussein. With thousands of guilty penitents literally whipping themselves into a frenzy, the wisdom of staying home and well clear of the marchers as they passed by was hammered into every expat.

Towards the end of my stay, I lived on the top floor (the penthouse already!) of a tiny three-storey apartment block that looked out and across Manama's wonderfully atmospheric *souk*. On the morning of September 15, 1986 (Muharram 10, 1407 in the *Hijri* calendar), I awoke to hear the terrifying

THUMPA!
THUMPA!
THUMPA!

the ground made as that year's march of atonement drew nearer and nearer to my front door. If the din the marchers' feet made was terrifying, the actual sight of them was even more so. A sea of red and white zealots liberally studded with costumed horses, the crowd was a textbook example of collective insanity. Even snatching brief glimpses of the madness from a hidden eyrie some 20 feet above was sufficient for one to feel the psychosis slowly spreading.

While *Ashura* gave Bahraini Shiites a much-needed outlet for their – let's be honest – largely justified frustrations, there was, even then, an understanding that deeper antipathies might soon fester into something far, far darker. Thirty-odd years later, the Arab Spring helped bring all that pent-up anger spouting forth like pus from a particularly painful abscess. Not that most of the rest of the world seems to have noticed or cared. Thanks to the efforts of Bernie Ecclestone and his money-grubbing mates in the Formula One industry, the only time most people think about Bahrain is when it hosts its annual Grand Prix.

Before the petrolheads started block-booking the local hotels once a year, banking was pretty much the sole *raison d'être* for what prosperity the country and its people enjoyed. As the lending of money for interest, or *riba*, was considered usury, banking was expressly forbidden; or *haram* as the Quran puts it.

With bankers already starting to enjoy their well-deserved pariahdom for being a thirsty, boorishly behaved bunch, a career in high finance was obviously a no-no for Saudi's great and good. Bahrain was only too happy to take up the slack and run with it. All that was required for such practices to become (for want of a better word) *kosher* were a few minor adjustments. So it was that the Middle East discovered that curse of every Westerner old enough to open a bank account – the service charge.

As with everything about life in the Middle East, the resultant 'only in Bahrain' absurdities weren't without their lighter moments. A good mate of mine – probably the only banker who's achieved the honour – called 'Clive Mycroft' once gave me an especially choice example. His tale involved an elderly Arab merchant who, although barely able to read and write, had astutely parlayed his trading skills into a vast fortune.

Aware he might be approaching the end of his life, the old man decided to put his affairs in order. He promptly popped into his bank and humbly asked to talk to the person in charge of his savings account – enter Mr. Mycroft. After clicking the old man's account details onto his computer screen, Clive was amazed to see a chorus line of zeros dancing before his eyes. He promptly cancelled all appointments and respectfully ushered the oldster into his bank's boardroom with a turn of speed not even the recently absconded Alan Carcary would have envied.

Blissfully unaware of the myriad complexities involved in multinational finance, the elderly Arab had apparently simply wandered in from the desert insistent on 'seeing' his holdings with my friend's bank. Taking the unlikely billionaire's use of the word 'see' as a request to take a quick look over his account balances, Clive quickly printed him off a lengthy statement. Perplexed by the page after page of telephone-number-length figures being passed to him, the old man, said, 'No, no, you don't understand. When I say I want to see what money I have here, I mean I actually want to *see* what money I have here.'

Silently cursing the Arabic Beverly Hillbilly and his progeny for several future generations, Mr. M sat his visitor down at the boardroom table while he made a few calls. Following the inevitable ordering, pouring, and drinking of several cups of cloyingly sweet Arabic coffee, our Clive finally managed to beg, borrow, and steal a suitably imposing mountain of cash.

Eventually, a pallet stacked some three feet long, wide, and high with large- denomination Bahraini Dinar notes was duly wheeled into the boardroom for the old man to inspect. Totally unphazed by the colossal riches his lifetime of hard work had helped him to accrue, the elderly Arab reached into the pocket of his grubby *thobe*. He then pulled out a sheaf of yellowing papers that Clive was about to discover contained the number of every note his guest had ever deposited with his bank. 'Mr. Clive, you tell me this is my money! Yet, when I check the bills you have brought here against the numbers of the notes I deposited here in 1962, I am unable to locate them anywhere...'

***

On those rare occasions when attempting to detox away the endless abuses Bahrain had perpetrated on one's liver, lungs, and kidneys seemed sensible, the Shaikh's Beach was just what the doctor ordered.

A committed Anglophile, Shaikh Isa (or 'Jack' as he'd apparently been nicknamed by Britain's senior royals) had reserved the seafront near one of his palaces as a private retreat for Western expats. With most people only getting Thursday afternoon and the whole of Friday off, the Shaikh's Beach proved very popular with the monarch's European, American, and Australian friends – well, the white ones, anyway. Non-Caucasians – even those smart enough to have packed their British, American, European, Aussie, or Kiwi passports inside their eskies – were simply turned away at the gate.

Ironically, those deriving the most pleasure from such rejections were the Pakistani guards who'd never have been allowed on the beach in a million years themselves. Those lucky (i.e. pale-skinned enough) to gain admission were then ostensibly free to sun themselves and enjoy ice-cold beers out of sight of easily offended/sexually frustrated (delete whichever appropriate) Arab eyes.

I say 'ostensibly', as the Shaikh was himself widely rumoured to be a priapic old letch of mythological proportions. Indeed, his allegedly bottomless fondness for Gulf Air hostesses – or insatiable fondness for Gulf air hostess's bottoms – was the stuff of legend. Command performances during which Happy Jack apparently squeezed his portly frame under a glass-topped coffee table while his latest Gulfie voided her bladder and/or her bowels were supposedly a particular royal favourite. Reputedly rewarded with top-of-the-line gold Rolex watches for their sexertions, those sitting atop the table(s) certainly weren't wasting any time complaining.

***

One of the few other pluses of working in Bahrain was the opportunity to whet my appetite for wanderlust at ADept's various other offices in Middle Eastern capitals. The first of these was Dubai in the United Arab Emirates (UAE), where I was seconded for several weeks not long after my arrival in Bahrain itself. Yet to mutate into 'the Switzerland of the Middle East' (is it just me, or is every self-professed 'Switzerland' of somewhere an irredeemable shithole?), Dubai was then a real backwater in every sense.

Skip to the next time I would reluctantly end up working there some 15 years later. Now the Emirate was globally renowned for its annual Shopping Festival's attempts at ever more inconsequential world records. Eager to see or hopefully even gorge yourself sick on giant-sized slices of the Earth's longest Swiss roll? Then 21st century Dubai's *the* place you want to be! But hey, back in the mid 1980s, the emirate's jam and artificial cream-slathered opulence lay far in the future.

In those nostalgia-tinged far-off days, Dubai and the ADept branch there were both tiny and insignificant in the great scheme of things. Indeed, so far down Manuke's to-do-list did the Emirate's office rank that its running had been entrusted to an old-school friend called 'Waleed Khajaf' (a.k.a. 'Squaleed Waleed').

As in other professions, one's colleagues in ad agencies can generally be stuffed into one of four pigeonholes:

1. Those who are good at their jobs and reasonably nice chaps (or chappesses).

2. Those who are so focused on their careers that they've morphed into monomaniacal bullies at work but remain good company and fun to be with outside office hours.

3. Those who are useless at their jobs but generally reasonably pleasant individuals. Category Three types will often ask for – and more importantly – get (and be pathetically grateful for) any help you can offer them in covering their arses.

4. Those who are not only lousy at their jobs but also happen to be crappalling human beings. We're talking people whose utter cuntishness during office hours is only outstripped by their totally groundless sense of self-belief and full-on obnoxiousness before, during, and after work.

Had Waleed fallen into categories one through three, it would have been possible to make allowances and rub along with him reasonably well. Unfortunately, God had seen fit to plant this buffoon's tent pegs squarely in the fourth and final group. His all-round ineptitude and unpleasantness ultimately made him a nightmare to deal with on every level.

That the man was in urgent need of a CD to sort out his office was no secret. Enter a suitable fall guy in the shape of J. Fuery, Esquire. Fresh off the plane from Jeddah, and having barely unpacked my bags in Bahrain, I was seen as being easily malleable. I was, in other words, a natural patsy to ride to the agency's rescue during a two-week trial in Dubai.

After enduring just a couple of days of the squalid one's utter disregard for anyone daring to venture an opinion different from his own, my biggest fear was that I'd end up jobless. My concerns quickly zoomed into the red danger zone the first time I went out to meet a client with him and his sour-faced Palestinian female henchwoman, 'Qhaba'.

The client we were off to see, 'Mr. Sharmouta', was a huge ('Significant!' as my long-time friend and former ADept workmate, Neil, would have called it) multinational soft drinks firm. Rarely having had to attend such a supposedly high-level meeting with so apparently important a client up to that point in my career, I was understandably a tad nervous. My pants would have been several shades browner if I'd had an inkling of what was to later happen inside the client's opulent – for Dubai in the mid 1980s, anyway – office.

Then as probably now, senior-level management positions in the Middle East/Arabian Gulf were the closely guarded sole preserve of the Lebanese. So impenetrable was this particular closed circle that Western expats had taken to flippantly calling it the 'Mafia of the Mediocre'. As a result, it came as no great shock that the man whose plush office we were ushered into was – hold the front page – yet another of Manuke's former classmates.

Momentarily abandoning his minute scrutinising of doubtless very important papers, Mr. Sharmouta imperiously waved me, Waleed, and Qhaba to our seats and ostentatiously pressed a button beneath his desk. As if by magic, a predictably prehistoric tea boy appeared to take our orders and, against all the odds, successfully – if rather shakily – deliver them.

That Mr. S had not bothered to enquire what we might like to drink did not matter in the slightest. The only hospitality on offer in offices the length and breadth of the Middle East – even in this bastion of the soft drinks industry – never varied.

You either suckled up mud-like coffee or horribly over-sugared tea, or you kept your gob shut.

Pleasantries exchanged and fraternal greetings done and dusted, the self-styled big swinging dicks got down to the serious business of hammering out a winning ad strategy. And what a plan Mr. Khajaf had lined up!

'Qhaba, if you'd do us the honours,' said Waleed in what he hoped were the sort of commanding tones he'd read about in self-help books whose first chapters he'd started but would never finish. Vacuum-packed into a sleeveless dress that caused every eye in the room to hone in on her unshaven armpits, Qhaba began working the flipchart like the off-screen assistant in an Al Qaeda video.

Quick as a flash, the not-so special K was on his feet and outlining his genius stratagem for driving the soft drink giant's sales for the coming year. At the heart of all great advertising ideas are insights. Squaleed's was based on the way in which all of Dubai's other small-, medium-, and giant-sized soda manufacturers seemed to splurge their entire ad budgets during the Emirate's unbearably hot summer months.

Leaving his host a moment to digest this coruscating observation, Mr. K moved in for the kill. Why didn't Mr. Sharmouta and his brands steal the march on the competition by blanket-advertising Dubai during its colder winter months?

Before the sugary Arabic tea (Mr. Sharmouta, Waleed, and Qhaba) and thick Turkish coffee (me) had time to drop to room temperature, we found ourselves descending in the lift. 'Well, I don't know about you two, but I think we left him with quite a bit of food for thought,' said Khajaf in the taxi back to the agency.

Hindsight has given me a slightly kinder overview of my prospective employer's unique marketing mindset. With most top brands now routinely rolling out their Christmas ad campaigns as early as mid-October, leading advertisers the whole world over would certainly seem to concur.

My less than successful trial over, I went back to Bahrain and made it very clear I would under no circumstances be willing to work for Manuke's chuckleheaded mate from Beirut's Class of '65. Happily, my ultimatum worked, and my three-and-a-half-year stay in Bahrain began in earnest.

About a year later, I and a colleague called 'Matty' were told to get our arses up to Kuwait. Although booze was supposedly prohibited, old Kuwaiti hands assured me local customs officers would generally turn a blind eye to Westerners carrying a bottle for personal consumption. To further grease the wheels upon arrival, it was recommended to carry not one but two bottles – one for yourself and the second as *baksheesh* (a back-hander) for the thirsty local jobsworths.

As with everything else in the Middle East, hanging on to the good booze involved a considerable amount of subterfuge on the part of thirsty imbibers such as me. Tired of destroying their livers with BD3 (£6) bottles of rotgut own-brand whisky, local customs officers had begun seizing the more expensive-looking tipples better-off visitors were saving for themselves.

Aghast at the idea of having to surrender high-end liquors to such undeserving and uneducated palates, arriving expats had begun decanting and swapping the contents of whatever bottles they were attempting to import. With levels of bluff and double-bluff worthy of the opening pages of Kingsley Amis's *Old Devils*, getting the good stuff past the customs desk remained something of a crapshoot.

The prospect of such shenanigans failed to trouble Matty, whose vital organs were hanging out of his arse after a thousand and one too many nights in Dublin pubs. With M's GP having expressly forbidden him from ever again touching another drop, I unselfishly stepped into the breach and offered to carry his supply of unwanted shorts through customs myself.

Throwing caution to the wind, I promptly bought four bottles of bog-standard Johnnie Walker Red. Miraculously, despite the loud chinkings and clinkings emitting from our hand baggage, both Matty, myself, and all four of our fellow travellers were waved through customs without a second glance.

***

The other benefit of working at ADept was that I got to shoot my first two or three TV commercials (TVCs). Showing a bored client the agency's photographic studio one day, Manuke performed one of his usual George Burns-like pauses and removed a tobacco scale model of New York's Chrysler Building from his mouth. Waving the stogie around expansively, Mr. K. summoned up his trademark *braggadocio* and boldly announced, 'We can – we have – shot several cars in here.'

'Really?' said the clearly unimpressed and itching-to-get-across-the-road-for a-drink client. 'And given that the "studio" we're in is on the first floor and you have no access to the street, how might that be?'

Filmed with a video camera we'd bought from a local department store, the first TVC we shot was for a Lebanese mate of Manuke (whoever would have guessed?) called 'Abu Reiha'. Mr. R's lot in life was to try and satisfy his Arabic target audience's insatiably sweet tooth with a range of unbearably saccharine-tasting sugared nuts.

Despite churning out and selling these heart attack starter kits in the hundreds of thousands, Abu was known for being ultra-tight when it came to parting with his money. So much so that even Manuke used to joke about his pal's ability to produce half-eaten *falafels* from the pockets of his impeccably well-cut Ermenegildo Zegna suits. The end result was that despite the huge potential upside (exposure to millions of bored potential snackheads across the Arabic-speaking world), Mr. R. was reluctant to spend more than BD500 (about £1,000) on producing his commercial.

With no budget for sets or talent, we came up with a simple one-shot spot featuring a well-known Arabic comedian (who knew!). The idea was that Bahrain's answer to Bill Hicks was too busy stuffing his face with the client's comestibles to tell the folks at home just how yummy they were.

With half-masticated mouthfuls of food splattering the camera lens, the finished film – should such a thing be possible – was even more unappetising than a covert nibble on Abu's nuts. The person most angered by me and my junior art director 'Calvin''s request for a reshoot was the agency's in-house cameraman/producer, 'Kounem'.

Fiercely proud of his Armenian roots, Kounem was consumed by hatred for everything that might have any kind of Jewish connection. When hearing that I was planning to visit New York on an upcoming holiday, his sole remark was. 'New York? We Armenians call that pigsty *Jew* York!'

The Levantine George Lucas's fuse burned

equally short should anyone be foolhardy enough to question his skills behind the camera – as poor Calvin was soon to discover. After very politely being asked to persuade our talent to refrain from emitting a barrage of saliva-slick nut fragments from his mouth during one of the day's many takes, Kounem's tetchiness hit Defcon 1.

His anger was so great he barely spoke to either Calvin or me again for the remaining year or so of our stays in Bahrain. A few years later, a similar TVC won a gold medal in the low budget category at the Cannes Festival, so we must have been doing something right.

***

By now, you'll probably have twigged that Manuke's preference for employing British creative staff failed to give him the grasp of UK-style irony and sarcasm he needed to deal with them.

Towards the end of my time at ADept, Manuke broke his UK-only hiring rule. Casting his net further afield, he began attempting to snare formerly undeniably brilliant but now irrevocably burnt-out expat CDs from Asia. The first of these was a once hugely talented man called 'Eamon Lowe'. Regarded as something of a genius for his 'uniquely Asian welcome' hotel campaign from a couple of decades earlier, Eamon had – like Joe at Clown – now been reduced to a shambling wreck.

Advertising can sometimes be a cruel business.

If you're coming up with ideas that win or keep accounts, no one really gives a hoot. Agency managements don't give a toss how much drink you consume or how many spliffs you smoke. Nor could they give a flying fuck about whatever additives make up the bulk of the white lines you shovel up your nose. 'Hey, Eamon's just another wacky creative who's just scratching his creative itches and/or blowing off some steam, right?'

Wrong.

Falter on the high-wire for just one moment, and all those questionable habits start to become first minor niggles, then nagging issues and eventually urgent concerns. In no time at all, you wake up in the morning to find just how far you've fallen and how highly unlikely it is you'll ever manage to climb back. By that stage, of course, you're well and truly banjaxed, and those running agencies whose lobbies you'd once peppered with awards are now papering their waste paper bins with your c.v.

His shaky hands barely able to grip a magic marker, the big E's days of running ideas up the flagpole to a sea of universal salutes were long gone by the time he eventually washed up in Bahrain. All that remained of his glory years was a prodigious albeit rapidly diminishing capacity for a drink (or three or ten). Farcically, it wasn't the sight of Mr. L struggling for inspiration at his desk or flailing around hopelessly in client meetings that ultimately led to his walking the career plank. It was his late wife Ruth's recently deceased pet dog, 'Flopsy'.

Cut to an early morning meeting in Manuke's office. Eamon – remarkably clear-eyed and clear-headed for once – had been told to present himself, me, and Calvin the junior art director for a meeting with a German client who'd just flown into town. Despite his earlier words to the now long-gone Jack, Manuke was a firm believer in the Arabic maxim that *kelps* (dogs) are somehow unclean and so was no great lover of man's best friend.

The client, however, adored all things canine and wasn't slow in producing pictures of his various family members and pets for Manuke, Eamon, Calvin and me to admire. 'Look at zis liddle chep, everyone! Izzen he edorable?' said the client.

Manuke cooed over the various images with all the enthusiasm of Winston Smith bidding a cheery good morning to the rats in *1984*'s Room 101. When handed the picture-stuffed wallet, Lowe emitted an anguished keening bray.

'He looks just like Flopsy! Poor, poor Flopsy! Poor, poor Ruth!' wailed the weeping CD. From the embarrassed silence that followed, it quickly became apparent that it might be a good idea if the former creative colossus absented himself from the remainder of the meeting. Still more misfortune befell the newly clay-footed saviour when Manuke later decided it might be an even better idea if Eamon absented himself from ADept's office for the remainder of his days.

Not long after, Mr. L found himself bundled back on a plane to wherever it was his ex-paymaster had conjured him up from. The following morning, Khara sidled into my office having adopted the irritatingly matey style he thought indicated he gave a toss about his staff. Long a firm believer in the warning inherent in the words 'there but for the grace of God...' I said, 'Sad news about Eamon.'

Telegraphing that he was about to make a profound utterance, Mr. K detached from his lips a steaming brown cylinder that looked like the last remains of the gone-too-soon Flopsy. Pausing only to tap his ash onto the carpet my BD2 monthly deduction was struggling so ineffectually to clean, he formed his face into a rictus of what he probably hoped resembled concern. Alas, the emotion he was striving for emerged looking more like the aftermath of a case of acute constipation.

'Ah, Eamon!' Manuke said with a level of false geniality that would have made a TV game show host cringe, 'A great creative talent laid low by his love of beer, wine, and whisky.' And then, hovering Donald Trump-like over my shoulder, he asked 'And you, John...which of the three will be *your* downfall? The beer, the wine, or the whisky?'

'That would really be entirely dependent on

whether it was you or me who was getting them in, Manuke.'

***

Having singularly failed to garner any last dregs of creativity from the desiccated husk that was Eamon Lowe, Manuke now decided to hire another geriatric CD. A portly and almost entirely bald creative greybeard called 'Toby Snead' was the chosen beneficiary of this latest leg of Manuke's one-man 'Help the Aged' campaign.

While I'm sure he was a splendid chap whilst at home or down the pub with his mates, once at the ADept office, Toby was an arsehole of the brownest stripe. His opening gambit of 'I'm not here to win any popularity contests' as a means of introducing himself to his new team was all one needed to know. Has anyone who's spouted such clichéd drivel ever come close to getting or deserving any kind of mandate indicating the opposite?

When it became apparent that his primary function was to get shot of as many of ADept's current crop of expats as quickly – and cheaply – as possible, Toby's stock unsurprisingly plummeted. No sooner had he manoeuvred his flabby gut through the agency door than he had been renamed 'Toady Greed', and that was the end of that. Who says there's no such thing as truth in advertising?

With Toady demonstrably devoid of the Machiavellian brass balls needed to implement a divide-

and-rule campaign, Manuke began looking for other ways to clear the agency decks. He eventually settled on a wheeze involving the introduction of clocking-in cards. While they may motivate drones in institutional grey-and-puce-green-walled offices to toe the nine-to-five line, such devices have no place in more creative environments. This is especially true in ad agencies, where writers and art directors desperate to expand their portfolios will frequently cheerfully work late into the night or over the weekends for no extra pay.

Although we all hated having to do so, we each obediently punched our cards each morning and again when leaving the office each night. Everything was running like clockwork until immediately before the first batch of cards was due to be processed. When Manuke's corporate lickspittle of choice and soon-to-be-jailbird company comptroller, Javid, went to collect the cards, they were oddly conspicuous by their absence. What he discovered in their place was a brief typed message saying 'Looks like time has run out, Mr. Khara!'

When Manuke pitched up at work the next morning, his rage knew no bounds. In a classic case of trying to secure the stable door after the bolted horse had left only soiled straw in its wake, he ordered immediate checks of everyone in the office. Straight out of Captain Queeg's book of decisive actions from Herman Wouk's *The Caine Mutiny*, the initiative might have been, but it proved too little too late. Following a repeat theft at the end of the following month, the offending time clock and its empty card racks did a Ferdinand Marcos-style vanishing trick and were never seen again. Despite his incandescent rage at his thwarting and the Wile E. Coyote-like zeal with which he hunted the culprits, poor old Khara never did learn who took the cards or where they went. All I know for sure is, it definitely wasn't me.

Another person it most certainly wasn't – he was wwwwwaaaaaaaayyyyy too driven for such juvenile pranks – was an account director called 'Neil'. Having helped agitate for my return to the agency after my disastrous stint at Clown, the poor fucker and his lovely girlfriend (and later wife), 'Sara', paid a terrible price for their support. They ended up having me foisted upon them as a flatmate. Happily, Neil was not one to harbour grudges and also came to my rescue by providing me with his spare room during my critical first few job-free weeks in Hong Kong. He remains a friend to this day.

Whilst generally an all-round good guy who made his mark in the career stakes almost everywhere he went, Neil had one major flaw. He could not structure or write a sentence of English to save his life. When asked, I would do my bit to try and repay him for his friendship by rewriting his presentations. Given that Neil's sentences sometimes weighed in at 70-plus words and were frequently free of grammatical niceties such as verbs, subjects, and/or objects, this was not always an easy task.

Making matters even worse was Neil's irrational desire to climb to the top of the greasy corporate pole. His discovery of Philip Broughton's random buzzword generator from 1968 (a variation of which is reproduced below) was just one more rung on the ladder:

Column 1	Column 2	Column 3
0. integrated	0. management	0. options
1. total	1. organizational	1. flexibility
2. systematized	2. monitored	2. capability
3. parallel	3. reciprocal	3. mobility
4. functional	4. digital	4. programming
5. responsive	5. logistical	5. concept
6. optional	6. transitional	6. time-phase
7. synchronized	7. incremental	7. projection
8. compatible	8. third-generation	8. hardware
9. balanced	9. policy	9. contingency

As Mr. Broughton said, 'While no one will have the remotest idea of what you're talking about, the important thing is they'll never have the balls to stand up and mention it.'

Another step in Neil's tireless one-man assault on the top came with Sun Tzu's *Art of War*, then very much the corporate speaker's go-to guideline of choice. In those days, even somewhere as off the beaten track as Bahrain was not free of this hyped-up tome's ubiquity. No surprise that Neil soon started adding little homilies about ancient Asian military strategies for dealing with one's enemies into his own presentations.

Unfortunately, like most new converts to Sun Tzu's view of the world back then, Neil hadn't the foggiest idea as to who those enemies might be. His colleagues? His clients? Other agencies sniffing around after the accounts he worked on? With Al Qaeda and ISIS still a blip on the CIA's radar, the overeager Pakistani labourer who rushed to clean Neil's car when we arrived at work each morning didn't seem worth counting.

One day, while giving a speech to gee-up the agency creative department ahead of a big presentation, Neil embarked upon some unfathomable epigram about attacking opposing armies while they were unprepared.

As Neil's oration reached its stirring climax, a stroppy South African art director called Colin decided he'd had enough. 'Why don't we just hunt the cunts down where they live, kick in their bedroom doors, and cut their and their kids' fucking hearts out, Neil?'

Soon after, Neil was to decamp to Hong Kong, closely pursued by me, Calvin, and another colleague called 'Cliff'. In common with those of you who've read this far, all four of us would go on to encounter varying levels of success and failure.

Given his all-encompassing drive, it should

come as no surprise that it was Neil who rose the highest. Unhappily for him, he was also to suffer – if not the hardest fall back to earth – then at least the harshest wake-up call.

Having got his heart's desire of a non-stop ticket to the top, Neil learned that life aboard the executive jets that whisked over-achieving execs around the world was anything but golden. Rather than insightful discussions of cutting-edge management strategies, Neil was horrified to find that the only conversations he was privy to usually involved rationalisations, downsizings, and outsourcings. Rather than visionary ideas that would transform lives and earn their originators squillions of dollars, the only numbers being bandied about were the large numbers of people who'd soon be 'let go'.

Be careful what you wish for and all that.

BOOK TWO:

Bleeding in the Gutter

'Of course he has a problem with authority,
he's the copywriter in an advertising agency.'

–Anon

Chapter Six

Good morning, Mr. Shittybottom

'Thanks, you've just called me a cunt.'

Or so said the BBC (British-born Chinese) CD of the first Hong Kong agency to grant me an interview after I bade him a perfectly innocent 'Hi.'

Luckily, my interrogator quickly assured me he was joking. But with each word in the Cantonese dialect boasting nine possible pronunciations and meanings – at least one of which always seemed to be obscene or offensive (and very often both) one could never be quite sure.

Culturally, it's true what the 'East meets West' cliché-mongers say, Hong Kong really *is* unique. Well, at least, it was before the Chinese got their mitts on it and began stealthily depriving Hong-kongers of their civil liberties. Still, back in 1986, when I did the old travelogue standby and first flew into Kai Tak Airport down Kowloon high street, such possibilities were still restricted to Deng Xiaoping's dreams. While I don't want to get into ever more trite descriptions (how's about 'a real melting pot of occidental and oriental cultures'?), the hokiest of hokey old platitudes really did – and frequently still do – apply here.

One of the early impressions that I found – and continue to find – most striking about the territory was the unquestioning acceptance of superstitious practices across all ages and educational levels. Even cynical, 'tell me something I don't know' expats who really ought to have known better weren't immune.

I know. I was one of them.

When I got my first phone line in Hong Kong in early 1987, I thought nothing of my new number's ending with three consecutive fours. At least, I didn't until a Chinese friend told me that, if wrongly pronounced with a rising rather than a mid-level pitch, four (*sei*) sounded exactly like the Cantonese word for death. As the locals considered such connotations to be extremely inauspicious, the number was naturally not in great demand by Cantonese speakers applying for phones.

Although initially dubious, I soon began to notice the elaborate lengths to which locals would go to avoid four in every corner of their daily lives. As one wag told me, while threesomes were OK, upping the erotic ante by just one person was simply not on. To this day, many buildings in Hong Kong not only skip their fourth floor but also their 14th, 24th, or 34th levels.

Initially absurd, such irrational fears eventually worm their way into even the most supposedly mature belief system via some kind of mystic cultural osmosis. They then remain cowering in the corner of your soul until Death's Big Four begins pounding on your front door.

A self-perpetuating prophecy? Perhaps. But to this day, I still find myself mentally urging digital clocks and car speedometers to accelerate past times or visual displays in which fours are repeated several times. Let's hope my car's digital milometer never clicks over to 44,444 as its dashboard clock hits 4:44 pm while I'm driving down the A440, or I could be in serious bother. Better pray you're not in the car behind.

In case you're interested, eight (*baht*), which echoes the Chinese word for rich, is a far more propitious and therefore desirable number to have on your phone, ID, or car number plate. You don't believe me? If you're ever fortunate enough to visit Honkers before China's Central Government irretrievably fucks it up, check out how many buildings proudly trumpet that their address is numbered between seven and nine. You'll also be impressed by the plethora of top-of-the-line Mercs and Beemers with eight-heavy personalised number plates.

As in so many countries, Westerners who adopted a sniffier approach to local cultural sensibilities did so at their own risk.

Take Fiat. When the carmaker was planning to launch its best-selling 124 model in the territory, its head office was apparently advised to change the name, which, when spoken in Cantonese, sounded like 'easy way die'. The company then supposedly turned a deaf ear to all pleas from their local dealer to reverse their decision. The end result? This otherwise-excellent car apparently endured a real struggle to achieve initial acceptance.

Once in a while, a client's colossal disregard for local feelings would actually pan out in their favour. When researching a possible Hong Kong launch in the early 1980s, Pizza Hut was apparently repeatedly told their sales would flatline like the base of one of their pizzas, the reason being that the Chinese are generally disgusted by the malodorous smell of cheese and the foreigners who eat it.

Abhor *fromage*, Hongkongers very well might, but three decades later, they continue to wolf down pizzas like there's no tomorrow. Which, given the amount of carbohydrates and artery-clogging fats lurking in each slice, there may very well not be for anyone over-indulging.

Transparent human figures, or even the most gossamer-thin hint of a possible phantom, were other unwanted ghosts at Hong Kong's marketing feast. As a Westerner, one quickly learned to grow accustomed to being called *gwailo* (literally white ghost man) or *gwaipor* (white ghost woman). While one's Chinese hosts would usually oblige the request, only the pettiest of churls would insist on being described as a *sai fan yan* (person from the West).

Still more obtuse was the cultural clodhopper (answers on a postcard to John Fuery competition...) whose suggested ads for a dietary product showed a lithe supermodel-type escaping her formerly Rubenesque curves. 'Hey, John, killed any *feipors* (fat women) lately?' came the gleeful shout from my colleagues – both Chinese and Westerners – for weeks thereafter.

***

Two Hong Kong habits I never could quite manage to get my head around were many locals' casual racism and total lack of consideration for colleagues suffering from some sort of personal problem.

The most glaring example of deeply ingrained racism I saw early on was Darkie (later renamed as Darlie) toothpaste. Featuring a crudely rendered caricature of a straw-boater-wearing black minstrel with dazzlingly white teeth, the brand's packaging remained prominently displayed in every pharmacy and supermarket until its late 1980s' rebranding.

Because it was most apparent in one's workplace, and frequently occurred on a regular basis, insensitivity to others' perceived physical faults or emotional sufferings was even more sickeningly obvious. The most telling example I can remember came during the Secret Santa gift exchange at an agency Christmas party I attended in the early 1990s. One female colleague who was still traumatised after a recent miscarriage unwrapped her parcel only to find it contained a horribly lifelike doll of a crying baby.

Another girl whose teeth had been ruined by Hong Kong's poor fluoridisation of drinking water in the early 1960s tore off her gift's wrapper to find several family-sized tubes of whitening toothpaste. As my present at the same party was a six-pack of Carlsberg Elephant Beer, there were no complaints about a lack of thoughtfulness from me.

But before I get too far ahead of myself, let's travel back to early 1986 and the first time I set foot in the city that would be my home well into the next century. As noted earlier, ten-a-penny anecdotes detailing perilous between-building landing approaches in which travellers could clearly see the inhabitants of apartment blocks scoffing meals or doing the dishes were actually eye-popping realities. Throw in the subsequent drive into town through the towering tenements of Kowloon, and it's easy to see why, like so many new arrivals before me and since, I was smitten.

Fascinated by the messy tangles of greenery and laundry hanging from each indescribably grimy building, one couldn't help but recall images of the dystopian cityscapes Ridley Scott had conjured up in *Blade Runner*. When watching one of Mr. S's numerous later 'Director's Cuts', it was no surprise to learn the movie's oft-kilter ambience had apparently been inspired by his own first visit to Honkers.

With Mrs. Thatcher and the wonderfully-named Percy Craddock's army of civil servants having just finished hammering out the then much-lauded 'One Country Two Systems' (OCTS) agreement, Hong Kong was buzzing back then. Disappointingly, far from being the promised harbinger of a bright future for the territory and its people, OCTS went on to prove itself 'not fit for purpose'. Barely had the Brits handed over the keys to the territory's new mainland masters a decade or so later than the Chinese had begun riding roughshod over everyone's basic rights. It was a classic case of that old Chinese torture the 'death of a thousand cuts', or as a journalist friend so eloquently put it, the 'death of a thousand cunts'.

With the grim spectre of the handover looming closer by the minute, the inevitable question Westerners heard everywhere they went in the late 1980s and early '90s was 'What's going to happen after 1997?' The only person I knew who had an answer was an Aussie mate called Andy Duncan (RIP – another victim of what 11th century Persian poet, Omar Khayyam, ruefully called 'the old familiar juice'). Faced with the oft-repeated question, poor old Andy always used to respond: 'I'll tell you exactly what's going to happen after 1997, mate.

Stupid twats like you are going to stop asking me about what's going to happen after 1997...'

***

Names were another huge potential pitfall for the unwary. Local Chinese people apparently chose their English first names out of a large book they were given at school. As a result, the handles one encountered in and around town were often absurdly comical. One agency messenger we had was called Mercury, appropriately enough. Even more amusing was the Foreign Correspondents' Club barman – a dead ringer for HK's then most prominent democracy activist, Martin Lee – who proudly sported the word 'Hitler' on his name tag.

Fresh-off-the-plane expats didn't have it any easier. One of the first tasks newly employed *gwailo* hires were given was to order a bunch of business cards with their Chinese name on the back. Time was when European arrogance was such that all the hard-pressed foreigner had to do was snap his fingers and summon his sexy Asian secretary to do the honours for him. Shrewder foreigners preferred to spread the task of finding them a suitable Chinese name across several people. Either way, it was vitally important that anyone in need of a name whose series of squiggles they couldn't begin to hope to read or even pronounce:

    a.) Made doubly sure their misplaced sense of superiority hadn't pissed off the local colleagues/underlings who'd been entrusted with the sensitive task of dreaming up their Chinese name.

b.) Checked, double-checked, and then treble-, quadruple-, and quintuple-checked any name bound for the back of their card ultra-carefully before having several hundred printed off to pass around at client meetings and functions.

The other Golden Rule for anyone doing business in Hong Kong or China has always been to avoid doing anything that might cause their local colleagues to 'lose face' in front of others.

Like so many expats before him, the newly arrived CEO of one agency where I worked in the early 1990s considered himself so exalted as to be absolved from respecting such common courtesies. To spare him from further embarrassment, let us call him 'Bob Seaforth'. While not his real name, the alias is phonetically close enough to his actual moniker for the purposes of this retelling.

Despite his bags and boxes having barely been unpacked in his humongous corner office and ostentatious apartment, Bob had already succeeded in pissing off several of his new colleagues. Anyone who's ever worked in the territory will be quick to tell you that the vast majority of Hongkongers work extremely hard and like to stay in the office very late. In a market where title rather than salary inflation is endemic, working after hours is ultimately a sure-fire way of climbing the corporate ladder and acquiring a new business card at each rung.

Ultimately, even the small minority of those afflicted with some kind of diligence deficiency or determination bypass do everything possible to remain at work as long as possible. Their reason for doing so isn't born of any altruistic desire to show solidarity with their colleagues. They're simply trying to delay returning home and having to spend any more time than is absolutely necessary with the big extended families who share their tiny, cramped flats.

While the branches of all of our various family trees invariably contain a toothless, gurning oldster or two, there's only a finite window during which they remain charming, right? In Bob's case, one got the impression any elderly relative who had outlived his/her usefulness was destined to brave winter's first serious cold snap on the porch outside the Seaforth family home.

Keen to give his new underlings time to mull over whatever pearls of wisdom he was about to impart, Mr. S scheduled his introductory speech late on a Friday afternoon. It practically goes without saying that early on in his proclamation, our new *tai pan* (big boss) let everyone know he hadn't – aarrrrrrghhhhhh! – 'travelled to the ends of the earth to win any popularity contests'.

Having effectively scuppered his already impressively long odds of taking home a 'World's Best Boss' mug, the Charles Saatchi *manqué* moved on to more pressing matters. Summoned to Bob's office, the studio manager was ordered to get a full set of business cards and letter-headed stationery sorted out a.s.a.p.

Having done the sensible thing and asked for two or three options, Bob learned that the Chinese name that stood out was pronounced *'Bo-see-fat'* in English. When asked what this meant, he was mollified with the usual old guff about 'he who is courteous, wise, and kind'. Presumably too tied up with work to solicit a sensible two or three confirmations from people outside the office, Bob hastily initialled the artwork, and everything was sent out for printing.

The few days after the cards arrived were a non-stop whirl of networking in the arduous round of lavish business lunches and cocktail receptions that are the Hong Kong CEO's lot in life. If anyone who received one of the hundreds of cards Bob passed out like fliers for a new gym during this period noticed anything amiss, they sensibly remained silent. It was only when Bob welcomed his first major local client to the agency for a 'meet'n'greet' the following week that problems with his name card began to rear their ugly heads.

Meeting convened, Bob went around the agency's boardroom table bestowing his new card to his recipients in the two-handed style all newcomers to Hong Kong are taught to adopt. His jumbo-sized inner egotist was probably secretly delighted with the shy smiles his new card elicited. Doubtless, recipients were greatly impressed by the lengthy list of letters and accomplishments the card's designer had shoehorned in beneath his name and title. Shortly after Bob sat down to chair the meeting, he slowly began to twig that something very curious was starting to happen. Every time the agency's new *capo dei capi* began flapping his gums, the various VIP guests present all began doing their level best to suppress sniggers.

Eventually, the meeting came to an end, and Bob walked the still smiling clients out to the agency's very swanky-looking reception. Having waved everyone goodbye, our by-now very red-faced and plainly extremely pissed-off CEO returned to the chaotic back-of-agency area visiting clients rarely saw.

'What the fuck was all of that about?' Bob demanded angrily. Happily, none of the *gwailos* present had an inkling about what might be the cause of his colossal mither. Unusually and ominously, of the Chinese staffers, there was no sign. For the first time in the agency's history, it seemed that every senior Chinese colleague had taken advantage of a rare opportunity to piss off home early. It was only after later getting hold of one of the mirth-inducing cards and surreptitiously taking it to the pub that I found out what all the kerfuffle had been about.

'You see these Chinese characters? Well, there's your mate's problem right there!' said one of my Cantonese friends.

I began to explain how the three characters that made up Bob's Chinese name were supposed to perfectly encapsulate the twinkly eyed wisdom and avuncular benevolence he wished to project.

'What these three characters are saying isn't "he who is courteous, wise, and kind". *Bo* means "big", *see* means "shitty", and *fat* means "bottom". So, what your boss's card actually says is "Mr. Shitty Bottom", as every Cantonese-reading person to whom he's given out one of these cards these last few days will have known.'

While no heads in the agency rolled, Bob soon got himself a set of new cards and never again spoke quite so condescendingly to the Chinese staffers who beavered away beneath him.

***

Before I could acquire a business card of my own, there was, of course, the small matter of my first finding a job. Amusingly – or amazingly, as today's hype-prone world would have it –reaching

Hong Kong ECDs via the phone without having to waste half your life listening to *Greensleeves* was still possible in those days. Not that the appointments you scheduled always took place as planned. Tired of constant cancellations and re-arrangements, I decided to approach a few of the territory's specialist advertising head-hunters for help.

Mobile phones and speed dialling capabilities still being little more than a meaningless squiggle on a Nokia engineer's notepad, the top name on everyone's Rolodex was a lady called 'Gail Derekson'.

While she might well have been the 'fast track to everyone who was anyone' in the local advertising industry, Gail's life was not exempt from more mundane concerns. With Christmas fast approaching, even top head-hunters had to find the time and money to buy turkeys, drinks, and presents. Naturally, any commission Gail earned from placing me would be a huge help.

Gratifyingly, Gail hit pay dirt with the first interview she set up for me – a copywriting post with a boutique medical agency. While sure to shoo creeping poverty away from my door, knocking out heavily footnoted copy for suppositories and trusses was not really the shot in the arm my career needed.

Keeping the Medicus offer in my hip pocket as a kind of 'get out of jail free' card, I did what everyone else with two brain cells to rub together would have done. I held back from signing a formal contract and resolved to carry on looking for something better – with or without Gail's help.

To build up my reserves of good will at the Bank of Gail, I pressed Calvin and Cliff into her tender loving arms following their arrival from Bahrain. Within days of putting themselves out and about in Hong Kong's job market, the pair had also scored jobs that earned my friendly neighbourhood head-hunter commissions. The scent of a third nice, fat fee in her nostrils, Gail was desperate for me to stick a pen in my arm and add my own bloody signature on the medical agency's dotted line.

Then, two things happened. First off, I met and became good friends with Sue Carver, the extremely nice woman who would be sacked were I to take the job at the medical agency. Second, I accepted the offer of a copywriting post with the more mainstream multinational ad agency which actually owned the agency Gail was so desperate for me to join.

Ironically, the female CD who ended up hiring me (Anita Haynes – still a friend to this day) was married to the CD of the agency which hired Calvin and Cliff. Confident she'd be so busy spending the two sizeable fees she'd earned from my referrals, I figured Gail would leave me free to choose the job

I felt was right for me.

Wrong.

When I eventually rather sheepishly summoned up sufficient courage to call Ms. D and inform her of my decision, she was not a happy joey. Visions of jeroboams of Champagne vanishing into thin air as fast as the insincerely scrawled greetings on last year's agency Xmas cards, Gail reacted as if I'd dumped a turd in her tinny.

Deaf to my arguments that it was my and not her long-term future rather that was at stake, Gail accelerated into full-on meltdown mode. 'You fucking people! All you think about are yourselves, you bastards!' she banshee-wailed down the phone in broad 'Strine. The rising Australian inflexion at the end of 'bastards' reached such high-speed dental drill intensity, one could almost picture the baubles on her office Christmas tree shattering.

Leaving Gail to loudly denounce me for my treachery in doing the unthinkable and daring to put my best interests ahead of her own, I sheepishly hung up the phone. Predictable as ever, I then fucked off down the pub to celebrate my new job.

Despite being home to some six million people Hong Kong is a small town, and Gail's ire soon burned itself out. She eventually served me up my just desserts by offering me jobs with the two least popular ECDs in the territory's advertising industry – one of which – surprise, surprise – I stupidly took.

The two men in question were called 'Jack Dillon' and 'Irving LaSalle'. The latter had been cruelly – but rather accurately – nicknamed Aunt Sally by any expat foolish enough to have ended up on the chain gangs that were his agencies' creative departments. The local Chinese had an even more unflattering name – they called him the Anorexic Ogre.

Unsure whether to sell my soul to Dillon's devil or jump head first into LaSalle's deep blue sea, I turned to a friend from another agency for advice. He happily shared a cruel but apparently unerringly accurate joke about Mr. D that was then doing the rounds in the local ad industry. The story goes something like this...

A man walks into the reception of the agency where Dillon worked as ECD and informs the receptionist he is here for his 11.30 am appointment. Taken aback, the lady behind the desk looks up and says, 'Oh, dear, I'm afraid Jack isn't here today. Nor will he ever be coming here again. Perhaps you hadn't heard, but I'm afraid Mr. Dillon, unfortunately, passed away over the weekend...'

Stunned, the visitor leaves the office, only to return the following morning to make the same request and receive exactly the same answer. This whole shebang goes on for something like three or four days before the receptionist finally snaps and says, 'Look, I've told you I don't know how many times that Jack died last weekend! Why do you keep on coming back here when you know he's dead and gone?'

'Because I like to hear you say it,' says the man.

Eventually, I decided to go with the Anorexic Ogre and his Client Servicing *compadre*, Henry Rufus's agency, 'KR&K', (inevitably renamed KROK by its permanently put-upon staffers). When I caught up with a second friend in the business shortly after I had made my decision, he said: 'Jesus, John, didn't anyone tell you the joke about Aunt Sally that's doing the rounds?'

'It's not the one about the man and the receptionist, by any chance?'

'That's the one! Bloody funny, isn't it? Glad I'm not working for the twat.'

The ultimate job of an ECD is to carefully nurture and inspire his team to originate work that wins accounts and (hopefully) awards by providing clear direction. Although an experienced ECD and commercials director, LaSalle was - for me at least – an abject failure in both areas. As mentioned earlier, one can generally forgive people who are horrible but brilliant at their jobs, or who are nice to hang out with but dreadful to work with. Sad to say, the Anorexic Ogre was all of these negatives rolled into one charm-free Manson Family-sized package.

As he and Rufus (a.k.a. 'Rufus the Doofus') were either too short-sighted or miserly to realise the benefits of investing in computers, the entire creative department toiled away on hopelessly outdated and inadequate equipment. In my case, this involved a dinky little Canon electronic typewriter similar to one I'd bought in Dubai *souk* and used at home. Although ideal for dashing off the odd personal letter or record review for the local rag, the machine was totally incapable of meeting the demands of a modern ad agency. And never more so than when the serfs chained to the desks in said agency's creative department were pinioned beneath the unfeeling thumb of Irving LaSalle.

Each morning at around 11:00 am, I had to report to Aunt Sally's office to present whatever copy I'd managed to write the previous day and revise again that morning. Typically, one of these creative review sessions would consist of his going through each ad's text word by wretched word, phrase by painful phrase, line by soon-to-be lifeless line. It was like an early prototype Dignitas Clinic for advertising copy.

Scouring each submission for something – anything – with which to emphasise the enormity of his knowledge against the paucity of my own, LaSalle would pounce on any perceived shortcoming that caught his eye. 'Buy one, get one free,' he would utter with the solemnity of an Egyptologist unravelling as yet unrevealed meanings in the Dead Sea Scrolls. 'I don't know, John, isn't that kind of old and tired nowadays? Isn't there some shorter and punchier way we can say this?'

'Well "buy", "one", "and", and "get" all contain only three letters each, Irving. And we're hardly talking a headline on a four-colour double-page spread. Just a shelf talker that has to communicate quickly to get noticed.'

Reasoned arguments such as this would inevitably cause Irv's face to collapse like someone who'd just discovered you'd suffocated his childhood puppy before he could reach for the pillow and have the pleasure of doing it himself. If your efforts to please him proved especially disappointing, his look of tortured incredulity was that of a man clinging to the top of a tall building whose fingers you'd just stamped on.

At this point, it was generally a good idea to remember that it was you and not LaSalle who was in danger of falling and try and fashion yourself some kind of parachute.

'How about "grab", "seize", "collect", "acquire", or "receive"?'

Before Irv had sufficient time to dismiss each suggestion out of hand, it made sense to further muddy the waters by lobbing in a few additional alternatives.

'Or maybe we could try "gain", "earn", "attain"; or even "avail", "secure", or "procure"?'

Oh, dear, the aggrieved, quasi-constipated look was back on my tormentor's mug once more. Time for one last desperate roll of the dice.

'If none of the dozen or so alternatives I've given you prove suitable, we might need to look at making the sub-head a bit longer and less likely to be read. In which case, our options include "pick up", "get hold of", "get your hands (or mitts) on"; or perhaps "invest in", "make a purchase of", or even "grab yourself some..."'

Visibly wearying of such trifles, the anorexic one would then call a halt to proceedings with a brusque 'Maybe you could just take the whole thing away, revisit it, and re-present it again at tomorrow's review.' The remainder of the day would then be spent in a futile attempt to patch up the rejected copy in readiness for another mauling. The following morning the resubmitted 'buy one get one free' message would go sailing through when another set of words caught Irv's eye and was dismembered in its stead.

Given LaSalle's maddening inability to make any kind of decision, my typed sheets quickly became so ridged with peaks and troughs of hardened Tippex they resembled relief maps of Alpine valleys. Successfully squeezing the three-dimensional paper into the toy typewriter the agency had given me frequently proved every bit as challenging as writing the copy itself.

While I've said it before on these pages and it's rarely ever any kind of consolation, there's always some poor sap in the gutter compared to whom you're happily swinging on a star. Slogging away even further below me in the bowels of the agency were KROK's unimaginably put-upon art directors and visualizers. Expected to churn out dozens of TVC storyboard frames and ad visuals to presentation standard at virtually no notice, these poor fuckers led lives infinitely bleaker than my own. Lugging around the huge number of coloured markers they needed to complete their work being totally impractical, they were also effectively tied to the office until well after midnight when working. Further adding to their woes was the fact that LaSalle rarely bothered to share the high aesthetics he expected to see first thing the following day before he buggered off home.

One night at around 4:00 am, I remember leaving the visualizers hard at work roughing up TVC storyboards for an important pitch just six hours later. When everyone assembled back in the boardroom for the Anorexic Ogre's inspection of the finished boards an hour ahead of the presentation, his business-like face quickly clouded over with its factory-issue frown. The cause of his displeasure? The fact that the colours the visualizers had used in the chequered tablecloth that appeared in almost every frame weren't the ones he'd mentally envisioned when briefing the job in.

***

August 1988 didn't just mark the only holiday I got to take from the deadening drudgery that was life at KR&K. It wound up being the last time I ever got to see my dad. Throughout that spring and early summer, my mum had been in and out of the hospital with what everyone feared was bowel cancer. Thankfully, it turned out to be a severe case of diverticulosis – no laughing matter in itself.

So worried about my mum that he neglected to take care of himself, poor dad looked and felt worryingly shrunken and insubstantial when we hugged after my arrival at Coventry railway station. Before I headed for my return train a couple of days later, I had one of those rare moments of clarity all grown-up kids must get. Strangely certain that I would never see him again, for the first and only time in my adult life, I told him that I loved him and embraced him more tightly than I ever had before. I'm so glad now that I did as, late that November, my qualms became actualities. As I was heading out of town one weekend, I called home on Thursday to say 'hi' to my folks. Dad had apparently gone up to the road to enjoy his occasional couple of pints, but no worries, I could always talk to him next time. Except there was to be no next time as my dad died in the early hours of that Sunday morning.

Horrifyingly, I later learned that as mum and I spoke, dad was actually lying on the sofa in pain so great his every move was agony. A big and powerful man in his prime, he was now too weak even to make it up the stairs he and my mum had climbed every day for nigh on 35 years. Having refused to make a house call because of foul weather, our family doctor had 'prescribed' nothing more than a few days' bed rest. Convinced that the man whose life she had shared and whose children she had raised would get better, poor mum didn't have it in her heart to burden me with her fears.

Signalling the start of days devoid of any kind of joy, few sounds in the world were more plaintive than the anguished howling the 5:53 am tram from Happy Valley. And never did its wheels wail more mournfully than when they squealed past my home on Morrison Hill Road on the morning of Tuesday, 25 November, 1986.

Having returned from a weekend away late the previous night, it was only then that I learned the dreadful news that younger children cannot comprehend and adult kids know must inevitably come to pass.

My father had died two days before.

With no dad to say goodbye to and my flight back sure to cause my mum unnecessary added worry, my sister, Mary, sensibly told me there was little point in my flying home. Reluctant to spend my day uselessly moping around my flat, I did the only thing I could and went into work.

What would be the first thing you'd say to a colleague/employee who was stranded thousands of miles from home and had just learned a parent had died? In my case, I would have asked, 'Do you need to take time off work to grieve? Do you want to fly home to be with your family? Is there anything – and I do mean anything – I can do to help?'

When I told LaSalle about my dad's death, he barely looked up from his desk, uttered a couldn't-give-a-fuck 'That's too bad', and carried on doing whatever it was he was doing. Stopped dead in my tracks by the man's lack of basic humanity, the few seconds it took my legs to recover from their paralysis and carry me out of his office seemed like an age.

Although already persuaded not to return home, an offer of time off to do so from Irving would have far outweighed the otherwise uniformly unflattering memories of him included here. Incapable of showing a more human side to his character (one hesitates to call it a personality), it turned out LaSalle really was the uncaring Anorexic Ogre his Chinese employees denounced him as being.

Still, not to worry! The Christmas and New Year

holidays were fast approaching. Perhaps the Ogre and Doofus were delaying ditching their Scrooge and Marley double act and saving their boundless reserves of bonhomie until KROK's annual 'Thank you!' staff shindig. Although seldom – fuck it, never – the obscenely hedonistic affairs immortalized on film and TV, such jollies are the only times agencies make an effort to push the boat out for their long-suffering employees.

Not that a once-yearly session with your nose in the corporate trough ever winds up being anything other than a tiresome chore. Sure, a night of free grub and grog sounds like fun, but don't forget the sort of wankers you'll have to elbow past as you home in on that last sausage roll. In KROK's case, this not only meant the Thin Ogre and Rufus the Doofus, but also the equally humourless drones who'd followed them over from the last agency they'd run.

The only real bright spot about the upcoming hootenanny was that KROK held the 'Caninberg' beer account. Surely, there'd be sufficient supplies of complimentary ale to wash away the last remaining vestiges of what had been easily the most wretched year of my adult life?

Used to seasonal celebrations that promised at least an imperceptible dusting of fun, everyone's collective spirits sank when they learned the venue in which Henry/Irving would tread the boards as

Santa. Rather than go the whole hog and splash out on a fancy restaurant as would most other agencies, KROK had booked the less salubrious surroundings of the South China Athletic Association canteen.

Upon arrival, I was disgusted to find that while the first two soft drinks were free, anyone who wanted any kind of alcoholic beverage would have to pay for the privilege. Resolving to spend as little time as was humanly possible attempting to smile along with the assorted glum-looking carousers, I ordered up a can (No bottles! No pints!) of Caninberg.

A Thumbelina-sized thimble of beer whose elaborately coiffed creamy top and HK$27 (about £2.70) price tag would have given my old Combe sparring partner, Jimmy, conniptions arrived moments later. Of the can and what must have been the sizeable thirst-quenching quaff of beer remaining inside, there was no sign. Given that 7-11s were then selling 440ml cans of Caninberg for the princely sum of approximately HK$5 (about 50p), I doubt I was alone in feeling a tad cheated.

Having had quite enough of Ogres, Doofuses and their progeny; and no longer giving a stuff about keeping my job, I downed the dregs of my munchkin-sized serving of Vitamin C and headed doorwards.

'Off so soon, John? I would have thought you

would at least have stuck around for Henry's speech,' said LaSalle. I paused in my journey to a waiting motherlode of cheaper booze in the nearby Kings Arms.

'Sorry, Irving. Unless he says anything other than the usual load of old bollocks about it being a hard year, I've heard it all before. I'm sure everyone else will tell me the bit about having to tighten their belts for an even tougher coming 12 months on Monday morning.'

Given the two (full-sized!) cans of Caninberg I had enjoyed at KR&K's expense during the miserable previous 12 months, I suppose I should really have known better.

Working late nights and long weekends unpaid is part of the rich tapestry that is agency life. As one famous ECD in Asia told his staff in the wee-small hours of Saturday morning, 'If you don't show up later today, don't bother coming Sunday, Monday, or indeed any other day after that.'

Early on in my servitude to the Anorexic Ogre, the entire creative department had been told to cancel their plans and spend their weekends helping out on a make-or-break Caninberg pitch. Having cracked the creative whip all through Saturday and Sunday, Irving seemed to momentarily enter some kind of mental fugue state.

Unexpectedly gifted a regular level of decency, he promptly gave everyone a 'take five' break before resuming full-on-bastard mode. Thirsty from my endeavours and wishing to study the brand's packaging (no, really), I went to the boardroom fridge. There, nestled amidst the various over-priced bottled waters and soft drinks bought in to mollify clients, were two – count 'em – two cans of Caninberg. I promptly grabbed one and, rubbing its refreshingly icy beaded exterior on what I hoped passed for my genius-fevered brow, returned to my seat.

Several – God knows how many – hours later, Aunt Sally came over all nice again and declared another time-out. Unwilling to leave a solitary can of beer lying in the fridge alone and helpless, I got up and rode to the rescue.

'Wow! You're going a bit heavy on the beer there, John! Do you have some kind of problem with alcohol or something?'

There are moments when life gifts one open goals so wide and welcoming that it'd be a sin to pass them by. Then again, there are times when it's far more judicious to keep on walking without ever once averting your gaze.

Despite the scores of suitably cutting ripostes regarding the likely origins of any problems I might have had that were dancing around my head, I took the wiser path and kept my trap shut.*

***

Eventually, Irving and Henry hired another ECD called Chas Moore to – ad agency press release cliché alert, ahoy! – 'take KROK to the next level'. Aside from saddling me with the well-nigh impossible task of having to write copy briefed in by one ECD and get it reviewed by a second, the rationale behind Chas's hiring remained a mystery.

Doomed to pinball helplessly between my two bosses with very different opinions, it was only a matter of time before I got told to clear my desk and clear off. Far from being a crushing blow, this first of what would eventually end up being one-and-a-half sackings in my career proved strangely liberating. The many, many beers I sank that night were probably the most satisfying I'd drunk in what had been an utterly abject twenty months.

The morning after my dismissal, I pitched up for work an hour and a half late armed only with a large Nike holdall to collect all my stuff. On the way to my desk to 'Just do it', I passed the Anorexic Ogre's office and was summoned in. Weirdly

---

* Happily, I did eventually get some small smidgeon of revenge. A couple of years later after I had dumped my memories of KROK in a mental incinerator, I was browsing in a bookshop. 'I didn't know you could read, John!' came the unmistakable sound of the Anorexic Ogre from behind me. 'Certainly can, Irving,' I replied. 'I learned all I needed to know by studying the Sits Vac ads at the back of *Media and Marketing* during the miserable year and a bit I spent working for you.'

unaware of my recent sacking, LaSalle's face fell when I informed him of my intention to absent myself from the agency before lunch.

'But Henry and I are still paying you, and as a result, we expect you to work out your full one month's notice, John,' he said.

When I remarked that a well-respected Chinese colleague called JB had left KROK the day he'd been fired, Irving shook his head sombrely. 'JB was let go because he was unprofessional, John. While you'll probably never be the writer I am, both Henry and I have both been impressed by your reliability. As a result, we expect you to come in and fulfil you professional obligations every day for the next four weeks.'

Seething, I returned to my desk. While I did end up showing my face at the office for more or less my entire notice period, I'm proud to say I did so with minimal grace and maximum uncooperativeness.

'Right, I need everyone to stay late tonight to prepare layouts for an urgent presentation tomorrow morning,' said our Irv to the creative department early on during week two of my notice. As crucial presentations rarely get arranged without more warning, it was typical of him to delay making an announcement until everyone had already arranged to see their families or friends.

'Enjoy yourselves, guys, and watch out for the

colours on any tablecloths, carpets, and curtains in your visuals,' I said cheerily as I shoved my chair under my desk and made to leave.

'John, can you come back? We need you here tonight,' said LaSalle to my retreating back as I ambled towards the lift.

What was he going to do – fire me? And why would I care if he did? I'd already lined up a senior copywriting gig with CPU. In two weeks, I'd start the purplest patch in a career not exactly overburdened by overachievement.

***

Two of the very few things that made my incarceration in KROK bearable were drink and dope. Drink would normally be taken in the sort of local one would seriously consider hanging out in anywhere in the world apart from Hong Kong. Dope – in the form of grass or hash – was an annoyingly less readily available ways of removing the angst from one's pants.

When I first moved to Hong Kong, Neil from Bahrain had kindly agreed to put me up at his flat in Happy Valley until I got a job and found digs of my own. It was one day while returning home after a fruitless Monday's job hunting that I wandered into my first Hong Kong local, Traps.

Located in a windowless basement (shades of the Omar Khayam!) at the bottom of Happy Valley racecourse, the pub was a magnet for hard-drinking local jockeys, trainers, journos, lawyers and policemen. I felt right at home before the head had settled on my first pint of Caninberg.

The Wednesday morning after my first sesh there, I opened the daily paper to see the man who'd pulled me that pint less than 48 hours before being escorted to Victoria Prison. It seemed that mine host had been involved in some race-fixing scandal and – I later learned – had apparently carried the can for his much richer and more powerful friends.

Gambling is, I am happy to say, the only vice not to have found a willing partner in crime in my hopelessly addictive and impulsive personality. While betting in other countries is freely available to anyone witless enough to want to throw their money away, gambling in Hong Kong is rigidly controlled by the Hong Kong Jockey Club (HKJC). Established in 1884, the not-for-profit institution continues to use the billions of dollars it earns from Mark Six lottery tickets and wagers placed on twice-weekly in-season races to benefit dozens of deserving causes. Although illegal betting rings do exist, anyone caught attempting to muscle in on the HKJC's action is stamped down on fast and hard.

Whilst largely law-abiding sorts, Traps' hardcore gamblers had wearied of interrupting their drinking to trudge the four hundred yards or so to the local HKJC off-course betting centre. As a result, they'd begun paying a local Chinese regular to drop off their wagers and later return with any winnings. As their gofer – chosen nickname Running Bear – was reputedly an off-duty cop, what could possibly go wrong?

Plenty, as it happens.

Despatched to collect the bar's sizeable winnings after one very lucrative 4:15 pm Saturday race at Sha Tin late in the season, the bear kept right on running and was never heard from again.

Left dangling from a loose end during the three-month June to September off-season, the guys were desperate to scratch their collective gambling itch. Some would attempt to salve their addictions by betting heavily on liar's dice sessions that stretched far into the night. More adventurous souls would try to find relief by betting big sums of money on a series of road safety TVCs from Hong Kong's Government Information Services (GIS).

As I was later to discover, GIS was ultra-parsimonious with its advertising budgets. Determined to squeeze every last drop of value out of their limited funding, the creatives behind this particular campaign had shot one accident from multiple points of view, *a la* Akira Kurosawa's *Rashomon*.

Each of the spot's six or seven variants would open on a busy city junction where a young mother was lovingly gazing down at a pram containing her adorably cute toddler. Busy doting on her offspring, mum failed to notice a labourer who was struggling to push a trolley dangerously overloaded with heavy construction materials across the road. Nor was she aware of the public light bus zooming by at a speed well over the legal limit. Rounding out each spot's *dramatis personae* were a taxi driver killing between-fare downtime by studying a racing form, plus a truck driver too busy examining his pager to focus on passing traffic.

The end result was an almost endless range of spots involving various forms of death, destruction and general mayhem. The version in which mum lost control of her pram and its precious contents and watched helplessly as it rolled into the path of the speeding light bus was a personal favourite. Swerving to avoid the future Darwin Award-winning mother and child, the van driver promptly crashed into the worker, whose newly released cargo further added to the carnage. Rarely, if ever, has the multi-stranded plot complexities of an arthouse cinema classic so effectively encouraged road safety or given so many gamblers so much bang for their buck.

As mentioned earlier, my other crutches during my internment at KROK were grass and hash. When these materials were available, joints would be rolled and smoked like a fiend every chance I got. All of which is not to say that the substance politically incorrect souls used to call 'the damnable wog hemp' was easy to come by in the Hong Kong of the 1980s. Not down my way, it wasn't. Ensuring steady supplies generally meant stockpiling worryingly large quantities of stuff in my fridge's under-sized (and otherwise under-used) freezer compartment at any one time. All well and good unless the police happened to come knocking with a cheery *'Jo san! Jo san! Jo san!'* (Hello! Hello! Hello!).

Eventually, steady supplies dried up about 18 months before the end of my third and final stay in Honkers. With dope having got stronger and stronger and more and more expensive, 'Mr. Fuery's Potent Old Shag' and I pretty much reached a sad parting of the ways from that point on.

What might have happened to me if the cops *had* come a-knocking and chanced a peek into the deeper recesses of my Lilliputian fridge-freezer? Hand on heart, I don't honestly know. Reluctant to think about the possible repercussions, I decided ignorance was bliss and never did check the local legal guidelines regarding minimum amounts.

It wouldn't have been that hard for me to find out. All I'd have needed to do was ask one or more of the several senior local police officers who'd become drinking pals at first Traps and now the King's Arms. One particularly close mate – let's let him off with a caution and call him 'Malky' (a.k.a.

'Inspector Coarse') – invariably taunted me re my bad habits. To this end, he'd make a great show of telling any fellow plod fresh to the bar of our shared local what exactly was hidden in my flat. Before I could finish jotting off a mental note to refrain from touching my toes in Victoria Prison's gym, Malky would begin deducing where my stash might be found.

If only Inspector Coarse had exercised similar levels of care and due diligence when it came to taking proper care of his police-issue revolver. Alas, said weapon regularly used to accompany my generously tired and emotional plod pal on his frequent early morning jaunts to the fleshpots of Wanchai.

After touring one or two of the hellholes there, Malky's end-of-the-night party trick involved folding his arms and 'assuming the position' on the bar. Laying his head down, the Coarse one would then drift off to do some wee-small-hour patrolling of the Land of Nod.

Inevitably there came the night where poor Malky left an especially sordid establishment called *'Cojones'* having forgotten to pick up his briefcase and the police-issue Smith and Wesson revolver inside it. Luckily, the bar's *mama-san* understood the importance of maintaining cordial relations with the police and returned our friend's thankfully unloaded and safety-catched belongings when he rather more soberly retraced his steps the following lunchtime.

While senior expat coppers didn't seem to give two fucks what I got up to in my spare time, regular beat cops were another story. Early one Saturday morning after starting work at my usual ungodly hour, I sparked up a spliff to try and get the creative juices flowing. Having achieved the desired effects about a third of the way down, I left the nubbins to fizzle out in an ashtray.

Suddenly, there was a huge commotion at our front door. Within seconds, my girlfriend and now wife, Belle, had let in a police constable and high-vis-jacketed and helmeted fireman. My eyes blazing manic red, I emerged from my room to discover the pair rushing around our flat as if the end of the world was underway.

It turned out a fire had broken out after some fuckwit (not me for once) had chucked a still burning cigarette butt down our building's central well from a higher floor. It was here that most homeowners – myself and Belle included – hung and dried their laundry. A quick sniff of the decidedly odd-smelling air in my room was sufficient to convince the two that the worst harm Belle and I might suffer was a lungful or two of smelly smoke. Their less than forensically detailed investigations concluded, Hong Kong's Starsky and Hutch hot-footed it to the next flat.

Equally fond of illegal smoking pleasure – although his chosen drug of choice, opium, was far more heavyweight than my own – was my former landlord Mr. Wing Cheung. In addition to being arguably Hong Kong's greatest living Cantonese opera singer, this tiny man had the unique distinction of being the territory's last remaining licensed opium addict. Renowned for his extraordinarily high singing range, local scientists were keen for Wing to donate his body for research so they could study how exactly he was able to hit such stratospheric notes. A refusal to release the old man's body was about the only thing that united his family during the bitter legal battles that followed his death in 1997.

By the time I got to know him a decade or so before, Mr. C was in his mid 70s although he looked a heck of a lot older. Perennially off his tits on the contents of his pipe and speaking little or no English, he had wisely left the running of the building to his son, 'Dickson'. One would, however, occasionally run into the old boy as he and his tattered silk smoking jacket took their late morning constitutional. Unfailingly polite, as all elderly Hongkongers invariably are, Wing would smilingly raise his ever-present trilby each time he and I passed in our shared building's entrance lobby.

My most memorable encounter with Hong

Kong's Caruso came when I was returning from a night's carousing in Wanchai at around 11:00 am one Saturday morning. As I entered the building, the lift doors opened, and out came Mr. C with two rather intimidating-looking younger men. Having exchanged our usual mute greetings, it was pretty much a case of business as usual at Wing Cheung Mansions, so off to bed I went. Only when I opened the following day's paper did I learn that two triad members had shanghaied and frog-marched Wing to a local ATM and relieved him of HK$10,000.

Triad members were also to feature heavily in my other most interesting experience during this period – jury duty. Fascinated by the chance to see Hong Kong justice being dispensed up close and personal, I rejected the usually successful tactic of pretending to be racist when the jury was empanelled. My reward was to join six other – Chinese – jurors on a juicy murder trial.

In pre-handover Hong Kong, those who'd had their collar felt for breaking the fifth commandment still faced the possibility of having their neck broken by a hangman's noose. What made my trial so emotive was that although both had still been under 18 when the murder had taken place, the two defendants in our case were now old enough to be tried as adults. Worse still, they were up on joint endeavour charges. With no hard evidence against them, they were effectively facing the death penalty for nothing more serious than failing to flee a crime scene as quickly as their gang member mates.

The trial dragged on for four days – most of which I and my fellow jurors spent sequestered in the jury room while the lawyers on either side argued the legal niceties. Brought back before the judge, we learned that as the defence had plea-bargained the murder charge down to the lesser offence of manslaughter, we were required to return a guilty verdict.

And who do you suppose got the pleasant task of announcing the defendants' guilt to a courtroom packed with angry family and heavy-set triad types? You guessed it, yours truly. Even the Machiavellian politics of life in an advertising agency creative department were a walk in the park after this particular interlude.

***

After the lengthy spell in hell that was my confinement in KROK, the three-and-a-bit years I ended up spending at my next agency, 'CPU' were a real breath of fresh air. Best of all, for one of the few times in my career, I actually got to work on a team and bounce ideas around with an art director.

So smoothly was everything running, I even survived one of those regime changes whose resultant round of musical chairs ends with the blood of 'terminated' creatives being sluiced out of the agency lobby.

For the first time, I also got roped into helping out on regional pitches, often getting flown off to Asian cities I'd not yet had the chance to visit. While flying around on work may sound great, it's actually nowhere near as attractive it's cracked up to be; there always being more travelling between airports, offices, and hotels than free time. A rare example of my wising up, I soon learned to insist on a couple of days off for exploration and relaxation at the end of each trip.

Adapting allegedly 'multicultural' concepts created by global head offices in far-flung places such as London or New York was all part and parcel of life in agencies in Asia. That most mandatories in the one-size-fits-all 'brand bibles' head offices despatched to the remoter corners of their empires were irrelevant to the consumers there didn't seem to bother them one jot.

Indeed, so inflexible were most of these glossy guidelines when it came to individual market conditions that local clients and agencies would dismiss them with a peremptory 'NIHS' (not invented here syndrome). All in all, it was hardly surprising when local communications experienced the occasional swerve between what head office allowed and considered to be well out of bounds.

To ensure that the coke-powdered noses of the

senior suits* in London or New York weren't put out of joint too often, agencies employed global CDs (GCDs). More often than note, these GCDs were once-valued wrinklies who'd toiled in the conceptual salt mines for so long that they had very little new or novel left to say.

In an atypical display of concern for the well-being of the staff who'd built their business-es, agencies generally wasted no time in booting past their sell-by date creative virtuosos upstairs. There, the oldsters concerned would eke out however few years remained until someone else took their place in the God of Creativity's Waiting Room – assuming their livers didn't roll over and give the white flag one last wave first, of course.

'Roger Thornhill' was one such GCD.

While a big-name adman during the 1960s and '70s, Mr. T was now better known for his unfeasibly Dickensian sideburns and pompous pronounce-ments in industry papers such as *Campaign* than any creative *chutzpah*. Having just Googled him, I'm delighted to learn that he's still going strong at the ripe old age of 80-odd and regularly writes books and gives speeches to elderly Americans about legendary UK and US crime writers.

Absurdly, this means that the old bugger would

---

* Agency creatives' contemptuous term for their water-carrying colleagues in account servicing who deal with the clients, write the briefs and frequent-ly fail to sell the resultant creative work.

have been a young firebrand of just 57 – some six years younger than I am now – when the events below took place. While Google images detail the cruel effects of ageing on our Rog's elaborate combover, those magnificent Mr. Fezziwig-style mutton chops continue to remain unruffled by what Andrew Marvell called 'time's winged chariot'.

By the time we met, the not-so-young Mr. T had managed to parlay his eroding creative track record from the days when three-hour lunches were *de rigueur* into a seat on CPU's global board. Unfortunately, one afternoon, he and his fellow fat cats had been roused from their post-prandial slumbers by alarm bells about how a key client's business was being handled out of Hong Kong.

One business class flight later, his magnificent sidies gently rippling in the air-conditioned breeze, Mr. T strode through the doors of the agency and straight into the office of our CEO, 'Jerry Lim'*.

Conscious of the need to impress his emissary from head office, Jerry decided a typically OTT eight-course banquet-style lunch was in order. As CPU Hong Kong's only *gwailo* creative, I was hurriedly roped in for the duration. My mission? To provide our VIP visitor with someone *sympatico*

---

* Chinese names can be very confusing! In the case of obviously Chinese names such as 'Kai Zi' appear, Zi is the first rather than the family name and is used when I am reporting conversations with the person concerned. Where a mix of Western and Chinese names like 'Jerry Lim' appears, Jerry is the first name and is used conversationally thereafter.

to chew the fat while attempting to chow down on chicken feet.

My late 1990 meeting with Thornhill occurred just as Mrs. Thatcher (whom I personally loathed) was about to face a – happily terminal – challenge to her leadership. With head office's concerns about our handling of the big global client deemed way above my pay scale and dealt with earlier, there wasn't much left to talk about on the work front. Assorted chitchat about the differences between agency life in London and Hong Kong over, an awkward silence quickly descended over the table.

A surprisingly large number of those who work in ad agency creative departments lean to the left in terms of politics – myself included. Assuming that Rog 'dressed to the left' himself, I recklessly took it upon myself to try and fill the gap.

'Well, it looks as though that vile Thatcher woman is finally about to get her comeuppance,' I announced confidently while narrowly failing to steer a chopstick-load of expensive Chinese food into my mouth.

'Let me tell you something, chum,' our prickly by name and suddenly prickish by nature lunch guest shot back. 'Margaret is a personal friend of mine, and when we were having lunch last week, she told me she had absolutely no intention of giving in to her party's wets and weaklings. And let's not make any mistake, when that lady says she's not for turning, believe you me, she's not for turning,' added Mr T. To make doubly sure I wouldn't misinterpret his words, our Rog banged the ends of his chopsticks on the crisp white linen tablecloth for emphasis. Happily, Thornhill was jetting off to Tokyo later that evening, so any opportunity to further explore our political differences in greater depth was effectively scuppered.

Less than six hours later, Mrs. Thatcher bowed to the inevitable and stood down. Doubtless necking an agreeable Chablis or three, Mr. T probably never spared either her or me a second thought before crashing out for the night in his business class stretch bed.

***

CPU's most high-profile successes while I was there involved taxpayer-funded announcements of public interest (APIs) for the Hong Kong Government's Information Service (GIS). For those who have never worked in advertising, winning awards has always been the surest way of being able to lord it over your mates at other agencies. Best of all, take home sufficient gongs, and potential employers are sure to come knocking with salary-boosting job offers you'd have to be clinically insane not to consider.

Despite having laughably low budgets and requiring endless rounds of pitches to anally retentive civil servants, GIS campaigns were an excellent way for agencies and creatives to heighten their profiles. Small wonder so many multinationals were clamouring to board GIS's potentially accolade-laden gravy train each time it puffed its way out of the station.

In my three or so years with the agency, CPU won five of the six GIS tenders in which it pitched work against much bigger and better-resourced rivals. Best of all, the campaign concepts via which we won each assignment ended up being showered with more than their fair share of local and international awards. Indeed, so pronounced was our dominance that one of Jerry's disgruntled former staffers (and lovers) falsely made accusations that he'd been providing corrupt backhanders to his GIS counterparts.

So seriously did the client take these baseless allegations, CPU was eventually temporarily removed from the government's list of preferred agencies. Not that I had anything to fear. Aside from one brief meeting with the representative of a Dubai production house many years later, I never encountered the slightest whiff of bribery at any stage of my career. Best of all, I ended up taking home about 15 awards certificates from various shows across Asia and around the world. Despite my wife's demands to the contrary, they remain unframed and unexamined in a dusty case in our even dustier spare room to this day.

The only bugbear in the pitching process was having to get up and explain our agency's work to panels of government time servers who could have bored for Hong Kong at the Asian Games. Once you'd finished doing so, everyone – and I do mean everyone – taking part on the client side had to be seen (and heard) to have their say.

The main part of each presentation involved each of CPU's creative team feverishly trying to convince the clients how brilliantly the agency's proposed ideas had met their brief. (Here's a handy hint: When presenting, be sure and get two bites of the cherry by talking through the work you're about to show before you actually reveal it).

There would then be a brief Q and A session in which the 10 or so people from GIS would get to 'share' their feedback. Given a totally free reign to chuck in his or her two cents' worth, the first person at the table – generally the most junior – would invariably make a reasonably sensible suggestion.

Afraid of looking stupid in front of his/her more senior colleagues, the junior's immediate supervisor would then make various remarks of his/her own. And so, up the organizational ladder, it would go; the fatuousness of the comments offered up increasing exponentially with every rung.

By the time the most senior client representative got to have his or her say, there'd not only be nothing left to find fault with, there'd be sod all left of the idea you were trying to sell. Reluctant to cause their juniors to lose face by over-ruling them, such seniors would invariably then toss a few irrelevant thoughts of their own into the pot.

My then new-to-Hong Kong Singaporean art director, 'Willy Tsang', got to experience a fatal dose of such idiocy when presenting TVCs for a GIS road safety campaign.

Skilled presenter that he was, Willy did a bang-up job of selling the agency's storyboards before expectantly sitting down to bask in the warm glow of universal approbation. Unfortunately, being new to Hong Kong, he was totally unfamiliar with just how quickly post-presentation Q and As with GIS had a habit of devolving into sheer stooopidity. Instead of the hearty praise he was expecting, our Singaporean senior creative was showered with the usual round of moronic remarks ('Don't like the colour of the man's jacket in frame four of the storyboard,' 'Why is this concept so different to the TVC we ran last year?', etc.)

Having gone around the table and reached the uppermost branches of the client tree, the last comment would fall to the most senior department head in the room. Thanking the agency profusely for its efforts, the man said, 'Thanks for all the lovely work. The only query I have is, what are the TVCs you've shown us doing to inform blind viewers?'

Far from being sightless, the good burghers of Hong Kong's Securities and Futures Commission (SFC) possessed some of the sharpest eyes in Hong Kong. At least, they did when I and Tsango came up with an even more audacious campaign for 'Kestrel Insurance'.

About halfway through my stay with CPU, the client's marketing manager – a splendid Irish chap called 'Thaddeus' – asked the agency to create a campaign focused on a savings plan tailored for Australian expats. With the country's cost of living going through the roof, and Aussies including Bob Hawke and Alan Bond mainstays on newspaper front pages across the region, we opted for what proved to be a dangerously ballsy approach.

Our launch ad featured a shot of then Aussie PM Hawke, head bent and snot gushing from his nose, during one of his well-publicized teary breakdowns on TV. The headline for our magnum opus? 'The cost of living in Australia is no laughing matter.' The morning our 'Blubbering Bob' ad appeared, my phone was ringing off the hook with calls from friends from rival agencies who knew an award-winner when they saw one.

Across town, the hotline in the client's marketing department was also glowing red hot. Unfortunately for poor old Thaddeus, not one of his callers was advising him to get his tux out of mothballs in readiness to have his back-slapped at upcoming awards show dinners.

Before the end of the day, the SFC had been on the blower to both agency and client to prohibit such an 'offensive' and 'insensitive' ad from ever appearing again. CPU had also been ordered to fax over the two remaining ads in the campaign for urgent review.

Executions featuring Ned Kelly ('Hands up every Aussie who'd like to improve their quality of life') and the freshly bankrupt Alan Bond ('As every Aussie knows, sound financial planning pays dividends') were subsequently banned before the ink on the faxes had dried.

One indiscretion the SFC was particularly pissed off about was the admittedly sneaky way we'd minimised and concealed the fly-shit warning type that must appear on all financial product ads in Hong Kong. While Kestrel banned us from entering 'Blubbering Bob' for awards, the prominence SFC caveats had to be given on financial ads continued to bring a rueful smile to my face for many years.

Of course, idiotic complaints weren't the sole preserve of civil servants. Expats being expats, the Westerners in Hong Kong always found moan-worthy topics that necessitated firing off angry missives to the *SCMP* or placing outraged calls to local radio phone-ins. Bored expat housewives (BEHs) whose husbands worked in banks and finance were the worst offenders. With nothing better to do while hubby was off gouging his bank's customers, they'd fix themselves a G&T, and open that day's paper to see what fresh indignity threatened their pampered lifestyles.

The trifling gripes that ruffled these good ladies' feathers were many and various. Ignoring the fact the poor women had nowhere else to go, the BEHs would rail against the number of Filipina maids who filled Hong Kong's Central Business District on their Sundays off. They'd also scream blue murder about how local supermarket aisles weren't as wide as the ones back in the UK.

Full of pensionable puns about eggs, as such communications always are, an Easter ad I once wrote for Hong Kong's biggest video rental chain proved to be a particular irritant. Tired of having to write 'eggscrutiating yolks', I paraphrased Groucho Marx and tossed in a throwaway remark about how tapes cost a 'poultry amount' to keep over the long holiday weekend.

Sufficient steam coming out of her ears to melt the ice in her bathtub gin, one BEH tremulously put down her half-empty drink. She then promptly dashed off a damning indictment of our use of a currency her financier husband had never heard of. Amazingly, Mother Ruin's literary effort actually got published in the letters page of the *SCMP* and she probably became the toast of the Ladies Recreation Club. Talk about laughing all the way to the bank.

A couple of years later, I once again found myself skewered on the *SCMP*'s letter pages. This time, I stood accused of 'treasonously' using footage of Queen Elizabeth II in a TVC for a high-end German carmaker. Arriving home from my nightly endeavours in the pub in my usually dishevelled state, I noticed the marque's cars had featured in all three headline stories on the nightly TV news. The next day, I sold the commercial I envisaged to the local client on the basis of nothing more than a sheet of hastily typed paper.

The only problem now was how to get hold of all the footage. This being about five years before the internet started to transform everyone's lives, sourcing archive film and video was far from easy. Thankfully, after firing off several voluminous faxes to the BBC and Pathé libraries and scouring of literally dozens of hours of time-coded tapes, we had the makings of our TVC.

Although an inexplicably disappointing (to me, anyway) performer at awards shows, 'Leaders' did manage to rattle the cage of an elderly local PR 'guru' called Ted Thomas. Seemingly resident in Asia since Marco Polo first hit the Silk Road, twinkly-eyed Ted seemed to be infected with the same misplaced sense of superiority afflicting most other expats of his generation.

The reason for his righteous indignation on this particular occasion? Our perfidious use the Queen of England to sell a German car. Either unaware of (or wilfully blind to) the Teutonic skeletons lurking in the House of Windsor's (née Saxe-Coburg's) closets, Ted fired off an angry fusillade that appeared in the next day's paper.

Years later, it emerged that Ted had fleeced internationally renowned veteran journalist Clare Hollingsworth (RIP) out of some HK$1,465,000 (then about £112,000) of her life savings in one five-day period in August 2003. When questioned about the size of these particular withdrawals, Thomas claimed it was for 'taxi fares and wet fish'. Whether or not the subject of my 'Leaders' TVC came up during one of the confabs for which dear old Ted used to bill Ms. Hollingsworth HK$400 an hour has yet to be established.

***

As my brief and unhappy stint with KROK demonstrates, getting hessian-bagged was (still is) just one thread in the rich tapestry of ad agency life.

The next time a sacking (not, I hasten to add, my own) was to affect me was at an agency called Cr8ive. But first, there was the small matter of applying for and being offered a job there.

Having heard from friends that the agency was

looking for an associate CD (ACD), I promptly fired off a written application. Should it prove successful, my direct boss at 'Masturb8', as the agency's perennially peeved former (and current) employees called it, would be a man called 'Kai Zi'. A rather anally retentive local HK Chinese chap, the Kaizer eschewed any cultural activities that didn't involve centuries-old classical music. With most successful admen determined to 'grab and squeeze the zeitgeist by the bollocks', Kai's stance didn't sit well with the many colleagues and consumers who did not share his tastes.

During our initial job interview in the summer of 1992, I discovered he was even less solicitous of the need for confidentiality when recruiting staff. Stuck in a rut after three-odd years at CPU, I was, to recycle a phrase the 'dynamic, self-starting' me used to regularly trot out while writing recruitment ads, 'seeking a new challenge'. Could I 'add a new dimension' to Cr8ive's 'successful, multi-award-winning team? I not only could, by golly, I would!

After reading my letter, the Kaizer invited me in for a preliminary interview for the ACD job. While I'm still in the dark about why such pow-wows succeed or fail, our get-together seemed to go reasonably well. We certainly discussed upping my existing salary from HK$40,000 to HK$44,000 a month (then about £3,300). Knowing the Hong Kong Chinese shunned the number four because it sounded like 'death', I should have stuck to my guns and demanded an extra thousand or four.

As we exchanged goodbyes, Kai said something along the lines of 'I hope you don't mind if I talk to Jerry at CPU about your potential move here.' I politely responded that it might be better for me if he held off until I'd signed (or at least been given) a legally binding contract. At this point, Kai's face turned fire engine red with embarrassment. In a sign that was later to become all too familiar, a small vein in his right temple then began a steady rhythmic pumping. 'Sorry, John, I don't think I made myself clear. I actually spoke to Jerry about your moving here yesterday before you came over,' my employer-designate said rather sheepishly.

That night, I went home to find a letter in my mailbox in which CPU informed me that they had awarded me a HK$5,000 increase – roughly double the raises I'd received in each of the previous two years.

Fuck.

I was set to become probably the only creative in advertising history to move from one agency to a more senior position at a second for less money. Thanks a bunch, Mr. K.

In addition to his tendency to screw up his potential employees' careers, the Kaizer was also in the habit of shucking off projects he wasn't inter-ested in like a snake sheds its skin. The messes he left would then have to be sorted out by myself and an Aussie art director called David Szabo. As he remains a good friend to this day (he even designed the cover of this book), I am sure Szabs won't mind when I call him a tad eccentric. Sadly, little foibles such as spreading peanut butter onto lunchtime slices of bread using a grimy, cow-gum-encrusted 18-inch plastic ruler drove agency CEO 'Lou Hai' ballistic.

The reason for Loopy Lou's colossal downer on Szabs remains a conundrum only he could explain but never properly did. Ultimately, I found Szabs to be – whilst sometimes maddeningly stubborn – easily the most gifted of the three really terrific art directors I've partnered for any appreciable amount of time. Within six months of our first putting our heads together, we had 11 pieces of work on the walls at the annual Hong Kong 4As awards show. While the distance from the wall to the list of category finalists was as far as all 11 putative *meisterworks* travelled, our shared creative trip was a blast while it lasted. Had Hai only acted sensibly and refused to allow personal foibles to undermine his professional attitudes, there's no telling what David and I might have achieved together.

Temporarily unmoored from reality by liberal helpings of pre-show beers and spliffs, I may have been, but that particular awards show marked the evening I made my local TV debut. In desperate search of someone quotable, local radio DJ and awards evening show host called Steve James grabbed my arm in the queue for the bar. Before I knew it (and against my better judgement), I was happily dispensing pearls of wisdom for the viewing masses. Well, at least those who were still conscious at 12:30 am five days later when the recording finally went out. Generously refreshed, I may have been, but Steve was so happy with what we got on screen that he persuaded me back for a repeat performance the following year.

But back to Hai's shitcanning of Szabs. One Friday morning after a lengthy spell of late nights on various pitches, I called in a 'mental health day'. With a bank holiday on Monday, four whole days of idleness and Biblical-level debauchery stretched ahead of me. When I did return to work the following Tuesday, Kai surreptitiously slid into my office and silently shut the door behind him.

'I suppose you've heard about David?' the Kaizer asked me *sotto voce*. Having spent much of Saturday and Sunday on the phone to Szabs, I had indeed heard what had happened. Not that I was prepared to let Kai off the hook lightly.

'No, I've not. Is he OK? I hope that nothing bad's happened to him,' I replied.

'Well, Lou came in on Friday afternoon and told me that I had to let him go.'

'"Let him go"? Sorry, Zi, but I'm not sure what

you mean. Was Szabs somehow unhappy here because he felt you and Lou were holding him against his will or something?'

'No, I mean he's been retrenched...'

Ignoring the way the small vein in the Kaizer's temple was beating faster than a hummingbird on crystal meth, I decided it was not quite yet time to throw a parachute to the falling man.

'Sorry, mate, still not with you...'

'What I'm trying to say is that he's been downsized...'

As Szab's sacking was sure to kick the legs from under a series of potentially award-winning ads we were doing for various clients, I wasn't down. I was fucking livid.

'Oh, you mean Lou told you to *fire* him. Why on earth can't you just come to the point and say what it is actually happened rather than try and nicey it up to the nines, Zi?'

While career defenestration was unlikely to prove more than a short-term blip for poor old Szabs, it was going to have rather more of an impact on the agency's second-string writer, 'Gary Poulson'.

Despite the year and a half that had passed since I had achieved the well-nigh impossible industry first of moving agencies for less money, my new employer had yet to review my salary.

With a pay freeze in place at Cr8ive (times were apparently 'tough!' – hey, whenever were they not?), it was most unlikely I'd be receiving any increase anytime soon.

Amusingly (hindsight always is), Hai had joined the female head of the sister agency in Cr8ive's shared group office, to announce an ongoing salary freeze to all staff. 'We are,' Hai gravely enunciated in the sort of voice that usually means the exact opposite of what's being said, 'all in this together.'

If alarm bells hadn't begun ringing by this point, they quickly started their disruptive clanging when his female counterpart helpfully chipped in that we were 'all one big family'. Looking at the pair gurning away at the front of the boardroom, one couldn't help but think of Fred and Rose West as they welcomed a new tenant to their home for dinner.

Pissed off by the callous way Hai had gone over his head and thrown Szabs under the bus, the Kaizer had apparently dreamed up a solution he hoped would kill two birds with one stone. Since Hai was justifying his sacking of David as part of a drive to 'make the agency leaner and meaner', Mr. K now counter-proposed pulling Szabs back and chucking Gary under another bus instead. I, ran his unspoken subtext, would then do my bit for the cause by hurling myself under a 16-wheel lorry and taking on all of Gary's workload for a third of his salary.

Much as I liked (and still like) Szabs, there is no way in the world I could take a salary increase funded by the firing of a colleague and friend (as Gary, like my errant art director, remains to this day). The end result was that Szabs got the heave-ho and Gary lived to write another day.

***

In those pre-permanent global financial crisis days, Cr8ive's most precious (and profitable) client was a high-end German car manufacturer. Regarded as the ultimate status symbol by almost every Hongkonger, the cars practically sold themselves without any outside help. Happily, 'Robert Chan', who headed up the marque's local distributor, was a firm believer in the power of advertising.

Like Coca-Cola inventor Asa Candler, who insisted on re-investing the lion's share of sales revenues in branding exercises aimed at cornering the soft drink market, Robert's faith was not misplaced. When I worked on his account, his car brand was shifting more cars per capita in Hong Kong than anywhere else in the world – Germany and the US included. All I had to do was help my team to consistently create ads and TVCs that underlined the cars' desirability as a means of 'getting to the top' and staying there.

A staunch believer that 'money was falling from the sky' in sales revenues, Robert was open to almost any suggestion that might burnish his brand's image. As a result, he was easily the best client I've ever had the pleasure of creating ads and TVCs for.

Believing I was a gobby spendthrift, his subordinates, 'Harry' and 'Lloyd', tried to pinch the pennies by squashing every idea the agency came up with. Happily, Robert rather liked my WTF attitude and was only too happy to splash the cash needed to actualize his vision.

Fresh from winning a prestigious European Touring Car Championship in the mid 1990s, the carmaker had entered no fewer than four cars in the road race at that year's Macau Grand Prix weekend. Certain their cars' victory was a mere formality, Robert's distributorship coughed up some HK$2,000,000 for Szabs (then still gainfully employed by Cr8ive), me, and our choice of director and film crew to shoot a congratulatory commercial in Macau. And with gaudy 'Access All Area' lanyards slung rakishly around our necks, that's exactly what we spent eight whole days doing.

With some splendid interview and dramatic pit team footage in the can, the Sunday of the race rolled around. As wonderfully mild, bright, and sunny as only autumn days in the South China Sea can be, all looked set fair for a great day's racing. Another victim of the overconfidence bug, I signed our victory ad off with a flourish and gave our just-in-case second place ad a contemptuous initialling.

Emitting an unbelievably loud shriek and leaving a huge plume of toxic fumes in their wake, off screamed the 20 or so cars in the race. Barely had the miasma begun to clear than God decided to throw a divine spanner into the works of our cunning plan.

While it would be tempting to write that the wheels started to come off big time, it was actually two of our four cars that spun off the track and out of contention instead.

One turn of the race gone and half our assault force *hors de combat*, we were faced with an agonising twenty-seven-and-three-quarter-lap wait. Eventually, our best remaining car limped home fourth. As if all this wasn't bad enough, it did so behind three cars belonging to our client's biggest rival.

Left with literally miles of apparently useless footage, both Kaizer and our chosen director on the project quickly lost interest. It was something of a minor miracle that Szabs and myself were able to reward Robert with not one but two commercials salvaged from the mess. In neither TVC were the words 'Macau Grand Prix Touring Car Race' ever uttered or shown on screen.

The only other memory worth salvaging from the entire sorry saga that was the spot's post-production came when I was working with the film house's producer, 'Emma'. The Hong Kong of the early 1990s was a huge cash cow for dodgy self-assertive therapy treatments such as EST and Exegesis. The one that was currently flavour of the month was called Life Dynamics, and Emma was one of the program's most zealous adherents.

While waiting for a local production house to toss another on what was now a high pile of rejected edits, I casually reached for a beer and asked Emma about her plans for the weekend. Eyes ablaze with the righteousness of a Moonie or modern-day ISIS member, she proudly announced she was off to scale the latest peak in the Life Dynamics mountain range.

Perhaps, she posited, someone like me could benefit hugely from signing up and taking a few classes myself. 'Emma,' I replied, 'while I would be the first person to admit that I am every bit the fuck up you think I am, there's one big difference between us.'

'Oh and what,' Emma gamely enquired, 'might that difference be?' I simply replied that I wasn't so screwed over that I'd reached the point where I had to keep paying someone a large sum of money to remind me of the fact.

My two other fondest memories of working with Robert's distributorship involved a Christmas press ad and a TVC about a wedding.

Created immediately after Szabs' pink-slipping, the undisputed star atop the tree of the several Christmas ad options we proposed to the car company consisted of two successive full-size broadsheet newspaper pages. The first read: 'We'd like to wish everyone who already owns one of our cars a very merry Christmas.' Readers would then turn the page to learn: 'We'd also like to wish those of you who've yet to achieve your dream an even more prosperous New Year.'

While day-to-day contacts Harry and his number two, Lloyd, both liked the approach, the former was a black belt-level skinflint who always wanted to cut corners and slash costs. Why, he suggested, could we not save on budget by combining everything on one page? Thankfully, Robert entered the room at precisely this point and sat down to look over the ideas I and my team had created for him.

Robert was nothing if not a gentleman and said he would be perfectly happy to run all five or six options the agency had presented. What was the opinion of everyone around the table?

I briefly outlined how the agency and Harry were deadlocked as to whether to run our recommended ad over one or two pages. 'And what do you think, John?' Robert asked.

'Well, as you always say, Robert, we're in the business of marketing Hong Kong's most sought-after motor car so let's not hide our light under a bushel.'

The two-consecutive-page format duly signed off on, the great man promptly exited the boardroom and left me to face the barely suppressed animus of his two stymied underlings.

My other fun memory of working with this particular client was bringing to fruition a TVC about a wedding (the one time every Hongkonger was sure to ride in one of the company's cars). The only problem was – for reasons known only to himself – the Kaizer hated my proposed commercial with a vengeance and refused to let me present it to the client. Thankfully, Mr. K was not going to be around forever.

In the run-up to the territory's 1997 handover to China, there was a uniquely Hong Kong phenomenon known as the 'astronaut'. Such spacemen were local professionals who, fearing for their post-handover lives, had emigrated to Canada with their families in order to keep their options open after 1997.

A Canuck passport in their back pockets, they were then free to either regularly return to earth (i.e. Hong Kong) on short-term business trips. Alternatively, they could simply keep their powder dry until an opportunity arose to start devising other, more permanent, plans.

Having parlayed his bloated salary into ownership of some five or six local flats, the Kaizer decided to go one better and move his family lock, stock, and barrel to Toronto. Despite having given the agency's biggest client two TVCs out of a pile of otherwise completely useless footage, I was apparently deemed 'too volatile' to be anointed as his successor.

Annoyed but not surprised, I resolved to use the gap between his departure and his replacement's arrival to beef up my portfolio and showreel. I then worked harder than *24*'s Jack Bauer to get clients to greenlight as many projects of mine that Kai had binned as was humanly possible. One of the TVCs I was especially keen to get on air was the wedding spot for the German car company

Two days after Kai left – all the time it took to get the script languishing in my desk drawer polished, storyboarded, and presented – Robert gave us a blank cheque to proceed.

When Kai's replacement, 'Terry Crawley', came onboard, he fell head over heels for the concept. With no ad agency anywhere having yet used a famous song a long-dead singer had named after the car brand in a TVC, he told me to beg, borrow or steal the rights. In those days, I was supplementing my income by regularly reviewing records and books for the *SCMP*. As I'd recently critiqued the singer's sister and executor's memoir of her famous sibling, I was in just the right place to negotiate licensing fees. We duly bought out local broadcast rights for US$30,000 – even then, a ridiculously low sum for such an iconic tune. Within a couple of years, agencies in Europe and the US were paying vastly inflated retainers to use the song themselves.

There is a syndrome in advertising called the 'Airfix Client'. The term simply describes marketers who, content with grey, partly completed models, cannot see any logic in adding the paint and transfers needed to lift their work to another level. Harry and Lloyd were dictionary definitions of this phenomenon. Unashamed tightwads when asked to invest in transforming solid creative ideas into spectacular executions, their vision would never extend past the uninspiring grey of their boxes' interiors.

Despite knowing full well we would be using a reinterpretation rather than the dead singer's original, Harry kept asking to hear the tune that had gobbled up such a sizeable chunk of his budget. Finally, two days before the start of the shoot, we were forced to slot a CD of the fatally drink-and-drug-ravaged songsmith's tune into his office stereo.

As he listened to the not-long-for-this-world blues legend slur her way through the song's 30-odd seconds, Harry seemed in imminent danger of joining her on the other side. Had the 'Thin and White Lips World Championship' been held in Hong Kong that particular evening, he would have comfortably seen off all comers.

***

Despite our inevitable subsequent falling out, it would be churlish of me to diss Terry as being anything but a world-class creative talent. The only caveat? Despite his proven ability to craft award-winning communications, he never seemed to fully comprehend just how important the whole loss-of-face business was to the local Chinese.

Despite having settled in Australasia, Terry remained at heart a dour northerner whose man-management skills could have used a little – strike that – lot of work. Having initially given me a welcome 25 per cent pay increase not to up sticks for another agency, Terry soon started attempting to reshape Cr8ive's Hong Kong creative department in his own image. The only problem was that, seemingly more focused on style rather than substance, his hiring policies left huge amounts to be desired.

This being the 1990s, when such practices were common, the most telling early hire he made was of an extremely attractive South African woman called 'Leeza' as creative secretary. As awesome a sight as she was whilst striding around the office in her impossibly tight designer jeans, poor 'Leeza' couldn't type to save her life. This caused huge problems in the wee small hours immediately preceding pitches, when frazzled creatives who should have been finessing concepts were tied up typing their own scripts.

Despite my having pleaded long, hard, and unsuccessfully for a proper computer system for the creative department, Terry felt I was being disrespectful in moaning about poor Leeza's all-round unsuitability. During his next trip to London, he started interviewing other copywriters and art directors. Especially impressed by one art director candidate, he promptly hired not only him but also – sight unseen – his copywriter. This despite the latter's apparently not even bothering to get out of bed and travel across town for the interview.

Where was the money for these high-profile new hires going to come from?

Simple. Terry embarked on the age-old strategy beloved of agency top dogs who want shot of their staff: he began muttering dark hints that I was somehow 'unhappy'.

Needing funds to pay for the dynamic duo from London, Terry had made the unilateral decision that the melancholia he had diagnosed in me was now manifesting itself in my work. Maybe Terry – now rather aptly nicknamed Tropical Depression Terry (TDT) – enquired sweetly if I might benefit by 'resigning and taking a few months off to recharge (my) batteries?'

After pausing to take stock, I remarked that

if the agency wanted me gone, they could pay me the three months' notice they owed me under my contract. Lips pursed to a degree of thinness and whiteness even our old friend Harry would have hankered after, TDT was not a happy camper.

Having effectively signed my own death warrant, I now had to endure months of Creepy Crawley pettily rejecting pretty much every concept I ran by him. Despite actively investigating moves elsewhere in Hong Kong or Asia, I was getting increasingly pissed off by TDT's offhand treatment. But as the old saying has it, 'everything comes to he who waits.'

Opportunity finally knocked one lunchtime. A zealous adherent of the 1990s 'New Man' trend, Terry was forever adding to his impressive armoury of skincredible lotions, potions, unguents, moisturizers, and multi-corrective creams. This particular day, he'd gone off to a client lunch.

Desperate to fill rather than pamper his face for a change, he'd foolishly left his office door wide open and several products in plain view on his desk. Amongst them was a bottle of very expensive facial scrub *pour homme*. Given all the acidity Terry had begun pouring into my life, I considered repaying the favour by recalibrating what the label called his skin's 'meticulously optimised' pH balance. While revenge may be best savoured cold, it can be equally satisfying when served up a hot, steamy yellow and garnished with generous lashings of justified animosity accompanied by a *soupçon* of moral outrage.

Did I seize my chance to surreptitiously pocket Tim's bottle and stroll to the men's room? Alas I did not.

In all the years since, have I ever felt even the most momentary pangs of conscience for contemplating doing the unthinkable? If I did, any feelings of guilt or regret instantly evaporated when I opened that year's local awards book. Flicking through its pages, I was furious to learn Terry had credited himself on the 'Leaders' TVC I'd written and bulldozed onto screen months before he'd arrived in Hong Kong.

Eventually, all my fishing around for jobs paid off. Offered CD posts in not only Singapore but also Jakarta and Ho Chi Minh City, I opted for Vietnam. Having finally freed up additional funds for the creative team he'd hired from London, Terry was all sweetness and light again. 'I really envy you in having the chance to go and work in Vietnam, John,' he said, the warmth in his smile not quite burning bright enough to illuminate his eyes.

'Terry, the Vietnamese people have endured thousands of years of oppression by the Chinese, French, and the US, followed by 20 years of communist re-education. Don't you think they've suffered enough?'

Shortly before I and my then girlfriend left for Saigon, I read one of those amusing collision-of-culture articles the *SCMP* occasionally used to fill up space in its pages. The story concerned a local shop owner who'd mistakenly been sent a 'With Deepest Sympathy for Your Sad Loss' wreath when opening his latest outlet. As the retailer ruefully pointed out, the mix up was a lot more distressing for the bereaved family, who'd received a cheery bunch of 'Best of Luck in Your New Location!' flowers.

Busy packing bags and boxes ahead of my move across the South China Sea, I hoped the story wasn't some kind of portent...

Chapter Seven

*All things are possible in Vietnam
(except for the things that aren't)*

When I got offered the sniff of a chance to go and work in Ho Chi Minh City (HCMC) for an agency called 'McNamara's' by my friend Colin Ruffell in late 1996, I leapt at the opportunity. Although 'the American War' had ended 21 years before, US sour grapes and restrictions on trading and investment meant the country's wide-open French-style boulevards had remained largely unchanged.

Still decorated in the gaudy functionality that Eastern Europeans thought of as luxuriously chic, central HCMC's legendary Rex Hotel was a case in point. Drink in the untouched cityscapes available from its rooftop bar, and you could almost hear the ghostly laughter of vanished photographer Sean Flynn and his long-dead pals as they caroused in corridors far below.

''Nam'. Having watched the movies, read the books, bought the records, and seen the bands, it was impossible to think of it any other way. When I moved there in early January 1997, the country was home to one of the world's youngest populations, with something like 60 per cent of its then 74,000,000 inhabitants aged 30 or under. Remarkably for a country that had been so badly brutalised and scarred by year after year of bombardment from the air and take-no-prisoners close-combat fighting, even older Vietnamese rarely ever mentioned the hostilities.

After enduring the French and American wars, followed by two decades of austerity, hardship, and harsh re-education policies, Vietnam was finally taking its first hesitant baby steps into the late 20th century. Marking a move away from a planned centralized economy to a less rigid and better-balanced alternative, 1986's introduction of a new policy called *Đổi Mới* (renovation) was vital for the country's future success.

Older clients who'd grown up in Saigon and lived through much of the war and its aftermath were understandably less than fully convinced. As in all hard-line communist countries, deliciously dark, mordant humour had been adopted as a coping mechanism. One client – let's call him 'Mr. Dit' in case he's still around and likely to end up in a cell– told us a joke that summed up prevailing attitudes perfectly.

On his deathbed, Ho, Chi Minh apparently called for his *aides de camp* and began speaking of his vision of his homeland's post-war future. 'I see a Vietnam,' said Uncle Ho, 'where there is nothing but peace, prosperity, and unlimited potential for all!' His discourse over, the elderly leader closed his eyes one last time, sighed, and died. 'Today, some 28 years after Uncle Ho's death,' Mr. Dit told us, 'Vietnam is a quarter of the way to achieving his vision. We have,' he concluded, 'nothing.'

What HCMC did have in abundance were tranquil, tree-lined city streets where the hands of time had preserved in amber the world when it was a purer and more innocent place. Thankfully, nature hadn't exactly been swinging the lead when it came to nurturing and replenishing Vietnam's endless tracts of beautiful, lush green countryside.

So recently reduced to charred wastelands by the American forces' relentlessly callous use of Napalm and Agent Orange, the fields and paddies were now luxuriously verdant once more. Soaking up the lushness, it was impossible to imagine the farmlands all around you concealed the remains of a bigger tonnage of bombs than had fallen in the whole of World War Two. While efforts were being made to clear up the unexploded shells, so fierce was the battering Vietnam had endured that no one knew for sure how many bombs remained buried. Nor did anyone seem to know the exact spots where much of the ordnance had fallen or quite how deeply it lay. More than two decades after I lived there and 43 years since the US slunk home in disgrace, the country is still struggling to make its agrarian hinterlands safe.

My failure to do more than scratch the surface of what this most magical, tragic, and fascinating of places had to offer remains amongst my biggest regrets. Two sights that I was lucky enough to see during the year I spent in 'Nam remain seared on the back of my retina to this day.

The first was the complex crisscrossing network of tunnels at Cu Chi. Too tiny for the average Western to clamber inside, the original tunnels had been recreated in heights and widths that would more comfortably accommodate fat bastards like myself. As with the rabbit hole in Lewis Carrol's *Through the Looking Glass*, the tunnels led to a mind-boggling alternate reality – in this instance entire subterranean towns equipped with kitchens, dormitories, and even hospital operating theatres and recovery wards.

Once safely back on *terra firma*, one could even purchase bullets at US$1 a pop and fire an AK-47 at a far-off target. I proved so adept at my only attempt at firing a gun that the armourer rewarded me with what he dubiously claimed was a sniper's hat. Despite my doubts about its authenticity and its failure to do more than perch comically atop my swollen head, I still have the titfer all these years later.

My second far less pleasant memory of 'Nam came at the American War Museum (now just the War Museum) on Võ Văn Tần. Just a few hundred yards down the road from McNamara's HCMC office, the facility was a ramshackle assembly of photos, medals, uniforms, and disarmed or destroyed ordnance. To peek inside the cockpit of the star attraction, a more or less complete F5A fighter jet, was to discover controls so rudimentary you felt you could fly the plane yourself.

Nearby stood an innocuous-looking hut whose inner shelves housed the harrowing sight of jar after jar of malformed foetuses. Once a symbol of hope for its proud expectant parents, each unborn child had been warped in unimaginably hideous ways by the Americans' merciless (over)use of defoliants such as Agent Orange. Not having lived long enough to be numbered amongst Vietnam's two million or so war dead, each exhibit was horrific testimony to the awful wrongness of America's attempt to stop the spread of pinkoism across Southeast Asia.

Despite the 1960's optimistic surface sheen, logic and compassion seem to have been in very short supply outside the US and inside its armed forces. As one unknown American officer said after hundreds of Vietnamese lay dead in the rubble of Bến Tre, 'It became necessary to destroy the town to save it.'

Despite its having suffered so terribly at the hands of Western aggressors, first France and then the US, Vietnam was unique in at least one respect. Unlike almost every other Asian country I visited, its language did not appear to have any derogatory words or phrases for Caucasians. Not in my hearing, anyway. More than making up for the shortfall in this particular form of noise pollution was HCMC's unimaginably large number of antiquated (and very noisy) two-stroke motor scooters.

As anyone who's ever stepped into the seeming chaos of a Vietnamese street will be quick to tell you, the country's love affair with humble put-put-puttering motorbikes results in some eye-opening sights. On any given day, you might see not only mum, dad, and three kids but also grandma and grandpa hanging on for dear life as their family's cherished bike weaves through traffic. Scooters laden down with baggage far too cumbersome and weighty for the bike's driver to be able to see over or around were equally common. Amazingly, given such a lack of control, serious accidents resulting from drivers' poor handling of their errant wheels were something of a rarity.

This, of course, was of scant reassurance to hungover expats about to embark on their first Indiana Jones-style early morning crossing of a major HCMC thoroughfare. To arrive at the kerb of a road in any Vietnamese city in the mid 1990s was to effectively perch on and peer over the edge of a vehicular Grand Canyon. With no traffic lights or pedestrian crossings worth a damn back then, negotiating safe passage across the street was ultimately a crossing even Hannibal and his elephants might have baulked at.

The first step you had to take was the ostensibly suicidal one of plunging headfirst into what was effectively a ceaseless eddy and flow of families and cargo consignments on bikes. Congratulations! Understandably hesitant initial steps taken, you'd succeeded in making it fully three feet from the pavement's edge without getting maimed or killed.

Before you knew it, you'd begin summoning up the courage to embark on what only a few seconds before had seemed an unthinkable second, third, and then fourth step into the sea of scooters. With no one paying you the slightest heed as they imperceptibly shifted course so as not to run you over, you'd soon feel as if you 'd become one with the flow.

In no time at all, you emerged unscathed and plonked yourself down on the kerb at the other side of the road. When you rushed to tell your friends and colleagues about your once-in-a-lifetime journey, they'd simply give a disinterested been-there-done-that-got-the-T-shirt shrug. Two days later, you'd be crossing and re-crossing busy streets as nonchalantly as free running pioneer Sébastien Foucan scaling and running along the foot-wide rooftop ledge of an 80-storey building.

Vietnam's police were every bit as singular. Having found a delightful old colonial villa a stone's throw down the street from Phú Nhuận district cop shop, my then girlfriend, Bing, and I weren't too worried about break-ins. When I told a Vietnamese colleague called 'Pho' about our choice of home and its apparent advantages when it came to dissuading housebreakers, he burst out laughing. An enigmatic 'Good luck with *that*' was all he'd say on the matter.

Pho knew of what he spoke, too. The first week after we moved in, several senior representatives of the local Police Benevolent Fund were around requesting we contribute to their coffers. One US$50 annual donation in the proffered box, and the cops left us alone for the next six months. Just as well considering the amount of potent Vietnamese grass I used to get through each week.

Freely available from a fast-food stall outside Saigon's Opera House, Mr. Fuery's Old Shag came in mini-packs of 20 beautifully rolled joints for just US$5. A few post-work beers in the nearby Q Bar, a quick visit to the deaf and dumb lady who somehow juggled running her retail empire with her role as Vietnam's Howard Marks, and you were in clover.

***

A little over two decades after Viet Cong tanks had overrun HCMC's American embassy, another – far less bloody and significant but no less intense – battle was being waged. This time, the struggle was taking place in the conference rooms and creative departments of the city's fresh-on-the-block ad agencies. Soon, I was to find myself cast as a kind of unwilling commanding officer in McNamara's reimagining of Hamburger Hill. Ladies and gentlemen, please take your seats as we begin the great Kola Kontretemps of 1997.

Generating massive revenues for major agency offices the whole world over, 'KoKoKola' (KKK) remained the jewel in McNamara's global agency crown. In an eerie reflection of US military advisors' now rightfully derided domino theory, McNamara's sole *raison d'etre* for being in Vietnam was to hang on to the KKK account at all costs. As the agency's fifth CD in less than four years, my main task was to keep the brand from defecting to the local office of their deadliest rival for the client's massive global billings.

Alas, KKK Head Office in the US had blundered rather badly in appointing a returning Vietnamese (sneeringly known by the locals as 'Viet Qs') called 'Đéo Biết' (ĐB) as its local CEO. At which point, a little background is in order...

The deepest scars left by the American War included an abiding repugnance for those who had elbowed their way onboard the last few helicopters that had fled Saigon's US Embassy in April 1975. With the gravy train of good times fast approaching Vietnam's borders, many of those who'd abandoned what had then been South Vietnam had slowly begun to drift back.

Contemptuously called 'Viet Qs', the prodigals' return was viewed as a contemptuous slap in the face by those who'd been left behind and forced to endure years of unimaginable post-war hardship. Welcoming to Westerners, they may have been, but the 'remainers' weren't in any rush to kill and cook fatted calves for those who'd pissed off and left them to their fate.

The fact that he was less than universally liked or respected by his staff and suppliers simply ultimately didn't appear to bother ĐB in the slightest. But then, so ingrained were his delusions of adequacy, he might simply never have been aware of the low regard in which local Vietnamese held him. If there was one thing that was mithering him greatly, it was a competitor's use of the Spice Girls as 'brand ambassadors' in what was proving to be a hugely effective TV campaign.

One only had to turn on one of the local TV channels during a commercial break to see that the little oik had a point. There, warbling their meticulously auto-tuned yet oddly tuneless way through TVC after TVC extolling A.N. Other Kola Kompany's charms was a semi-naked assemblage of Posh, Scary, Sporty, Ginger, and Brad Dexter Spice. To make sure no one was at risk of misunderstanding the threat KoKoKola was facing, we studied the Spice Girls TVCs for the rival brand for the next half an hour. Needless to say, the fact that the sight of scantily clad Western hussies on Vietnamese TV was as rare as prime-time showings of Sylvester Stallone's *Rambo* had absolutely no bearing on our decision.

'Something has to be done about this and fast,' ĐB demanded with a decisiveness of which short-lived South Vietnamese leader Ngô Đình Diệm of three decades earlier would have been proud.

Once every few years in an adman's life, the stars align, and every utterance that comes out of his or her mouth assumes a lustrousness worthy of unspun gold. This particular creative meeting gave me one of those fleeting 24-carat open goals.

'Why don't we mount a letter-writing campaign to local TV stations and the country's various censorship boards?' said I.

ĐB's ears immediately pricked up. 'Sounds good to me, John, but how exactly would we go about doing such a thing?'

What I suggested was that I and the rest of the creative team go away and churn out 15 to 20 template letters. Each and every missive would denounce our enemy in the Kola wars for unleashing wave after wave of offensive capitalist smut we were sure the censors would agree had to be stopped. Once the drafts had been approved, staff from KKK and McNamara's could get their friends to sign and send out pre-prepared letters to those with sufficient clout to pull the Spice Girls off-air.

In the end, we came up with some 15 variants of righteous moral indignation that would not have disgraced the letters page of the *Daily Fail*. A typical self-righteous screed from 'Disgusted of Điện Biên Phủ' would read not unlike the draft below:

Dear Sir,

The other night, my family and I were watching TVN and were shocked to see a bunch of shameless, barely clothed Western trollops disporting their cheap sexuality for all the world to see. As someone who lived through the American War, I am appalled by how quickly our once-noble motherland is rushing to embrace capitalism and its hollow promises. Neither I nor anyone I know who reveres sound Communist values believes we should allow such effluent to continue polluting the hearts and minds of our youth.

For the sake of my wife and children and other similarly defenceless creatures the length and breadth of Vietnam, I implore you to remove this corrupting filth from our country's TV screens this instant!

Yours, etc, etc

It eventually took our battalion of paper-tiger

correspondents just under a month to get A.N. Other Kola's campaign pulled off the air. Only after the spots had been re-edited to the point of emasculation were they once again deemed fit for broadcast.

My mate 'Geoff' over at 'BlackAd', whom we will eventually meet up with again later in Kenya, was not nearly so lucky.

As the Vietnamese authorities viewed advertising to be the thin and unacceptable end of a fat, un-lubricated capitalist wedge, actually getting TVCs passed for on-air broadcast was a Kafkaesque nightmare. Generally, an artfully folded US$50 – or, in rare cases, US$100 – stuffed into the video case was usually sufficient to get a rough-cut VHS past censors at station level. Unfortunately, the official with ultimate power of life and death over your TVC was probably far less open to corruption. Either that or he was just wwwwwaaaaaayyyyyy more expensive to bribe.

Geoff's tale of woe involves the production of a TVC aimed at marketing affordably priced canisters of liquid petroleum gas (LPG). Despite already being hugely popular with families in big cities, such new-fangled conveniences remained unimagined luxuries for the millions attempting to eke out livings in Vietnam's vast rural hinterlands.

Vietnamese-style communism still being very much of the old-school '2 + 2 = 5' variety in the

1990s, getting storyboards officially greenlit before proceeding to the horrifically expensive business of filming was a must. As already noted, local-level rubber-stamping usually entailed little more than the surreptitious slipping of a few foreign banknotes into the itchy palm of a time-serving jobsworth. Only available from humourless hard-liners presented with finished, ready-to-broadcast films, national-level go-aheads were infinitely harder to obtain – as Geoff was shortly to learn.

Fresh off the plane from shooting, editing, and post-producing his locally approved concept in Australia, Geoff arrived at the government censor's office to leap his one last hurdle. He duly slotted his VHS into the bigwig's video player and rolled his tape.

The next half-minute was a blur of heart-warming images of smiling rural Vietnamese family members returning home after a fulfilling day of tilling their fields for the glory of the motherland. Remarkably unsoiled by their hours of sweaty toil, in true TVC style, dad and the kids watched adoringly as mum turned on their LPG stove. After a few mandatory shots to establish how simple LPG was to use and how beautifully it cooked food, the spot cut to mum serving up a delicious, nutritious dinner. With barely a scantily clad Western slattern to disrupt their reverie, everyone sat down to share a dish that would not have disgraced the tables of Saigon's leading *cordon bleu* restaurant.

All set to bask in the healthy glow of official approval for his Vietnamese cultural value-affirming efforts, Geoff promptly sat down himself. The censor behind the desk, a 'Colonel Nguyen', simply tossed his video back at him and uttered a curt 'Approval denied!'

While usually unwise to question the reasoning of dyed-in-the-wool Communist Party officials, an envelope stuffed with filthy capitalist lucre was sometimes sufficient to grease and get the wheels of censorship moving. After carefully appraising the mood of the stumbling black sat opposite him, Geoff sensibly decided this was not one of those occasions. That said, he wasn't about to let all those precious large-denomination US$ notes the spot had cost slip down the drain without a fight. 'Could you perhaps tell me what is so contentious about our commercial that you've decided to stop it from being screened, Colonel Nguyen'?' he asked politely.

Adjusting the rimless, half-moon spectacles that are the uniform of underqualified and overly powerful government lackeys the whole world over, the Colonel looked up at Geoff and glared. 'If cooking on a wood stove was good enough for my mother and grandmother, it should be good enough for the rest of the country,' he snapped. 'Now, if you would be so good as to vacate my office, I have matters more deserving of my time and attention.'

It was, Geoff told me later, the most expensive pack of matches he'd ever bought.

Given the sort of monkey business many agencies and clients brazenly chanced in what was effectively the advertising world's Wild West, Col. Nguyen's reaction actually doesn't seem that unreasonable. A recent Australian ad showing Dove Soap's creamy, dreamy suds washing a native aborigine girl white demonstrates that such cultural insensitivities weren't confined to Vietnam or, indeed, the dark ages of the late 1990s.

Yet while everyone moans about admen and women flim-flamming facts, it's all too often arrogant clients who insistent on doing the distorting despite their agencies' vociferous warnings not to. KKK Vietnam's great racing bike giveaway of 1997 is one of the most brazen cases I've ever seen of a household-name client being 'economical with the *actualité*'.

The top prizes in this particular promotion were a hundred – if the client was to be believed – top-of-the-range BMX-type bikes. All KoKoKola drinkers had to do to claim one of the giveaways was to collect 10 bottle tops showing different cycle parts that, when put together, effectively formed a whole bike.

Ever collected Panini football stickers or,

indeed, anything offered by a brand in such a promotion? Then you'll know from painful past experience that there's always one card or piece that is almost impossible to find. Most companies get around this by ensuring that the missing part differs from marketing territory to marketing territory.

Of course, ĐB being ĐB and magically immune from the risks inherent in pissing his customers off, his promo omitted to take this simple step. With high-profile ads, posters, and TVCs hitting consumers everywhere they turned and sales starting to head towards the stratosphere, our old chum was happiness made flesh. Not even Mc-Namara's oft-repeated warnings that KKK needed to start fairly distributing the promised prizes or trouble would ensure was enough to slam the brakes on his sugar rush.

Failing to share ĐB's mile-wide smile of delight were the countless thousands of Vietnamese KoKoKola drinkers who'd collected multiple sets of tops bearing all bar one of the bicycle parts. The only component no one could seem to get their hands – actually backsides – on was the saddle. And as any cyclist will be quick to tell you, it's bloody painful sitting down and trying to cycle somewhere on a bike with no seat.

Ironically, given ĐB's earlier embracing of my suggestion of an anti-Spice Girl letter-writing campaign, it was the sacks of mail sent by disaffected customers out in the sticks that eventually did for his promotion. Before you could say, 'Lance Armstrong,' the wheels had begun to first wobble and then fall off the promotion big time. When Bing and I flew off to Bangkok for a weekend break, everything had started to look a little shaky. By the time I bought a copy of the *Asian Wall Street Journal* (it was either that or a weeks'-old *Women's Weekly*) to read on our return flight, KKK Vietnam was up to its handlebars in the doo-doo.

Towards the top of one of the paper's inside pages was a painfully explicit piece that skewered the brand for its sharp practice regarding the unequal distribution of the bike part bottle tops. Illustrating the piece for all the world to see was a large photo of Vietnamese government workmen ripping down one of ĐB's expensive roadside billboards.

Undeterred by the scandal, ĐB ploughed ahead with his continual request for new TVC concepts despite his never having sufficient funds to actually shoot and screen the damn things.

Having toured the cafes where young Vietnamese gathered to chew the fat over a post-work coffee, I'd seen how popular animated films such as Tom and Jerry and Looney Tunes were. Why, I suggested at our next client review, don't we film and broadcast an animated TVC?

'Vietnamese people don't like animated cartoons' – or so ĐB's deceptively boyish-looking mini-me, the appropriately named 'Mr. Phat' (pronounced with an 'r', in case you're interested) would have us believe. Each time we proposed a new concept, our flatulent friend promptly shot it down for the same reason.

'Vietnamese people,' the baby-faced enforcer would drone imperiously, 'don't like new things.' Nor, it later transpired, did they like 'old things'. Spots showing people in cars, on scooters, or playing with animals also stood tall in the Vietnamese people's massed ranks of mystifying no-nos. Tiring of the dance (a romantic meeting in a disco was another idea the omniscient Mr. P had earlier rejected out of hand), I asked what it was he thought that Vietnamese people *did* like?

Mouth turned downwards like Sylvester Stallone's whilst reviewing the Vietnamese box office returns for his latest under-performing *Rambo* sequel, Mr. Phat was extremely aggrieved. Clambering down from his high chair and puffing himself up to his full five-foot-two-inch height, he disapprovingly denounced me as a racist in front of the entire meeting.

'Chinh, mate,' said McNamara's CEO, 'Peter Seaton', 'I think you can and probably will accuse John of many things. But given that his long-term girlfriend, Bing, whom you actually met at the agency's Tet spring dinner, is from the Philippines, I very much doubt racism is one of them.'

***

With many major household name brands having received generous seed money from head office and hot young local talents wanting to prove themselves, shooting TVCs in Vietnam should have been a breeze. Unfortunately, most of the dosh sloughing down the corridors of these clients' regional offices came in the form of Vietnamese Đồng, or 'VD', as many Westerners infectiously called it.

Like the collective noun for STDs that inspired its nickname, VD was universally unwelcome both inside and outside Vietnam. And like any unwanted (are there any wanted ones?) dose of clap, it had to be got shot of the moment its unpleasant stigmas started to become apparent. When it finally came to getting a TVC approved for shooting, finding a way to transform those useless đồng notes into user-friendly US dollars thus became everyone's top priority.

While the skill sets (such as they are) of writers/CDs like me are many and varied, money laundering is generally not high on the list.

Enter 'Zak Lister', an Aussie film director, who I worked with for most of the time I was in Vietnam.

While Zak's grasp on day-to-day truth was –

let's be uncharacteristically charitable here – less than rock solid, he was granite personified when you needed to get tightly budgeted TVCs shot and on air. He achieved this double whammy by dealing with a Russian guy called 'Lev', who was going out/staying in with a Western McNamara's staffer called 'Cathy'.

There is a saying amongst those who move in such circles that the US mafia will only kill defaulting debtors after first chivvying them along by breaking a leg. Unfettered by any such moral handbrake, the Russian mafia generally fast-tracks debtors from late payer to killed-and-dumped-in-the-river status before the words 'the cheque's in the post' can exit their mouths.

Wisely, neither I nor anyone else at McNamara's was ever enough of a numpty to ask Lev to loan them money or request he talk them through his impressive array of tattoos. That said, if someone – doubtless Lev himself – held a gun to your head and ordered you to identify his place on the spectrum of extreme violence, you'd unhesitatingly indicate the red danger zone.

Each time a VD-rich McNamara's client needed to shoot a TVC, they'd shuffle through the agency's front door weighed down by a large case stuffed with greasy high-denomination local banknotes. After painstakingly counting out the money and leaving the cases with Zak, the client would then exit the building. Awaiting the all clear, either Lev and/or one of his henchmen would enter the agency via the back door and give the director a smaller and lighter holdall full of US currency. The deal done, Lev and his mate would bugger off to God knows where, and Mr. L would hightail it to the airport and the next flight to Sydney with me not far behind.

My first experience of producing a TVC in Vietnam involved a kind of samizdat 'Q and A' we shot on the streets of Saigon for a two-stroke moped called Love. Although no award winner, the spot – a *vox pop* in which we stopped and asked various likely looking locals what Love meant to them – should have been as cheap as chips to produce. Indeed, the rough cut we shot with a home video cam for just over US$100 certainly got the bike's Vietnamese distributor smiling.

Just one thing was stopping us from airing the TVC.

Totally lacking the technological hocus-pocus needed to turn out vaguely professional-looking commercials, most local production and post-production facilities were positively Flintstonian in their primitiveness. Able to set their own prices, production houses boasting more recent equipment were, of course, eye-wateringly expensive.

The local production company we contacted asked for a ridiculous US$25,000 to reshoot the perfectly serviceable rough cut we'd filmed ourselves for little more than the cost of a decent lunch. In the end, we told them we'd pay them a maximum of US$5,000 to finish everything up to broadcast standard. Faced with a choice between nada and a small amount of cash to begin with, followed by more dosh from other clients later, the production house meekly rolled over and complied.

The most bittersweet aspect of being an expat CD/ECD in an emerging market is the eagerness with which its newly well-off citizens wish to abandon the centuries-old values that underpin their cultural identity. Like Saudi Arabia before it, Vietnam's initial replacement of choice took the form of bland, modern superficiality.

Awestruck to be able to work in such a genuinely extraordinary country, I did everything possible to encourage local creatives to rediscover and rein-terpret their shared heritage for their countrymen and women. As a result, the best of the ads and TVCs I and my teams created while I worked as a CD in places such as Vietnam and Kenya all have a strongly local flavour.

The best of the six of seven commercials I helped create during my year in Vietnam was undoubted-ly the water puppet spot we shot for a Malaysian cooking oil. The story was about a fisherman who catches a fish and is offered a wish to set him free. Rather than take the talking fish to the next round of *Vietnam's Got Talent* auditions, our fisherman requests a lifetime's worth of delicious food and is rewarded with a bottle of cooking oil. (I know, I know...)

If you've read this far without binning your book or burning your kindle and have never seen a water puppet show, they're amongst the most enchanting of Vietnam's many unique traditions. Originally used to entertain the 11th century peasants who broke their backs labouring in the rice paddies of the Red River Delta, the puppets had made the American War Museum their home.

I was instantly smitten when I saw my first show after a fascinating afternoon spent touring around the museum's grounds while searching for inspiration. Best of all, with a budget of about US$25,000 from the client, supplemented by a similar sum from another company, we could post-produce everything to world-class standards in Sydney.

Vietnam being Vietnam, getting filming greenlit by the various authorities – one of whom was a former officer of very senior rank in the Vietnamese army – was inevitably a total nightmare. Happily, delighted with my present of a bottle of very expensive rice wine he then generously proceeded to share with me, 'Major Do Mo' signed off on our request with a wobbly flourish. Clutching the paper like Neville Chamberlin returning from Berlin, I went back to the office a blissfully happy, if unsteady and slightly nauseous, ECD.

Given that the theatre was full of tourists until the museum had been closed and cleaned each evening, the only time we could shoot was late at night. Lights set and cameras all ready to roll, Zak suddenly noticed something crucial was missing. There was no dry ice to give the spot that touch of ethereal mystique all modern-day fairy tales are crying out for.

'No worries,' said Pho, who promptly got on his mobile and called up a few friends. Within half an hour, said mates were heaving the first of the several large blocks of ice they'd ferried to the museum into the pool that was our soundstage. Evocative mist failing to swirl across the water *a la* a Deep Purple video, Zak was disappointed to discover the freshly arrived blocks emitted less vapour than the cubes in his hotel mini-bar.

A lack of dry ice was, of course, the very least of our worries. Given the way every high-voltage camera and klieg light had been stuffed haphazardly into ancient-looking sockets – often with matchsticks – it was a wonder none of us wound up fried to a crisp.

***

The only gremlin in the convoluted financial arrangements involved in shooting TVCs outlined above was the company accountant – actually, an unqualified bookkeeper called 'Paul Burrows'.

While I'm no threat to Warren Buffett, it was glaringly obvious something was out of whack the first time I visited Paul's office. My reason for doing so was to chase up what would eventually prove to be the almost permanent late arrival of my monthly salary.

When you spend the bulk of your career in what economic analysts call 'the Developing World', getting paid late is something you learn to expect and accept on a regular basis. Although no saint, I always did my utmost to ensure my teams got their wages before I did, as they had families to feed and I did not.

With most company finance people, one would seek redress by barging into their office and indulging in a bit of shouting before walking away with a small advance. Cupboard shelves already been stripped bare? You could always try and put a rocket up the agency bean counter's arse by giving his office door a good, hard **SLAM!** on the way out.

Not with our Paul you couldn't. He was unique amongst comptrollers in actually *wanting* impoverished and pissed-off colleagues to heave his office door shut.

When initially quizzed about the whereabouts of my salary, Mr. B. jack-knifed up and out from behind his desk and threw an arm across his office doorframe to prevent me from entering. On my many subsequent visits, I learned that rather than dramatically banging the door, the most effective way to antagonise McNamara's 'Dr. No' was to leave it swinging wide open.

What dark arts was the agency's monetary Merlin performing on that ancient vanilla computer whose screen saver he was so quick to conjure up whenever anyone came within four feet of his desk?

And, more importantly, how long could he continue to keep them hidden?

For the best part of the year I was at McNamara's, no one had the slightest clue as to exactly what it was our under-qualified comptroller was making such a hash of trying to conceal. The only person who did was his Vietnamese girlfriend, 'Phung'. It later transpired that Burrows was funding this latter-day Madame Nhu's beauty salon in HCMC's bustling (sorry, but this is another of those occasions where only a cliché will do) Bến Thành Market.

Inevitably, the stage supporting Paul's extended audition for a Vietnamese retelling of Patricia Highsmith's *The Two Faces of January* eventually came crashing to the ground. Scheduled to meet me for a quick pint before he went away on holiday towards the end of my year in 'Nam, Paul simply failed to show up. Never having been especially big mates with the man, I chalked it up to apathy and ordered up another beer.

The next morning, I arrived at work to be summoned into the agency boardroom by what *Private Eye* would have called an 'ashen-faced and white-lipped' Peter Seaton. Paul, I was told, had spent the bulk of the previous evening 'fessing up the full extent of his embezzlement and was now down at the local nick.

There are times in life when levity just isn't appropriate, and this was undoubtedly one of them. As a result, I bit my lip and avoided the temptation to remark how Paul had effectively been robbing Peter to pay Phung. At the end of the day, though, Paul's greed and stupidity really were no laughing matter. By delaying his colleagues' access to money they had earned and needed for their wives and children, he had been systematically stealing from people whose only crime was misplaced trust.

This doesn't mean to say I didn't retain just a smidgeon of pity for the hapless Burrows. Vietnam's treatment of corruption in those days was draconian with a capital 'D'. The position, as explained to me, seemed to be that death was the standard punishment, with the best-case scenario of life imprisonment viewed as being a namby-pamby slap on the wrist.

Oh dear, poor Paul's prospects were beginning to look even less appealing than one of the 'before' pictures atop the two-for-one weight loss products section on Phung's thriving market stall. The fact that he – like me and every other expat in the agency – was open to all kinds of punishments for effectively working illegally was equally unlikely to help his cause.

Happily, McNamara's eventually took pity on Paul and agreed not to press charges if he agreed to give them sole control of his passport. With Phung vehemently denying all knowledge of his financial support, and not the slightest chance of his making restitution, Mr. B's sole remaining option was to sell his soul to the agency store.

When I eventually did meet Paul for our understandably overdue drink, I asked him why he hadn't simply fucked off to Tân Sơn Nhất Airport and fled the country. He sighed and told me he simply couldn't take the pressure of leading a double life any more.

On a more upbeat note, he added that he was determined to pay back all he owed and retrieve his passport from McNamara's. Perhaps I might like to help him get started with a small loan...

***

As obtaining each of us visas to legally work in Vietnam was proving beyond McNamara's capabilities, I and my four expat colleagues were all tripping the light fantastic on very thin ice. Too full of themselves to remember their hosts were dab hands at getting shot of unwanted foreigners, other companies' expats were labouring under the misapprehension they would never get caught or punished. The Vietnamese government's apparent shortcomings in this area were all due to its departments' inability to link up their various in-house computer systems – or so the visa-free execs had convinced themselves.

In inimitable Vietnamese style, the truth was a little more inscrutable. While I can't speak for any other employers, the Vietnamese Labour Department (VLD) certainly seemed fully aware of the various Westerners who were flying beneath the radar at McNamara's. So much so that entire teams of their Immigration Department counterparts used to hit the office and mount the occasional 'surprise' spot check to see if they could catch anyone in the act.

The only thing stopping them from making arrests was their thoughtful habit of telephoning Peter Seaton's secretary, Ngong, 24 hours before each secret swoop. Duly tipped off, Peter would follow immigration officers' advice and order his foreign staff to get out of Denver until the danger had passed.

Our office about to swarm with officials, we expats were simply free to down tools, pick up towels and lounge by a hotel pool until it was safe to return to work.

***

McNamara's only other major client of note –

and a major bone of contention with KoKoKola – was an internationally best-selling coffee brand called 'Javac'. As Vietnam has long been a major producer and exporter of coffee, its people were proving annoyingly resistant to whatever charms the brand professed it possessed. This may well have been because Javac's in-country head was a humourless Swiss gentleman called 'Cava Oubien'.

Failing to remember previous Swiss clients' insufferable dullness, dourness, and sourness, I immediately marked my card by jokingly requesting a cup of coffee from Javac's biggest competitor during our first meeting. The only coffee I was likely to be offered whenever I had the misfortune to run into Javac's reigning king of comedy thereafter would probably come in enema form.

The only way our initial meeting could have gone worse is if we had brought along our art director, 'Quyen'. When asked to share his opinion of Javac's flavour and aroma, he'd turned up his nose, saying he'd rather have a real cup of coffee than the *ersatz* shit Javac had on offer.

You think I'm joking about my Swiss mate's anal retentiveness? While overseeing Javac's business across the Indian sub-continent, Mr. O had become synonymous with nuclear particle-level nit-picking. One famous story recounted how he used to take books of pristine Pantone colour chips and benchmark them against his brand's colours on sun- and rain-lashed outdoor billboards. He was rewarded for his endeavours by being not-so-affectionately nicknamed 'the Swiss Hitler' (TSH).

Being seconded to Vietnam appears to have done little to lighten TSH's mood when reviewing concept after concept the agency presented for his brand's TVC. Eventually, he grudgingly approved an idea called 'Lightbulb Moment', in which animated lamps flickered into life over the heads of a group of tired executives after they drank cups of freshly brewed Javac. Storyboards, casting reels, and lighting references all approved by Oubien, and suitcases full of VD packed and ready for Lev's laundry to wash and press, Zak Lister and I headed down to Sydney to shoot.

While everything on the production went just fine and dandy, TSH was less than effusive about the results we showed him once our finished spots cleared customs. To say Mr. O was unhappy is to actually do him a considerable disservice.

Recognizing the extra branding our recommended coffee-coloured lighting treatment gave him, TSH had carefully studied and OK-ed the frame-by-frame shooting boards and samples he'd seen in our final pre-production meeting. With everything finished to broadcast standard, Oubien now decided he hated the effect. Worse still, he was insisting on a full reshoot, the total cost of which he expected the agency to bear.

Weary of dickhead clients, anally retentive officials, and money-laundering gangsters who'd kill you as soon as look at you – if not sooner – I began considering a move back to Hong Kong. It ended up being a move too far; a relocation that was to not only cost me a happy relationship but also most of my sanity for the next two and a half years.

***

When masterminding Warner Bros' wondrous 1930s, '40s and '50s cartoons, Chuck Jones captured Einstein's definition of insanity as futilely repeating an action in the hope of obtaining a different outcome more perfectly than anyone before or since. Just ask John 'Wile E Coyote' Fuery who at the start of 1998 opened his latest parcel from Acme Inc. to find a job offer from a Hong Kong agency called 'Bristol & Bagley' (B&B).

The agency was run – actually more of a directionless, zombie-like shuffle – by a pair of unrepentant high-functioning alkies and died-in-the-wool dopeheads called 'Bob Bristol' and 'Barry Bagley'. The two are amongst that increasingly rare bunch of characters of whom (bar a brief obituary of Bob from 2000) one can find barely any mention of on Google. Ancient-looking even back in the days when I worked with him, Bob, I was staggered to learn from his obit, was four years younger than I am now when he fired up his final bong.

Although they were amongst the earliest advertising professionals to set up shop in Asia, Bob and Barry's love of legal and illegal highs meant they had long since toped and toked their way to creative irrelevancy. 1950s' industry 'authorities' such as Vance (*Hidden Persuaders*) Packard and Wilson (*Subliminal Seduction*) Bryan Key might have begged to differ. Both ended up building lucrative careers warning credulous consumers that the Bobs and Barries of this world were twisted geniuses who hid subliminal triggers in their ads.

If the words 'sex' and 'power' were secreted amidst the ice cubes in the booze ads B&B's founders used to create, the pair were too intent on necking the drinks being advertised to bother looking.

Despite its founders' – uh – less than professional habits, B&B had managed to hold onto a big-bucks client in the form of a leading Asian hotel group called 'Forrest Hospitality'. Scenting blood and anticipating rich pickings, a high-profile agency called 'Clarion' had quickly bought Bob and Barry out lock, stock and barrel. As is normal in such cases, Clarion ensured continuity at the newly acquired agency by tying its founders to their apron strings for something like three years. Once this 'golden handcuffs' period was over, Bob and Barry's former agency and its accounts would be swallowed up and operate under the more successful Clarion name.

Asian cities have never been the cheapest places in the world to live if you don't have a job. Nor was I then the most detail-focused person when it came to weighing-up long-term considerations after a contract was dangled in front of my face. Having half-listened to Bob and Barry's spiel, I foolishly bought into their promise that my hiring as CD would be the first step in B&B's post-take over shake-up. A few more essentially meaningless reassurances about how we'd snatch a shitload of accounts and awards later and I was practically sticking the pen in my arm to sign on the dotted line.

Unfortunately, as is usual with agencies who 'talk the talk', actually 'walking the walk' proved rather different. In B&B's case, any kind of forwards motion consisted of the sort of queasy tottering that resulted from over-indulgence in post- (and increasingly pre- and during-work) drinks or spliffs in Barry's office.

Taking apparent pleasure in doing all he could to stick a spoke in the wheel that was the Forrest Hospitality account's smooth running was dear old Bob. While the Bobster's ability to multi-task as art director, photographer and illustrator had once been a valuable commodity, advertising had morphed into a highly specialised business. Like the jaded adman in the *Twilight Zone* episode *A*

Stop At Willoughby, B&B's Bob-of-all trades very much liked what he had seen in simpler times and had decided to stay put.

The reason Bob was so loath to relinquish his deathlike grip on the creative reins? One would imagine he simply couldn't countenance surrendering the extra income he was coining in from illustrating and photographing all of the client's work himself. Ultimately, Bob wasn't just sticking his head in the sand for the fun of it, he was digging a grave for his agency, staff and major client one paycheck at a time.

As loudly and often as my art director 'Alan' and I tried to warn Bob and Barry of the rocks that lay ahead, the less they listened and the harder they partied. The only thing keeping Forrest coming back for more was a senior marketing manager called 'Cal' who adored his trips to Barry's 21st floor eyrie as much as Alan and I dreaded them.

As those of you who've read this far will appreciate, I'm hardly in any position to cast the first stone at anyone who likes their beer, wine, hash and grass. That said, with my bad habits having become an occasional pastime rather than an enduring passion, even I was reluctant to answer Barry's increasingly early calls to join him, Bob and Cal for a 'quick confab'.

The working week would start with me reaching the office at around 10:00 am on Monday morning to try and clear the alcoholic fug from Sunday night with a few strong coffees. Bob would pitch up an hour or so later preparatory to heading off early for a long lunch from which he'd invariably arrive back late. Before that could happen, he would grab the lift up to Barry's office where the pair would more often than not uncork their first bottle of wine of the day. The week was pretty much in the express lane downhill from there on in.

In fairness, Bob and Barry weren't all bad. Old and creatively toothless they might have been, but the pair had accumulated quite a treasure trove of priceless stories along the way to extinction. The most salacious of these tales involved the nocturnal activities of legendary *Steptoe and Son* star, Wilfred Brambell.

It turns out that sometime in the early to mid 1970s, B&B had invited the infamous old queen to Hong Kong to shoot a series of press ads and TVCs for *The South China Morning Post*. Whilst this is hardly the time or place to talk specifics, our Wilf apparently really *was* the 'dehty owd mehn' his hapless son Harold regularly accused him of being in the much-loved sitcom. This is certainly a hypothesis that would find favour with the Malaysian airline captain in whose cockpit the surprisingly dapper and dandyish Steptoe senior once attempted to urinate.

Years later *The Guardian* ran a story about

how wee Wilfie and his wrinkled winkie had been on very good terms with a local Hong Kong radio personality called Ralph Pixton. Another larger-than-life character who is now sipping a pink gin in the great Green Room in the sky, the safari-be-suited Ralph provided my TVCs with top notch voice overs on several occasions.

A magnet for every disaffected expat in Hong Kong, Ralph's Saturday morning *Open Line* show on RTHK Radio was an especial hoot when it came to sloughing off a hangover. ('Ralph, I'm calling to express my not-inconsiderable dissatisfaction about the shocking narrowness of the aisles in my local Bag&Go supermarket!' would run a typical refrain). Always the consummate professional, Mr. P was invariably a pleasure to work with – if understandably rather taciturn when it came to discussing his post-work lifestyle.

***

Although once undisputed dab hands at spotting talent (hey, they ended up hiring me), Bob and Barry seemed to have totally lost the plot when it came to recruitment. About halfway through my B&B career, the pair belatedly figured out that since Hong Kong had now reverted back to 'the Mother-land', adopting a higher Chinese profile might just be a shrewd business move That it took fully 30 years after their arrival in Asia for this particular penny to drop perfectly encapsulates their pitiful grasp of the realities of late 20th century business life.

Desperate to beef up its profile, the agency hired a journeyman Chinese CD called 'JJ' whose library of reference books consisted almost entirely of slender tomes on lateral thinking by Edward De Bono. Joining Barry on the agency's upper floor as New Business Director and CEO designate was an odious expat called 'Marvin Hellman'.

Having only pitched for six fairly small accounts (four of them successfully), Alan and I couldn't help but wonder how the agency planned to pay for these sizeable extra salaries. As my increasingly frantic attempts to save my crumbling relationship with my then girlfriend meant I was less and less interested in getting wasted in Russ's office, I had a pretty shrewd idea.

Not helping matters was my somewhat difficult relationship with Hellmouth as Marvin had quickly become known around the creative department. Lording it behind his 21st floor desk, Not-so-Marvellous-Marvin would gleefully rip everything Alan and I prepared in our office five floors below to shreds.

Most creative people are well used to having their work bowdlerized by their empty suit colleagues in account servicing. The problem is that Hellman would routinely dismiss work out of hand without ever having bothered to properly digest the briefs he'd supposedly penned himself. A few 'you're asking why we've included this point, Marv? Well on page five of your brief, you've specifically made it a mandatory' questionings later and Mr. H began measuring me up for the chop.

Unfortunately for B&B, I wasn't the only person who'd soon be taking a one-way trip downstairs in the lift. Inevitably, there came the terrible day that Forrest announced that, having reviewed the agency's recent work, they had decided to put their account up for re-pitch. When clients ask their incumbent agencies to go head-to-head with their rivals in an attempt to hang onto their business, it's generally a harbinger of a sundering of their relationship. Ultimately, regardless of how solid your last ditch attempt to save your skin, you'd be well advised not to let the door bang your arse as you back slowly out of the client's office.

Perhaps the best story ever about a re-pitch involved the legendary David Ogilvy. After sitting down in the client's boardroom, Ogilvy and his team were told they'd have 15 minutes to state their case before a bell rang to announce their time was up. Pausing only to put his papers in his briefcase, Mr. O stood up and indicated his colleagues should follow him out the door. 'Ring the bell, gentlemen, ring the bell,' Ogilvy said to the client over his shoulder as he and his teammates headed for the pub.

Given that one generally has a pretty strong sixth sense about such things, my own exit from B&B was rather more prosaic. Late one Friday afternoon, I was summoned up to Marvin's office by what he grandiloquently described as his 'PA' (in actuality the junior typist cum secretary he shared with Barry). Of the doped-up, dipsomaniac duo there was, of course, neither hide nor hair. Once inside, Hellman's office, I was bade to shut the door and take a seat.

'John, Bob, Barry and me've been crunchin' sum numbuhs...'

As at KROK, rather than insisting on my leaving there and then as would have been the case with many agencies, B&B expected me to stay on and work out my three months' notice. In the end, I argued them down to 30 days on the proviso that they would give me time off to go to interviews.

As he made a great show of weighing up the merits of my request, Hellmouth looked at me like I was a fluff-encrusted lump of cow gum that someone had dropped in his coffee. 'Ah suppose ah'd be amenable to giving you the odd hour or two off, but just don't try and come the cunt wi' me, mate.'

'What exactly do you propose doing to me if I do "try and *come the cunt wi' you*", Marvin? Fire me?' Given my general lack of enthusiasm and abundance of obstructiveness over the next month,

B&B probably came to wish they'd gotten shot of me there and then.

The two first business sectors to be hit by a recession (and the last to recover) are advertising and construction. With Asia reeling from its worst financial crisis in years, jobs in the ad biz were as scarce as Marvin's nominations for the Hong Kong branch heats of the mythical 'World's Best Boss' poll. Lacking sufficient savings to tide me over for the minimum three months it would take to get paid for freelance jobs (assuming there were any), I started casting my net a little wider.

Chapter Eight

'Welcome to National Fuck Up Day, now in its 1,867[th] big week'

'At the third pip, it will be African time precisely. Don't expect anything to get done,' said my fellow Vietnam vet Geoff when my flight touched down at Nairobi's Jomo Kenyatta Airport in September 1999.

The next three and a half hours were spent in mounting panic as I vainly waited to reclaim my portfolio. It being the only copy I had, I couldn't risk losing it as I still needed to show it when applying for jobs back then. Given that no potential full-time employer ever asked to see it again after that trip, perhaps my anxiety was unfounded.

If so, no one had bothered to inform the poor fuckers behind the scenes who were presumably peddling bikes furiously to keep the airport's antiquated baggage carousel moving. As the elderly contraption endlessly wheezed and strained its way past with no hint of my bags, I was beginning to appreciate that Geoff might just have a point.

With the previous three months having been spent bending over backwards and getting royally reamed by a Lebanese chancer-cum-agency-CEO called 'Tel Hastizi' in Dubai, I was desperate to escape somewhere – anywhere. Luckily for me, having occupied his time since he left Vietnam as ECD at 'Kenyada', the Nairobi office of a major multinational agency group, George was heartily sick of all things African.

If only I'd read up on my fairy stories before I caught my flight. Like the genie who can't wait to grant you the wishes that'll condemn you to replace him in the magic lamp, Geoff was only too happy to recommend me as his successor. And I was only too happy to accept.

This isn't to say Geoff neglected to advise me about his own experiences there. He very kindly did but with the very important caveat that I should not be solely swayed by his words and took the time to assess the lay of the land for myself.

Surely to God, I thought, working in this most beautiful of countries couldn't wind up being any more frustrating or soul destroying than my stint in Dubai? With an old Clown mate called 'Ben Morgan' having helped secure me a three-month trial period as ECD at 'CADabra', Dubai, (a.k.a. 'Cadaver'), everything in the emirate had started out so promisingly. Frustratingly, as is often the case, situations that initially look that bullish rarely ever end up in the same hemisphere.

Despite my quickly managing to unite creative teams across five or six mutually loathing nationalities and personally win three awards for radio commercials, my 13-week Cadaver 'career' was effectively one long nightmare.

With days at the agency starting at around 10:00 each morning and frequently not ending until 14 or 15 hours later, there was little chance of any kind of social life. As a colleague told me over our umpteenth cup of coffee before lunch, 'Days here aren't just bad, they're 80-to-90-cigarettes bad.'

I was – as always – infinitely better off than I believed myself to be at the time. The poor wretches slaving to erect Dubai's dozens of new buildings suffered treatment so harrowing even Charles Dickens would have struggled to write about it. Flown up from unimaginably deprived corners of India and Pakistan on the promise of immense riches – breadline wages for you or I – they'd be instantly stripped of their travel documents on arrival.

Crammed on top of one and other in prefabricated huts, they'd then be forced to work 12- or 14-hour days – often hundreds of feet above the ground without a stitch of protective clothing or equipment. Those who survived their contracts more or less intact would eventually attempt to collect their pay packets and tickets home only to find that their employers had inexplicably declared bankruptcy. Broke and homeless thousands of miles from their loved ones, it was usually them rather than their unscrupulous former employers who wound up behind bars.

With its glossy veneer of wealth and culture concealing a cesspit of cruelty and greed stretching to the centre of the earth, Dubai was ultimately the worst kind of septic tank. It was also a hotbed of corruption and the first and only place where I was ever offered a bribe – a pretty impressive landmark in a career stretching back almost 40 years and taking in some of the shadiest places on earth.

For me, the cracks started to show when Ben advised me to pull my not-inconsiderable gut in when sitting opposite Hastizi, during my interview. Not exactly Karen Carpenter when it came to waving away approaching restaurant sweet trolleys himself, the Terry-Thomas lookalike was carrying a bigger complement of spare tyres than an 18-wheel truck. Not that this lessened el Tel's pathological mistrust and dislike of anyone who was carrying an ounce of excess flab – or, in my case, several stones of the stuff. Inevitably, my interview ice-breaking joke about paunching above my weight ended up being the third belly flop of the morning.

Luckily for him, my only rival for the newly vacant ECD's post following the former incumbent's throwing of an enormous wobbly sent even more bathroom scales into meltdown than I did. My 'prize' for winning the creative heavyweight championship was the dubious accolade of a three-month trial with Cadaver at US$5,000 a month.

Like everyone else I've found myself on the wrong side of during my career, Hastizi seemed to have had anything resembling a sense of humour surgically removed early on in life. More worryingly, he also came across as having been positioned at the very back of the queue when airline snack-sized portions of integrity and trustworthiness had been handed out.

One day early on during my probation, the big H dragged me into his office and indicated I should join him behind his desk. Gesturing underneath, he proudly pointed out the banks of CCTV monitors via which he surreptitiously monitored staff throughout the agency. Forewarned, as they say, is forearmed, so it should ultimately have come as no surprise when rumours began circulating that Tel and 'Sri', the previous ECD with whom he'd rowed so badly, had kissed and made up.

Sri – or so the agency scuttlebutt went – had accepted his former antagonist's invitation to resume his old position. If true, this meant that regardless of how well my soon-to-end trial had gone, I would imminently be surplus to requirements and 'Abra CADabra', my putative Dubai posting would disappear.

As the clock ticked down towards the end of my probation period, I decided to 'reverse the stress' and sit down with my new boss to clarify my situation. Given the huge problems I'd had getting my then girlfriend back into Hong Kong after leaving Vietnam, obtaining formal visas for us both was my top priority. Without them, it was virtually impossible to open a bank account, get a flat or obtain anything more than a pay-as-you go mobile phone. Hastizi listened to this and the remainder of my – perfectly reasonable – concerns about my role as ECD designate and rewarded me with the briefest of brief approving nods. Obviously quite busy, he told me to come and see him the following morning to dot the i's and cross the t's on my formal contract.

Remembering my previous bad experiences with Lebanese-style management in Bahrain, I conscientiously plonked myself down in front of Hastizi's door fully 20 minutes ahead of schedule. Predictably, el Tel failed to materialise. He'd simply snuck off to London the previous night on a trip I later learned had been scheduled several weeks beforehand.

When Hastizi returned almost a week later, I politely knocked on his office door to ask for his overdue clarification regarding my various visa issues and position as CD. While Dubai is always hailed as a gleaming, ultra-modern metropolis, its bureaucratic processes remain rooted in the 19th century.

As processing the necessary paperwork for staff was a complex and expensive undertaking, several of the other expats in the agency were listed as ancillary workers, such as toilet cleaners. Having reluctantly had to put up with various visa issues in Vietnam, I was keen for everything to be above board in Dubai. As anyone who's ever spent any time in the Arabian Gulf will tell you, the last thing you want to happen is to fall through the cracks in a Kafkaesque system through no fault of your own.

When I attempted to remind Hastizi of my hardly Faustian demands, he zoomed up from his chair faster than Dubai's slave labourers could erect one of its many jerry-built residence blocks. 'What right does a nobody like you have to come in here and speak to an important man like myself in such a way?' he blustered.

Spotting an easy way to wipe US$5,000 off his monthly wage bill, el Tel promptly announced that he'd had just about enough of my bolshie attitude. 'Clear your desk and get out of my agency right this minute!' he yelled, his face assuming a worrying shade of beetroot red.

Presumably absent from Evil Boss School the day 'Trampling Over Employee Rights 101' had been taught, Hastizi had been hasty in extremis, and neglected to calculate the expiry of my trial period. Had he staged his little outburst during our initial meeting, he'd have been able to get shot of me there and then. Now, a week later, I was five days past the expiry of my trial period and legally entitled to a month's salary in lieu of notice.

When I informed Hastizi of this, he started to waffle about how he was perfectly within his rights to backdate my termination to any day of his choosing. Really? I said. Perhaps the local labour department might be willing to investigate my case in rather more detail.

While they were at it, perhaps the authorities might find it worth their while to double-check the visas of AA's dozen or so other Western expat employees. The dawning look of horror that slowly crossed Hastizi's face as he realised he had involuntarily fucked himself over was almost worth all the unnecessary misery he'd caused me. Out of the agency on my arse, I happily added a few days holiday to the long weekend I'd already arranged for my interview to replace Geoff in Nairobi.

Appreciative of what I'd managed to accomplish within such a short period, poor Ben was a mess of twitching hands and nervous tics when we subsequently discussed my sacking over drinks. Was there no way I'd be willing to apologize to Hastizi and perhaps stay on as, say, head of English copy? Unwilling to say 'sorry' for something I hadn't done, or announce Ben's proposed Mickey Mouse title to clients who'd only just met me as ECD, the answer to both requests was a big 'no'.

If Ben really wanted to make amends for dropping me in it, I suggested that he try and persuade el Tel to honour his initial promise to reimburse me my repatriation expenses from Hong Kong. With whatever balls he used to possess long since cut off and left to moulder beneath the bank of CCTV monitors under Hastizi's desk, Ben never did. Oh, well, there's another Christmas card he and Mrs. Ben no longer had to worry about finding space for on their mantlepiece.

***

Funded by the windfall month's salary CADabra had unwittingly provided me with, my trip to Kenya proved to be a success on every level. Best of all, with two months before I had to start, my new job allowed me the sort of breathing space no other move had ever given me before.

While flying up and down from Europe to Asia, I had plenty of time to reflect on what a soulless dump Dubai really was. The recent case of a Scottish electrician who was gaoled for sexual impropriety shows that things do not seem to have changed a lot in the intervening 17 years. The man's crime? Simply brushing against his well-connected Arab accuser in a hotel bar.

Could have been worse, I suppose. The poor fucker might have run into and been forced to spend an evening listening to unfunny racist comedian and long-term Dubai resident Jim 'Nick Nick' Davidson.

Although I didn't know it at the time, Kenya

proved to be the final destination in my globe-trotting career. For the lazy travel writer, there are always quick soundbites ('Where East meets West!') that can be used to sum somewhere up for their even more lethargic readership. In Kenya, that soundbite would read something along the lines of 'where corruption meets chaos'.

If unchecked venality ever became an Olympic sport, Kenya's politicians would run rings around their rivals as silkily as its athletes routinely do in each Games' 3,000 metres Steeplechase. The reason why they were allowed to get away with theft on such a grand scale? Hardly anybody in the country could be bothered to lift a finger to try and stop them.

When I started studying at Hull Uni in October 1975, I was just in time to catch the fag-end of the 1960s protest movement. As such, I was always amongst the first to man the barricades on almost any political act open to me during what was a febrile time for debate.

Wearying of the usual cast of *faux* radicals during one occupation of the University Admin block in the summer of 1977, I and a friend called 'Malcolm Fine' went outside for a crafty spliff. While we were talking, Malcolm, who helped edit the student newspaper, was approached by an anonymous-looking but unfailingly polite gentleman.

The self-effacing chap turned out to be none

other than Philip Larkin.

Despite his apparently being a real stud muffin with as many as three 'lady friends' on the go at around this time, the poetic champion was refreshingly free of airs and/or graces. Years later, I read an interview in which Mr. L was asked why he didn't embark upon reading tours as had his equally lauded if arguably more 'glamorous' fellow poet Ted Hughes. A quizzical look on his face, big Phil had replied, 'But why would anyone want to pay to see me pretending to be myself for a couple of hours?'

Right now, Mr. 'they fuck you up, your mum and dad' was primarily concerned that the sit-in Malcolm and I had abandoned might spread to Hull's impressive university library, which he then ran. After reassuring him this was unlikely to happen, Malcolm kindly introduced me and told the perpetually harried-looking Mr. L that, like him, I had moved to Hull from Coventry. I'd love to be say we spent ages shooting the shit about the fortunes of our shared and now terminally declining hometown and its football team, but he didn't seem remotely so inclined.

Our offer of a toke of the spliff politely refused, Mr. L did, however, take time to subvert his image of having no time for undergraduates. Graciousness itself, he kindly took a few minutes to talk to us about poetry. As he hadn't published anything for quite some time, I took my life in my hands and asked him if he still wrote. He replied rather mournfully that his only waking thought as he grew older was his own imminent death.

Eight years later, when I was in Bahrain, the writer of the immortal lines 'All that survives of us is love' finally succumbed to cancer at the age of just 63.

One of the obituaries of his death I read mentioned *Aubade,* the last major poem he apparently ever wrote. True to his word to Martin and I all those years before, it was all about waking up in the morning and thinking about what little time was left to him. Looking back more than 40 years and realising that I am now the same age as Larkin was when he died , I can honestly say I know just how he felt.

Being young and therefore bulletproof, death was understandably the last thing on the minds of the students at Nairobi University when they took to the streets in June 2000. Regrettably, while the whole country was drowning in a sea of sleaze, corruption was equally low down on their lengthy list of real and imagined injustices.

The extent of Kenya's leaders' dishonesty and greed in the 1970s, '80s and '90s was – and still is – the stuff of legend. Take the poorly paved road outside a client's office locals laughingly called the 'Superhighway to Shit Creek'. The 'link' had cost some well-meaning NGO millions of US dollars in grants and yet was full of Sea of Tranquillity-sized potholes and petered out after a couple of hundred yards. Like the shell-shocked victims who'd spent the last 22 years being steam-rollered into submission by Daniel Arap Moi (a.k.a. "*Nyayo*', or 'Footsteps'), this particular road was going nowhere.

And what were the students who were being filtered into the fast lane to a brighter future on this truncated thoroughfare doing to right this particular wrong? In the Paris of 1968, pausing only to write witty despatches such as 'Underneath the tarmac, the beach', they'd have been tearing up the paving stones to erect barricades, or throw at their hated capitalist oppressors.

In the Kenya of the first year of the 21st century, the students' concerns were a little less vague and a whole lot more pressing. They'd downed pens and taken to the streets because the TV in one of their dorms had packed up ahead of that night's live match from Euro 2000.

***

Nairobi newbies wishing to own a phone or drive a car frequently found their desire to do so worn threadbare by Kenya's byzantine bureaucratic processes. Those who actually made it behind the wheel were frequently given instructions that, written down, resembled upturned bowls of alphabetti spaghetti. 'To get to the mall, you drive down Uhuru Highway and turn left at UNESCO. You then carry on straight past KANCO and MSF until you reach OXFAM.' Nairobi's city centre itself was so dilapidated that wittier locals had taken to referring to it as 'the Fourth World'.

Of course, the real cost of endemic corruption isn't just evident in the suppurating sores that are apparent everywhere you look. It's at its worst in the unseen nooks and crannies where it's free to fester unchecked at every twist and turn.

Cowering in the corner of the neglected room that was Kenya in the late 1990s was an even grimmer spectre – a medical condition only Westerners dared to call by its true name – AIDS/HIV.

In the sub-Saharan Africa of the then still bright and shiny new millennia, it was conservatively estimated that roughly one in four locals had been infected with the virus. That most of these sufferers would ultimately end up dying was largely due to the way amoral officials had sucked the life from their country's educational and healthcare infrastructures. With sex the only activity that didn't require any financial outlay, hardly anyone outside the big cities seemed to bother wearing – or even know about the need to wear – condoms.

The tragic end results were most vividly apparent in the scores of death notices that took up the last 20-odd pages of each day's *The Nation* and

East African Standard newspapers. The fact that such notices took up around a quarter of each day's paper eerily mirrored the then oft-quoted statistic that about 25 per cent of East Africans were now HIV carriers.

Each tiny ad featured a photograph of a loved one and a brief message about how that person had withered away as the result of 'a long illness bravely borne'. It's heart-breaking to imagine how desperately families who could ill afford to put food on the table must have struggled to afford to say their goodbyes.

When it came to matters sexual, Kenyans – in common with the citizens of many poorer countries – tended to lust after more generously proportioned women rather than their thinner counterparts. Ultimately, a woman's size and weight symbolised the success and wealth of any man who was lucky – no, strike that – rich and vain enough to marry and feed her.

Possessed of legs that stretched all the way to next Wednesday, many of the women left for Westerners like myself to fawn and sometimes fight over often resembled supermodels. Only the most foolish or drunken lothario would disobey older Kenyan hands' you-can-look-but-you-better-not-touch directive, though. Worryingly large numbers of these stunning women had gravitated to Nairobi from roadside truck stops where sex was cheap and plentiful and protection was non-existent.

While it was impossible not to be horrified by the gut-wrenching stories these girls sometimes shared, it was literally a matter of life and death that you never, ever took one home. I used to try and avoid the problems inherent in doing this by buying the girls drinks and leaving them lavish tips at the end of each night. Should such abstinence fail, a visit to the local clap clinic for an AIDS test was essential. Happily, it was one appointment I never had to make.

***

Its birth right stolen and its coffers the personal piggy bank of amoral leaders, Kenya's commercial sector unsurprisingly lagged far behind my other Asian and Middle Eastern ports of call. Its advertising industry was especially backwards in this respect.

Matters weren't helped by Kenyada's head-in-the-sand attitude when faced with the need to accept and adapt to changing times. Once the go-to agency in Nairobi when publicising your company or applying for a career, Kenyada spent more time living in the past than a battalion of Jethro Tull tribute bands.

Where other agencies had invested in high-tech office facelifts, Kenyada remained stuck in an era when rotary-dial Bakelite phones were considered cutting-edge. Worse still – through no fault of his own – was poor old 'Obadiah', the elderly Kikuyu gentleman who manned the phones and welcomed visitors in our reception.

Walk into almost any other ad agency worldwide, and the chances were you'd be greeted by a stunning 'It' girl. Step inside Kenyada, and your first impression was of a grey-haired coffin-dodger whose yellow-brown teeth were the colour and consistency of a Wolverhampton Wanderers strip from the 1950s. As nice and helpful as he was (and he genuinely could not have been nicer or more helpful), poor Obadiah was never going to convince clients they'd entered a dynamic modern ideas factory.

Perhaps joint-agency CEOs 'Edward' (a natural-born Kenyan) and 'Christine' (a white settler) had made an abortive attempt to replicate Allen Brady and Marsh's (ABM's) legendary 1977 pitch for British Rail (BR).

Desperate to reverse BR's seemingly terminal decline, BR Chairman Peter Parker had put his account up for pitch at several of London's most sizzling creative hot shops. One can only imagine his team's displeasure when they arrived at ABM's reception to be greeted by a mess of discarded newspapers, half-empty plastic coffee cups, and foul-smelling, overflowing ashtrays.

After waiting for what must have seemed like an eternity, Parker despatched a junior to quiz the surly-looking receptionist about the endless delays and absence of any kind of attention. When asked to provide an explanation, she simply shrugged her shoulders in the universal 'why would I know, why would I care, and why would I bother telling you if I did?' gesture. Just as the BR party had had enough and were getting up to leave, agency head honchos Peter Marsh and Allen Brady burst through the doors to tell them that this was exactly how BR's customers felt. ABM apparently won the account on the spot without even having to show any creative work.

Clients foolish enough to wait in Kenyada's reception were simply rewarded by a dubious-looking smile from the agency's domesticized Kikuyu tribesman.

The knottiest problem I faced at Kenyada came about halfway into my stay when Christine promoted a senior account manager (SAM) called 'Dorothy' to implement a swingeing cost-cutting drive. Knowing the best way for the agency to start turning itself around was to begin churning out top-notch creative, I fought tooth and nail to hang onto as many creative staff as I could.

Despite being far from excessive and frequently paid late, my US$5,000 per month (about £3,800 or 503,745 Kenya Shillings (KS)*) salary was next

---

* An exchange rate of approximately KS1,000 = £8 has been used throughout this chapter.

up in the firing line.

Dizzy with the possibilities bestowed by her new role as Christine's number two, Dorothy swept imperiously into my office and asked how much of a pay cut I would be willing to accept. When I told her that I would agree to exactly the same reduction as she'd taken following her recent promotion, she left my office pretty sharpish. The matter of my salary's being lowered was never raised again.

That Dorothy was a recovering alcoholic whose reliance on 12-step programmes left her totally intolerant of those who did like a drink (i.e. first Geoff and now me) didn't help matters.

Please don't think that the above means I am trying to detract from Alcoholics Anonymous (AA). While the organisation has been of huge benefit to friends with substance abuse problems in the past, I personally have never really gone a bundle on higher powers. Nor have I ever had a great deal of time for the 'my way or the highway' ethos with which more militant AAers like Dorothy 'work' the 12 steps.

Having been rather patronisingly given a copy of *The Little Book of Calm* as a gift by Ms. Sobersides, my predecessor shared my scepticism. Scorning the bland, contradictory advice contained therein, Geoff had one morning simply opened his office window and skied the insubstantial tome onto a nearby garage roof.

That he had done so at precisely the moment his benefactor entered his office to discuss some ads was unfortunate. Geoff subsequently confided that the look on Dorothy's face after she realised how insensitively he had disposed of her book had apparently been far more uplifting than any of the scores of trite truisms contained on its pages.

Having agreed to the culling of two of the most moribund pieces of deadwood in Kenyada's creative department, I thought the remainder of the guys would be safe. Dorothy, unfortunately, had other ideas and simply waited until I was away for a couple of days on a shoot before firing two of the hardest-working members of my team. With the agency having deprived me of the chance to do the decent thing and talk to them personally, both staffers must have gone away cursing me for my cowardice.

A good strong whiff of the intoxicating effects of power rather than booze filling her nostrils, Dorothy now started trawling for new business. And, my, what wonderful leads she had lined up to chase!

On one occasion, I was dragged along to meet a potential client who needed his company letterheads, envelopes, and business cards revamping with a new logo. Could we, he asked, improve on the efforts he'd had an office junior knock up in-house?

Exasperatingly, where I saw designing and printing of stationery as the start of the agency's devolution into a glorified branch of Kinko's, Dorothy saw it as the cornerstone of a new communications empire.

When your agency starts listening to – or worse still – believing clients who insist they can perform specialist tasks better than the professionals you employ, it's time to start milling around by the lifeboats.

***

Another wonderful thing about living in Kenya was simply being able to experience the majesty that is, was, and hopefully always will be Africa itself. Come Friday afternoon or a long weekend, I was out of the office at 4:30 and barrelling down the runway at Nairobi's domestic Wilson Airport within three-quarters of an hour. One bumpy turboprop flight later, and I'd find myself dwarfed by some breathtakingly endless expanse of exotic animal-packed grassland.

The last and most awe-inspiring of the four trips I made while in Kenya was to Masai Mara during the great autumn migration. The sight of wave after wave of wildebeest diving off impossibly high riverbanks into broiling waters filled with crocodiles and circled by hundreds of famished vultures still sends a privileged shiver down my spine. As do my memories of the moment our guide, who having made sure the coast was clear of dangerous animals, allowed us to step on to the savanna and immerse ourselves in indescribable silence.

The best thing about living in Nairobi itself was the sheer space. After spending years cooped up in a 700-square-foot apartment high up in a Hong Kong residential block, or more recently being hemmed in by the concrete canyons of Dubai's 'flatlands', how could I not? Before I eventually bowed to the inevitable and took over the flat in the compound Geoff had called home, I had a good look around the city and its outskirts.

The loveliest place I saw was a bungalow with shared access to a swimming pool on a family estate about 10 miles out of town. Eager to find out more, I arranged to go and see the owner – a man called 'Harry Powell' at his office. I subsequently found myself on the wrong side of one of the most bizarre conversations I've ever been involved in.

Mr P, as he couldn't stress early or often enough, was – groan – a committed 'born again' Christian (BAC). While I personally incline to atheism, I was brought up by Irish immigrant parents in a proudly Catholic home in Coventry.

Welcomed to the UK of the 1940s with clumsily written signs saying 'No Blacks, No Dogs, No Irish', my parents had developed an unshakeable respect for other people's beliefs and ways of life. No matter how absurd or unsavoury I personally might find others' attitudes and behaviour, broad-mindedness and tolerance had been hardwired into my genes from an early age.

Like many – too many, if truth be told – BACs, Saint Harry seemed to possess no such options on his spiritual control panel. You either believed unquestioningly what was written in The Bible or you were on the fast track to the fieriest corner of Satan's cellar.

Well-intentioned thoughts and kindly acts were no defence.

Fail to slavishly follow the Ten Commandments or any other Old or New Testament imperatives, and you wouldn't even get to stop off at the pharmacist to stock up on factor-50 sunblock on the way.

'What', I hear you ask, 'about those weak souls whose lives of grinding poverty had left them with no choice other than commit the sin of theft to feed their families?' I know I did.

'Surely,' I said to the beatific one, 'the merciful God that Jesus talks of in the New Testament would understand that such sinners' acts of petty theft were born of desperation? As such, would He not pardon transgressors for preventing far, far greater wrongs such as the death of multiple family members?'

Mr. P's face resembled that of a verger who'd

just discovered mice had been nibbling at his church's stock of communion wafers. 'Thievery,' he said, banging his desk for emphasis, 'is thievery and, as such, is punishable by God's Law!' There was, Mr. P believed, ultimately no, zip, nada excuse for bending or breaking a Commandment under *any* circumstances. Rolling his chair back to the filing cabinets behind him, our Harry opened a drawer and – yea verily – brought forth a multitude of comic-book-style tracts by the legendary Jack Chick.

While you probably think you don't know Mr. Chick's beautifully illustrated ravings, you'll almost certainly have been exposed to them at some point. Like me, your first introduction probably came when you were walking through town, minding your own business. Before you knew it, up popped some mad-eyed God-botherer to buttonhole you about his good close friend Jesus.

That tiny leaflet The Bible basher thrust into your hands as you steamed past was just one of countless religious pamphlets Chick churned out in a career dating back half a century. Check (or should that be 'Chick') them out at http://www.chick.com. Whilst his tone is unintentionally hilarious (read Harry Potter, and Heaven's doors will be forever locked and barred to you), his draughtsmanship is every bit as impressive as that of, say, Robert Crumb.

As a lapsed Catholic, the most interesting – and distasteful – of the sheaf of stuff Mr. P handed me was entitled *Do Members of The Church or Rome Really Deserve to Call Themselves Christians?* The answer, in every hard-line BAC's world, was a resounding 'No way, Jose!' Flicking through the hate-filled treatise, I wondered how distraught my devout 80-year-old Catholic mum would have been had she been handed this particular slice of 'Good News from on High'.

Worryingly, embracing Christianity and 'praising the Lord from the rooftops every chance one got' wasn't the only step my prospective landlord had taken on the highway to heaven. In deciding to cut all ties with his old life, he had also seen fit to renounce his initial religion, which was, as luck would have it, Islam.

Unfortunately for Mr. P, disavowing one's beliefs, or apostasy, isn't just a minor slight that's politely frowned upon in Sharia society. Hard-line Quranic scholars tend to regard it as an offence punishable by death.

Unwilling to offer myself up as kindling for an angry mob of fundamental Moslems in some Saint Harry-inspired theological spat, I abandoned all thoughts of moving to his family compound there and then. Even assuming I escaped ending up as a pile of ash, there was the real risk of Mr. P's sure-to-be-less-than-understanding attitude towards my then still quite hefty daily marijuana intake.

With packs of 20 pre-rolled mini-joints available outside most bars for just KS1500 (about £12), many expats – myself included – smoked like chimneys.

Amusingly, my stay in Kenya was the only time that implausible 'sure you did!' excuse about 'buying weed off a black man in the pub' was unlikely to be questioned. Likely to pose one or two more difficult questions were the various members of the Powell family who'd surely end up knocking on my door and staging some kind of intervention. Even less attractive was the prospect of Harry himself picking up the blower and dobbing me into Kenya's finest in an attempt to 'save me from myself'.

So, sorry, thanks but no thanks, Mr. P. Hope you managed to fill your vacant cottage with another, more compliant happy-clappy type. And that yourself and your family have all gone on to live happily ever without having been torn limb from limb by a fundamentalist mob.

***

The skies having shut up shop and embarked upon one of the worst droughts in recent years, Kenya's economy had been going from bad to worse since the moment I arrived. Indeed, so serious had the resultant water and power shortages become that the government implemented drastic countrywide energy-saving measures.

What this meant was that Kenyan households lucky enough to actually have an electricity supply would only be connected for 24 hours in any 48-hour period. The only dwellings free from the new 18 hours on and six hours off and six hours on and 18 hours off regimen were those in close proximity to President Daniel Arap Moi's official residence. Happily, while never quite being matey enough to pop around and borrow cups of sugar, Danny boy and I were nextdoor neighbours. The razor-wire-topped back wall that separated my gated compound from the first family's heavily curtained windows was as close as I ever came to real power in my life.

I'd love to say that the Arap Mois sometimes lowered their dog-eared copies of *Hello* ('Kenya's presidential couple share the lowdown on the Nairobi high life!') for long enough to give me a cheery wave. Alas and alack, such an exchange never came to pass.

Despite our living in each other's pockets for the best part of a year, I only ever saw *el presidente* up close and personal once. Given the man's far from universal popularity and rumoured reliance on body doubles to take a bullet on his behalf, it may not even have been him.

The encounter occurred one lunchtime when Moi (or his lookalike) was in the back of a disappointingly unstatesmanlike but doubtless heavily armoured Toyota, and I was riding shotgun in a decrepit old taxi. Swerving off the road to free the way for the man he assumed to be his leader, David the driver reverentially announced, 'That was Mr. Arap Moi.'

'He doesn't look a bit like he does on the stamps and banknotes,' was all I could manage by way of a riposte. Like Moi, a member of the Talenjin minority tribe, David remained singularly unimpressed by my insufficient showing of respect.

The only power brownout that affected me personally came when the electricity went off-grid for three or four hours one Saturday night towards the end of my stay. The reason? The pylon via which neighbouring Uganda helped supplement Kenya's energy needs had fallen over and ceased functioning due to unseasonably strong winds.

While whatever minor inconveniences affected me don't deserve to be mentioned in the same breath as the daily hardships afflicting regular Kenyans, the power crisis was a huge headache professionally. Always eager to cut costs and corners wherever possible, clients simply slammed their cheque books shut and froze any advertising expenditure for the duration. With only a handful of people ever likely to see them, TVCs were especially hard hit. As I'd been hired with the express task of improving Kenyada's profile and billings across

Eastern Africa, I was effectively Donald Ducked from almost day one.

During the entire year I spent in Nairobi, I worked on four 15- to 30-second films with a combined budget of less than US$15,000. Shot in Addis Ababa for the princely sum of just US$1,000, my side-by-side spot for 'Sudso' washing powder was probably the most notable of these. While in the Ethiopian capital, I stayed at the city's Sheraton Hotel – then apparently the chain's third most luxurious establishment worldwide. The sight of its ornate façade towering over an ocean of squalid tin and cardboard lean-to huts is not something I will soon forget. Nor were the dead-eyed stares of the children to whom I futilely tried to give money during a daylong taxi drive aimed at getting a feel for the city.

As doomed as it might have been, my attempt at experiencing the 'real' Ethiopia wasn't half as dispiriting as the indescribably bleak faces of the scores of youngsters who crowded around our cab. Distressingly, no matter how much you could afford to give or how fast you could pass it out, one visitor's efforts were never going to dent the country's all-pervasive sense of despair.

On a more superficial note, the higher-ups at Sudso's huge multinational parent company were so impressed by my Ethiopian TVC they promptly commissioned the agency to redo it all over again in Nairobi. The budget for the remake? A whopping US$5,000. Strangely, Stephen Spielberg never seemed to be around to take my calls when I phoned to ask if he might be interested in working the clapperboard.

Unimaginably poor and screwed over they might have been, but the people of East Africa were incredibly fastidious about their appearance. Ultimately, even clothes you or I would have thrown out long ago were cherished as if they'd arrived freshly pressed from the cutting and stitching rooms of a Saville Row tailor.

Faced with the morally bankrupt task of trying to soft-soap mums whose every waking moment was spent worrying about where their families' next meal was coming from, Sudso adopted a 'we care' approach. The fact that their willingness to flash the cash was dependent on their scoring a seat aboard the corporate social responsibility (CSR) gravy train was, of course, neither here nor there.

Generally dismissed as cynical 'we give a fuck' positioning by hardened seen-it-all-before creatives like myself, the client's CSR wheeze involved donating up to KS2,000,000 (then about £16,000) to a local orphanage.

As in all 'irresistible' advertising offers, the keywords here were 'up to'. Sudso's new-found compassion for its fellow man was ultimately solely dependent on how many sachets of soap powder it might sell. In other words, the more units Sudso shifted, the more money it would donate to the sad-looking kids whose faces appeared in each ad.

The only fly in the ointment – and a large and insistently noisy fly it was, too – was that Sudso's media budget was way more than the sum it was willing to donate. Not so generous after all – unless, of course, you happened to be selling or advertising soap.

***

One of the few rays of light for Kenyada during my stint there involved a huge pitch for a French company called Vivendi, who had just been awarded Kenya's first mobile phone network. Despite minor hiccups such as Dorothy's having decimated the agency's creative department, we gave the pitch our very best shot.

Adopting an audacious – for Kenya anyway – platform based around the idea of 'freedom of speech', we eventually managed to produce some 10 TVC storyboards and 20 press ads. While receptive and appreciative of the raft of ideas we had shown them, Vivendi eventually let us know that they were going with – oh, the delicious irony – an agency with 'more creative resources'.

Worn down by Dorothy's senseless gutting of my team and our fruitless efforts in pitching for an agency-revitalizing account we coulda, shoulda, woulda, and very nearly did win, I'd hit a brick wall.

Making matters infinitely worse – assuming such a thing was possible – was Kenyada's finance department's consistently late payment of my salary.

While always willing to defer my monthly paycheck until team mates who urgently needed money to feed their families had been looked after, there were limits. Having endured the misery of late salary payments with McNamara's in Saigon, I'd resolved to call time when the delays reached three months. This limit had been reached just weeks after we'd narrowly lost the Vivendi pitch. Then there was the fact that, despite my pulling out all the stops to get her a ticket and a visa, Bing had refused point blank to even come to Kenya for a look-see.

As anyone who's ever been messed around by an employer will tell you, the more accepting you are of their continual delays in paying you, the more the company concerned will take advantage. Or as my mum used to pithily advise the young ad exec she raised, 'Give 'em an inch, and they'll take a mile'.

At Kenyada, the inch-mile ratio had expanded into a fissure whose width and depth were in inverse proportion to the agency's survival prospects. Rubbing salt into the wounds slashed open by the agency's constantly late payments was Dorothy's continual bleating about staff 'streamlinings' and salary cuts.

Chuck in her focus on snaring no-mark clients who would only end up accelerating the agency's terminal decline and, goodness me, if it wasn't 'get the fuck out of Kenya o'clock' already! And what possible move remained easier or more attractive than yet another trip to the apparently inexhaustible well that was good old Hong Kong.

Given its agonisingly slow slide down the razor blade to oblivion, you might be forgiven for assuming Kenyada was due to be put out of its misery during its next visit to the advertising vet.

Quite the contrary.

While I don't know who had dangled the possibility in front of Edward or Christine or why, fate had one last card to play. It all came to pass one day during a meeting in Big E's office. The inevitable round of polite, Developing World-style pre-meeting chinwaggery out of the way, Edward proceeded to outline the real reason for summoning me along the corridor. Would I, he asked, be willing to create some pre-emptive political posters, TVCs, and radio ads announcing Daniel Arap Moi's likely candidacy during Kenya's 2002 presidential election campaign?

Like many other things in this most wonderful yet horribly fucked up and fucked over of countries, elections in Kenya rewrote the rule books on bald-headed duplicity. The prospect of Danny Boy *not* adding to his then 22-year stranglehold on

Kenya's coffers was about as likely as my running as his Vice President.

Leaving aside my personal repugnance for Arap Moi and his rapacious cronies and the multiple rods they had created to beat their fellow Kenyans' backs, the decision was not an easy one.

In the balance sheet's positives column was the fact that such high-profile work might just provide the kick up the backside Edward and Christine's once-respected but largely passé agency needed to revitalize it. On the 'thanks, but no thanks' side, there was my reluctance to stay in Kenya for a moment longer than I absolutely had to in order to collect the sizeable sum of money that I was now owed.

What ultimately decided matters was my aversion to helping inflict still more misery on my blameless and undeserving Kenyan colleagues and neighbours. For all my sins, there was no way I could have lived with being even partially responsible for their having to endure four (and probably more) years of Arap Moi and his fellow African mafiosi.

Although hardly delirious with delight, Edward at least had the good grace to accept my reasons for effectively trashing his agency. Happily, despite Dorothy's best attempts to turn the operation into the Nairobi branch of Rymans, Christine and Kenyada were still gamely plugging away gamely as late as 2014.

Chapter Nine

Take the money and limp

Like the proverbial dog returning to its vomit, I was back in Hong Kong for what quickly became the most emotionally draining move of my agency career. What last few dregs of it were left, anyway.

The klaxons should have started their insistent ***ARRRROOOOOAH, ARRRROOOOOOOAHing*** the moment I realised the all-round awfulness of the agency, 'Gordon Comstock' (GC) and the account (supermarket chain 'Bag&Go' (B&G).

But no. Ultimately, not even the names of those in charge – 'Phil Koh' (PK), 'Kao Yao' (KY), and 'Che Dan' (for the agency) and the terminally misanthropic 'Oliver Misrell' (for the client) – were sufficient to dissuade me. Before I knew it, there I was at the head of the queue at the B&G Megastore's '10 items or less' check-out for the soon-to-be professionally extinct.

Advertising is one of those careers where there's no real or lasting shame in finding your arse on the least stylish end of your employer's fancy footwear. A legendarily po-faced CEO, PK was famed for discarding creative talents as fast as quirky TVC storyboards zoomed over his head preparatory to clanging uselessly into his wastepaper bin.

At the end of the day – assuming you lasted that

long before getting the boot – being shafted by GC was generally seen as a badge of honour rather than a black mark. ('PK gave you the heave-ho? Take a number, stand at the back of that never-ending line over there, and join the fucking club!')

I touched down at Chek Lap Kok airport for what would thus far prove to be my third and final stay in the Territory on the Saturday afternoon of a long holiday weekend in September 2000. Barely had I arrived at my hotel and kicked the shoes off my jetlag-swollen feet than the agency was leaving messages badgering me to get my arse into the office.

I simply took the phone off the hook and stuck a 'Not to Be Disturbed' hanger on the door of my room. Knowing how quickly (fuck it, let's be honest, happily) I fell into bad habits when staying in hotels on overseas secondments, my top priority was to get myself a permanent base a.s.a.p. Unwilling to piss my new employers off, I did what I could to fast-track my living arrangements. As a result, I ended up making the basic *Renting a Property for Dummies* error of signing a two-year lease on an apartment that, while well within my means, was way too expensive for my needs.

No matter. I'd secured digs that would keep me out of the bars and trouble – during the week at least. Well, that was the theory, anyway. In actuality, working on B&G was some kind of freshly discovered tenth circle of the advertising industry's equivalent of Dante's Hell. The cans of Caninberg on the cold shelf of my local 7-11 have seldom looked in more desperate need of a warm embrace. Nor I in need of the fleeting conviviality they promised to deliver.

An old pro I used to work with once told me that careers in advertising consist of 'days, one of those days, and one of those fucking days'. My brief (albeit not brief enough) time at GC consisted almost entirely of the third of these categories.

Our working week would start at 10:00 am on Monday and rarely if ever finish before 12 midnight on any given weekday. As the time for our Thursday morning trips to Lowu near the Chinese border for our 7:00 am meeting with B&G drew nearer and nearer, these hours grew longer and longer. By Wednesday night finishes were so late it was simpler to try and crash out at your desk than to waste valuable sleeping time taking taxis to and from home.

A quick 6:00 am visit to the 18/F toilet to splash one's face, roll on some underarm deodorant and change shirts, and it was time to take the 50-minute taxi ride to the client's office.

The work – if writing copy for supermarket shelf-talkers, banners, and dump bins can be dignified as such – was mind-numbingly stulti-fying. There are, after all, very few ways – none of them new or novel – of saying '79c off' ('Save 79c!' 'Was $2:00, now $1.21!' 'Enjoy a mega 79c discount!' etc.). The only person who seemed to thrive on this procession of pap was my fellow CD Che Dan (doomed to remain the Dantichrist in my mind forever).

A journeyman art director whose artisanal aspirations had not made it out of his mother's womb, the Danster was a martinet who wasted no opportunity to diss every idea I had the temerity to suggest. While some of his criticisms were justified, his failure to elaborate on why he'd found fault or refused to explore my proposed directions further was frustrating in the extreme. His continual issuing of the sort of tired sigh one might use in dealing with a slow child when failing to back up his opinions was another characteristic that grated.

Shove my face down in the shit, the Dantichrist surely often did, but there were moments when I had the satisfaction of landing a blow or two of my own. 'These are *lapsap* (rubbish). Take them away and bring me something better,' said my alleged co-CD when I tried to discuss a set of headline options one morning.

'Sorry, mate, not at my best today.'

'Not at your best, Johnno? You should try and be like me, mate! I'm always at my best!' said the Dantichrist, obviously blissfully unaware of Oscar Wilde's definition of mediocre.

Che Dan was equally unmoved by my observation that a major electronics client's 'Let's Make It Better' tagline was perhaps a little wishy-washy. 'Well, they've written brand guideline a half-an-inch thick outlining their rationale for using the phrase,' he sniffed. 'Yes, and Hitler wrote a 600-page book attempting to justify Nazism called *Mein Kampf*, and that didn't work out too well either,' I shot back.

Targeted at the wealthier expats who breathed the rarefied air at the very top of Hong Kong's food chain, B&G's ambitiously named Gourmet line was the high point of what might laughably be described as my 'career' at GC. Regardless of how absurdly hyperbolic our target consumers' opinions of themselves might be, crafting once-monthly themed ads and seasonal full-pagers for them was a joy to do. I wonder if this was because I usually worked on these projects with another art director?

Providing a rare shaft of sunlight into what was fast becoming the darkest corner of my agency career, even the perennially impossible-to-please Oliver Misrell grudgingly conceded my ads were rather good.

Dishearteningly, even this creative safe space was not free of the congenital idiocy of B&G's in-house marketing team. Come Christmas, the chain's advertising drive went turbo, and we were asked to create a series of themed ads selling assorted – cliché alert ahoy – 'festive fayre'.

Aimed squarely at cash-flush expats, the series' star ad focused on how B&G made Xmas shopping easy and showed a turkey leg under the headline: 'It's a Piece of Cake'. Studying the layout with the puzzled intensity of a freshly awoken coma victim asked to count his surgeon's fingers, Misrell's Aussie wingman helpfully piped up, 'Jarn, meyt, thiz izen a slarce ef keyk. Et's a chekken dremstik...'

The presence of Oliver Misrell was so malevolent, rumour had it GC's receptionist had to check the man's feet for cloven hooves each time he manifested himself in the agency's office. During a suck-it-and-see trip across from Kenya for a weekend-long trial, I briefly met an art director called Annie who'd handed in her notice after barely a month on the B&G account.

In a quiet moment, she told me that her sole reason for leaving was Misrell's habitual red-faced rages at the agency's inability to give him the work he wanted. Doomed to forever fall several miles shy of his exacting standards, Annie had regularly been reduced to tears in less time than it took to zoom through an aisle crowned with '50c off' bunting.

The victim of exactly the same sort of torment from Irving LaSalle a decade or so before, I knew how she felt. I also stupidly believed that I'd now developed skin sufficiently thick to help me survive the most outrageous slings and arrows life at GC could chuck my way.

More fool me.

My first task when I took the plunge and joined the agency full time was a far-from-appetizing foretaste of the shape of things to come. The Dantichrist and I were given the absurdly tight deadline of six weeks to come up with a 'Big Idea' that would provide the foundation for B&G's advertising for the foreseeable future. Making an already intimidating task even more daunting was the fact Misrell also expected us to create, cast, shoot and air his new campaign's first TVC within the same schedule.

Why did we have to accomplish all this within a timeframe that left so little wriggle room? Simple. Because Oliver Misrell said so. Any illusions I might have harboured about appealing to the man's more reasonable side went tits up the moment I suggested that getting everything right was far more important than meeting some arbitrarily imposed airdate.

At this point, let's do one of those wavy screen things from the 1960s as we travel back, back, backwards in time to the GC Hong Kong boardroom in autumn 2000. As a fly on the wall, you are about to witness, first-hand, a re-enactment one of the most hackneyed scenes from every ancient film about advertising ever shown as a

Sunday afternoon matinee.

The story about to cause your roast lunch to reflux this particular weekend concerns an implausibly drop-dead gorgeous housewife who's joined an agency to help pay her son Chip's way through college. Bizarrely, and for no other reason than it advances the plot, the Grace Kelly-lookalike newbie is sitting in a crisis meeting with the agency's most demanding (i.e. borderline sociopathic) client.

Dramatis personae established, Chip's Mum feels honour-bound to poke her head above the trenches and speak out after hearing one of her bosses make a particularly witless suggestion. There follows a 120-decibel collective intake of breath followed by the loud clanging of veteran agency staffers' jaws crashing onto the boardroom table.

'Well, I don't think this is the time or place for your input, Mrs. College Fund,' the 1950s equivalent of PK huffs and puffs.

At this point, all eyes swivel to the usually satanic client, who removes a smouldering cigar from his mouth (hey, this is the 1950s after all) and starts to speak. Expecting the man to fire off a few pithy put downs, the collective bigwigs are amazed when he says, 'No, wait! Let her have her say! I rather like the cut of her jib. And let's be brutally honest here; it's been way too long since any of you stuffed shirts have dared to stand up to me!'

Predictably, Misrell's Sunday afternoon TV movie viewing habits were somewhat more selective than my own. Either that or he was too busy in the back garden pulling the wings off flies.

'Don't waste my time moaning about the deadline you've been given! Just get the fucking spot on air when I tell you to!' he snapped.

We eventually presented a concept called 'Mother knows best'. Although hardly an earth-shatteringly original way to shift groceries, our campaign starred a 'typical' Hong Kong mum who 'broke the fourth wall' and spoke directly to her fellow shoppers. With the scope to set spots everywhere from local homes and B&G Superstores to country parks and beaches, we were sure we had hit upon a fun and memorable way to talk to 'homemakers'. I know, I know! 'Homemakers' *is* the wankiest kind of PC word it's possible to get. But having seen the clients' faces turn apoplectic after I said 'housewives', B&G's targets remained 'homemakers' ever thereafter.

I concluded my presentation by stressing that the success of the entire campaign was dependent on our casting an easy-to-identify-with 'Everymum' whose sassy personality would lift our TVCs to another level.

Nuttier than a row of unflushed toilet bowls in a vegan restaurant, Misrell simply could not be persuaded to listen to reason. The female talent he insisted on using possessed none of the qualities our TVCs needed to rise above the mundane herd. Worse still, in yet another of those capricious decisions clients love to make, he flat-out refused to countenance pushing back the new TVC's air date until we'd resolved the inevitable pre-production hassles. The end result was a suicidal schedule that left us nowhere near enough time to coach and coax a winning performance out of our proposed 'Housewife Superstar'.

The following weekend, Che Dan and I spent two consecutive 14-hour days watching the blunt instrument that was our charm-free talent woodenly bludgeoning our script. The most worrying thing about her non-existent acting chops was the maddeningly slothlike pace at which she doled out the words and phrases she was given in our TVC's allotted 30-second timespan.

The big indication that your TVC or film is several miles up shit creek without a paddle invariably comes when some inexperienced idiot pronounces, 'Oh, don't worry about *that*, we'll fix it in post!'

There's a famous story about the shooting of Michael Cimino's catastrophically expensive *Heaven's Gate* being two days behind schedule after just one day on set. Barely had we a frame of footage in the can before it became obvious that all the post-production expertise in the world wasn't going to keep our own filmic turd from going the same way. When Misrell saw our hastily edited rough-cut of whatever raw footage was usable later that week, he worryingly walked – rather than stormed – out of the screening room.

Amazingly, despite my eventually carrying the can for costing an agency I'd worked at for a matter of weeks something like US$100,000, I survived. But my, didn't my name look nice in the looping cursive script my mind's eye had started to see appearing on the agency wall.

The first black cloud took up residency over my head just after Christmas, when B&G decided to yank all English-language advertising for the 'foreseeable future'. I was then left struggling to summon up any enthusiasm for writing endless variations of 'save 79c'-type messages long into the night.

The skies darkened still further three months later during an especially rainy night just ahead of 2001's four-day Chinese New Year (CNY) holiday. Returning home from the pub predictably unsteady on my feet, I slipped and painfully barked my shin while climbing a flight of rain-slicked stairs. Before the four- day break was over, large angry-looking bruises had begun to spread outwards from my right tibia. Within a few days, the discolourations had vanished, but unbeknownst to me, the injury had begun developing into a full-blown compound fracture.

In the wee small hours of one Saturday morning some three months later, my ankle cried 'enough!' and finally gave up the ghost in one of Hong Kong's less clean-cut 'nite spots'. Unceremoniously dumped in a heap on the grimy booze, fag ash, and chewing-gum-gooey floor of Wanchai's Boracay disco, I couldn't help but wonder how much lower my life could sink.

It goes without saying that my two weeks in the hospital and four months of thrice-weekly physio sessions did me no favours with GC. A man who seemed to have gotten out of the wrong side of the bed every morning of his life since he took his first step, Che Dan couldn't have been less supportive. His sole trip to see me in the hospital came on day two of my stay, when he tossed me a sheaf of scrap paper that looked as though it had been rescued from the bin beneath his desk. 'Just because you're in the hospital doesn't mean you can skive off,' said GC s reigning holder of the Mr. Empathy title. 'When I broke my leg in a kick about at my last agency, I was in and out of A&E in two hours. There was none of this nancy-boy poncing around with physios either,' he added glibly.

'Your words and deeds are, as always, an inspiration to lowly mortals such as myself, Dan,' said I. 'Alas, the 14 titanium screws and 12-inch steel plate holding my ankle together indicate I might require a level of care rather more substantial than that available during a quick two-hour visit to A&E. If you think I'm willing to spend the rest of my life riding a mobility scooter so B&G can shift a few more cans of beans, I suggest you think again.'

With four ever-more backward steps in succession – the last of them executed on crutches – my agency career was ready to be boiled down for glue in advertising's knacker's yard. There was only one avenue left open to me – to go freelance.

For once in my life, I'd actually gone about preparing for this quite methodically. Painfully aware of the thin ice that I was now hopping on rather than treading, I'd spent roughly half of my time at GC preparing personal cards, letterheads, and a website.

With 'Mother knows best' having crashed and burned so spectacularly, PK was understandably wary of any other ideas I might dream up. With a replacement concept needed and a long weekend in the offing, he called everyone in to the office to submit ideas for in-agency review.

In the unlikely event that your cherished initial thoughts survive several rounds of such scrutiny with their balls either wholly or partially intact, their emasculation is passed on to market researchers. As a result, much of my time at GC was wasted attending focus groups – or 'fuck-us' groups, as they are often accurately – if facetiously – called. Ask almost any creative ad person, and they'll be quick to tell you just how much they despise these pointlessly negative exercises in 'taking on board consumer feedback'.

To further rub everyone's noses into it, the various focus groups the B&G team was press-ganged into attending were almost always scheduled at 8:00 or 9:00 at night. There you'd sit, in a tiny room gazing out of a two-way mirror similar to the ones you see in cop shows. In the rather larger room on the mirror's other side would be a 'representative' group of 'typical' Hong Kong punters, or opionated tits with no brains as they are known by industry insiders.

After a stealamatic (rough cut) of the sort of images that would eventually make up your meticulously crafted TVC had been shown to the group, your storyboards would be despatched around the table for dissection. As with all such group presentations, a pecking order would quickly establish itself, with comments becoming increasingly crass as everyone pitched in their two cents' worth.

Pissed off by how often his agency's recommendations were trashed by overwhelmingly negative reactions from market research studies, one famous client decided enough was enough. He then simply binned the research findings and told his agency to run with the concept they'd proposed and he himself had loved. The end result? Doyle Dane Bernbach's legendary 'Number two tries harder' campaign. Having delivered year-after-year of bumper sales for Avis, it remains one of the most revered campaigns ever created. Predictably, B&G lacked any such backbone, so back to the drawing board and another round of focus groups, everyone dejectedly traipsed after each rejection.

***

While my agency career was busily circling the plughole at ever-higher speeds, mobile phone ownership in Hong Kong was heading in exactly the opposite direction. Despite almost every Hong-konger owning four or five of the things, I had always despised and shied away from buying or owning a cell phone. My refusal to do so remained a massive bone of contention between myself and GC's senior management. Every time the agency's phone list was updated, which, given its huge turnover, was roughly once a fortnight, there were only two names on the list who had no mobile phone number. The first was agency CEO, PK, and the second was, of course, yours truly.

When PK's chosen attack dog, KY – in actuality, more of a toothless *Shih Tzu* – told me I had to get a handset I had no use for, I asked why. The answer I received in return was that it would enable the agency to get in touch with me 'during emergencies'. I replied that since I was already spending so much of my life at the office, KY might find it easier and more cost-effective to simply bang on the wall that separated our offices. Alternatively, if GC continued to insist I needed a phone solely for agency business, perhaps they might like to pay for my mobile themselves.

KY sighed theatrically and announced 'John, Phil, Che and I can't help but feel that you're not really doing enough to fit in here.'

How odd. There I was routinely putting in six- and sometimes seven-day weeks with shifts that were rarely less than 10 hours long and yet I was still somehow 'not doing enough'. It was only a matter of time before KY reached into his well-stocked bag of banalities and pulled forth the inevitable 'and it's beginning to show in your work'.

Push having embarked on the last leg of its journey towards its final showdown with shove, I began preparing for what former Sex Pistol John Lydon memorably called: 'my grand finale, my goodbye'. Come lunchtime on Thursday, July 12, 2001, I finally surrendered to the inevitable and forked out for that long-overdue mobile phone.

The look on KY's face as he saw me struggling to programme my new Nokia's various bells and whistles features was almost worth the handset's absurdly expensive price on its own. Still, never mind; he and the Danster only had to wait an hour to put me back in my place when they gleefully stomped my latest proposed TV script into the dust. The last vestiges of my confidence having finally disappeared around the U-bend, I went home and awaited the inevitable descent of the hessian bag over my demoralised head.

When the next day – Friday the 13th appropriately enough – rolled around, I fell out of bed and got my sorry arse into work. The axe finally did its falling thing shortly after lunch. Far too grand to attempt the arduous eight-step journey to the office the Danster and I shared, KY despatched his secretary to summon me into his presence. There to witness my downfall was my old mate, Che Dan himself.

After beckoning me to take a seat, KY's Paul Daniels handed the Dantichrist's Debbie McGee an envelope, which he then passed over to me. The briefest of glances telling me all I needed to know, I made a great show of folding up the letter, replacing it in its envelope, and sliding it into my pocket.

'Cat got your tongue, Johnno?' said Che Dan, barely bothering to try and conceal the unmistakable traces of a smug smirk on a face in serious need of a good fisting.

'Not really, "Danno". It being Friday afternoon, raining, and me still being on crutches, I'm sure you'll understand if I leave it until Monday morning before coming back to clear out my desk.

Once I've done so, I'll hand in my door card, say my goodbyes, and we can all get on with our lives.'

'What do you mean say your "goodbyes"?' asked a confused-looking KY.

'I mean 'bye as in "bye bye", and good as in "gone for good" and never coming back. Given your and PK's reputation for going through creatives like shit through a goose, I'm sure you don't need me to elaborate.'

'No, no, you misunderstand. We're paying you two months' notice, and you're legally obligated to work out every day of your termination period,' said the Danster.

'Sorry, Che, but unless you've been sneakily acquiring enough stock to earn a place on GC's board, you personally are not paying me anything. As for you, KY, despite firing sufficient writers and art directors to illuminate next year's Chinese New Year fireworks display you've never learned how to write a letter of dismissal.

What you've put down here doesn't say whether I've been sacked or made redundant. Either way, you can colour me gone at 5:30 pm on the dot. Look at it this way, if you're firing me, it's because you consider me to be useless and it's not worth your while keeping me around. If you're making me redundant, it's because I'm surplus to require-ments and my services no longer justify my salary.

So, just pay me the two months' notice and all of the holiday money the agency owes me. Once you have, I'll be out of what's left of your collective hair forever.'

'Not so fast there, John,' said KY. 'Given your attitude, I'm personally going to make sure the finance department deducts any outstanding holiday money from your two months' notice.'

'Go ahead and try,' I laughed. 'Every time I've applied for or booked a holiday here, you've emailed me to tell me that I had to cancel due to a mysterious sudden influx of work. Would you like me to send you back the emails? Give me a couple of minutes to go to my computer, and I'll be happy to ping them back to you. When I do, I'll cc each message to the labour law solicitor I spent a couple of hours talking yesterday evening. Given what I've told him about the shitty way GC treats its staff, I'm sure he'll be only too glad to saddle up his coach and horses and ride them through this sad excuse for a dismissal letter.'

The following Monday, I went back to the office, collected my stuff, and left GC for the last time. Never again was I to ever enter an agency office on anything other than a strictly part-time basis.

With little to show for my previous two decades getting screwed every which way from Sunday by agencies, it was time to start making some serious money.

Chapter Ten

What time would you like it to be?

Like everything else in life, going freelance has its pros and its cons. On the upside, you get to work from home and schedule your working week however you like. On the downside, you soon start putting in all the hours that God sends and quickly lose any inclination to go out to meetings.

Actually, hold that thought. You can't stomach even the idea of having to go out to meetings. Nor are you willing to waste any time on anyone who expects you to be on call 24/7, and to jump every time they ring with an inane this'll-only-take-a-minute request.

As with so many ostensibly illogical decisions about my freelance career, there was some method in my madness here. Most people who wanted me to visit their office for a briefing, or to talk to me on the phone about some piddlingly insignificant grammatical point were generally a colossal waste of time.

'Can you come across to Taikoo Shing to discuss a new press ad 'Big Co.' is thinking of running?' AEs would invariably begin.

'Well, before I waste precious time and money taking a taxi to your office, maybe you could tell me something about the job the client is "thinking" of running.'

'Weeeeeeel, it's kind of complicated…' (Wasn't it always?)

'OK, let's start off with the budget for the ad. How much money does the client have in mind?'

'Um, about HK$1,000…' (about £80)[*]

'OK, so you expect me to break off from what I'm doing, jump in a taxi, and spend half an hour and HK$120 each way travelling to and from your office in heavy traffic. When I arrive, you'll probably keep me waiting for a further 30 minutes. You'll then take an additional half an hour to explain something you could easily have told me in the time we've just spent on the phone.

'Let's just tot this up. Start with HK$240 in taxi fares to and from your office and then add in HK$550 an hour for my time. That's effectively HK$1,340 in actual costs and billable hours I've had to outlay before I put pen to paper. All this to "talk about" an HK$800 job the client hasn't even committed to running yet?'

'Well, when you put it like that…'

'Favours' entailing unpaid editing/writing trials or 'on-spec' visits to clients' offices were yet another rod with which clients would attempt to beat freelance backs. 'Alison', a lady I knew from

---

[*] An exchange rate of approximately HK$100 = £12.5 has been used throughout this chapter.

Bahrain, once enquired brightly: 'John, how would you like to join us on a trip to Shenzhen for an exploratory meeting with a large multinational hotel group?' I actually fancied this about as much as having a drunken proctologist with late stage DTs conducting a colonoscopy with a rusty scalpel during a power outage.

A quick mental calculation was all it took to establish that getting to and from Bumfuck China for such a meeting would take me away from my desk for at least 72 hours. Obviously feeling that I should be pathetically grateful for the huge favour she was doing me, Alison instantly pooh-poohed my query about payment and sounded most aggrieved when I respectfully declined her kind offer.

Hopefully, she had better luck finding a replacement writer after calling the number of the local psychiatric facility I now kept handy to pass along piss-taking clients such as herself. With every dealing with this woman sure to require sky-high levels of service at rock bottom rates, I sure as shit wasn't going to start wearing jackets that fastened at the back.

***

As anyone who's ever decided to become self-employed or sub-contract their services will know, freelancing is essentially three jobs in one. Before you can actually start doing any work, you first have to seek out potential clients. Involving nothing much more demanding than sourcing addresses and sending out mailers and cards, this first part is simplicity itself.

Happily, once you've successfully announced your presence and taken care of a few projects, people (I hesitate to call them satisfied clients) will often pass your name along to their friends and colleagues.

After you've completed assignments and their attendant rounds of revisions, comes the third and trickiest part of your job – trying to collect the money you're owed.

Even after you allow clients a window of three months in which to settle their invoices, most bigger agencies will continue to do everything possible to dodge paying their dues. This invariably meant a round of emails (almost every one of which will go unanswered) followed by dreaded chase-up calls – a frustrating and time-consuming process I continue to put off until the last possible minute to this day.

The standard response from late-/non-payers was 'You'll be paid when the client pays the agency.' The simple answer to this was that the agency whose staffer had commissioned you was, in fact, your client and therefore owed you for whatever work had been done. In other words, any relationship the hiring agency had with the company running the ad was not your concern.

Predictably, even this most easily comprehensible of truths failed to achieve any traction in the tapioca-thick mind of the AE who'd initiated the job you now so unreasonably expected payment for. At which point, I would enquire sweetly: 'When did your agency last pay you, and how long would you continue to work there if you didn't get your salary at the end of each month?'

An especially choice example of the latter *genus* of AE involved a B&G job I'd taken from my much-hated former employer, GC. (I know, I know. You'd be amazed how flexible those previously inviolate standards become when the prospect of a juicy payment rears its ugly head.)

Despite payment for the job being so late it might require the debt management finesse of Lev in Vietnam to collect, GC's AE pleaded the usual nonsensical gubbins about how B&G had not yet paid the agency. 'On that basis,' I told the AE, 'I'll put down the phone and head right over to my nearest B&G Superstore to stock up on groceries for the coming week. I wonder how the staff there will react when I breeze past check-out saying that Oliver Misrell will deduct the cost from whatever his marketing team owes me.'

Should the above steps fail to produce any kind of movement on the payment front, it was time to change tack. I would now sigh mournfully and say that if the overdue payment was not the agency's fault, why didn't they simply tell me who I should get in touch with at the client's office? Appalled by free-spending clients' likely reaction when learning their agencies were offloading work they considered *infra dig* to freelancers, the AEs would shift from hemming and hawing to full-scale panic attack mode. What made this threat especially delicious was that while only a tiny fraction went to the freelancer, agencies charged clients' obscene amounts for copywriting.

Absurdly – they weren't the ones who were being asked to pay what they owed – agency staff could get very defensive about their employers' unwillingness to settle their bills.

Take the senior account manager (SAM) whose employer had owed me around HK$12,000 on a huge job for a major credit card company for over five months.

After repeated unanswered emails, I finally managed to corner the woman on the phone. She then trotted out all the usual by-the-book bullshit excuses to which I responded with the standard responses outlined above. Rather than agreeing that I might have a point and offering to do what she could to help, the woman turned around and snapped: 'If that's your attitude, you won't be getting any more work from us!'

'Let's get this straight,' said I. 'You're threatening to stop giving me jobs that you'll do everything possible to get out of paying once I've done the work. What kind of ultimatum is that?' Annoyed, the SAM started to witter on about how her company was inundated with requests for freelance work from upstarts like myself. Her attempted parting shot was that she was a very busy person and I should refrain from disrupting her daily routine by bothering her with such trifles again.

At which point, I completely lost it and told the SAM – quite truthfully – that having previously worked together several years before, her agency's CEO and I remained on very good terms. I went on to say that as soon as I ended our call, I'd be contacting her boss to clarify the agency's policy regarding sourcing and paying freelancers. 'Go ahead, then!', the surly SAM snapped. So go ahead, I did.

The moment I put down the phone, I reached for my copy of *The All Asia Agency Guide* and found the email address I was looking for. I then started writing an email detailing the SAM's totally unjustifiable nastiness and unprofessionalism. Before I hit send, I idly wondered whether or not I should check to see if the woman had had second thoughts about the unpleasant way she had treated me.

Nah! I thought and forwarded the email to not

only the SAM's direct boss, but also every other high-ranking agency official – in Hong Kong, Asia, and around the world – whose contact details I could find.

Unfortunately for our sullen SAM, not five minutes later, I made one of my habitual (i.e. anally retentive) checks of my inbox for newly arrived jobs. There, nestling third message from the top, was the abject apology and promise of prompt payment I'd sought a half an hour or so earlier. If only this stupid eejit had come to her senses a little earlier. When I emailed to thank her for the long-overdue settlement two days later, my unread message came bouncing back with a lengthy 'no longer employed by this company' rider.

The other great agency con was asking for reductions in fees when clients waved through jobs that – try as they might – they could find nothing wrong with. 'As the client didn't use any of their three agreed rounds of amends, everyone over here at the agency was wondering if you might reduce your charges a bit...'

'No, I most definitely might not,' was my unvarying reply to such pleas. Follow-up requests asking me to transfer the remaining rounds of revisions to future jobs received similarly short shrift.

When asked to justify my 'lack of co-operation' in such matters, I always used to ask the person who expected me to cut my fees to imagine how many late nights I'd saved them. Had I been a painter and decorator who'd transformed their flat ahead of schedule, I would remind them, wouldn't they be inclined to pay me more rather than less money?

Asking for sizeable discounts on first-time jobs because – wait for it – there would be an avalanche of high-paying assignments 'later on' was yet another fast one agencies and clients attempted to pull. While all very well in theory, the antici-pated stampede of jobs invariably never material-ized. Even when the odd job did trickle your way, its issuer would get all pissy if you failed to offer them the 'one time only' trial rate they'd received on their initial job.

The fact that freelancing's biggest advantag-es were also its most sizeable drawbacks was yet another frustration. Although free to pick and choose when and where you worked, you soon found yourself attempting to stretch time's apparent elasticity to its breaking point. While fighting for rush-hour taxis in the rain was a thing of the past, clients/agencies felt entitled to contact you at any time of the day or night with the most asinine requests. On more than one occasion, agency AEs called after midnight to thoughtfully inform me they'd be sending me over some minor, easy-to-accomplish job the following afternoon.

Despite weekends eventually becoming the busiest sections of my week, this was far from the case when I first set out my stall in 2001. In those endlessly sun-dappled summer days, I used to fill any empty late Friday afternoon hours before hitting the pub by going to the cinema. While they necessitated interrupting movies because you had to exit the screening room to answer them, phone calls were a necessary evil back then. They ultimately not only brought news of jobs, they effectively ended up covering the cost of each weekend's cinema tickets and post-film meal and beers.

One Friday afternoon while I was killing time at the flicks, I received a call from a pompous-sounding gentleman called 'Lan Yeung'. My caller apparently urgently needed my help in writing a speech he had been asked to deliver to the American Chamber of Commerce (ACOC) that Sunday.

One of Hong Kong's more charming idiosyncrasies is how even the tiniest, most insignificant Chinese companies saddle themselves with ridiculously grandiloquent trading names. Mr. Yeung's enterprise, for example, bore the modest moniker 'Top Wealthy Prestige Industrial Fasteners'.

'You are Fuery, yes?' Mr. Y began as if he were talking to someone incapable of drawing breath without the assistance of an iron lung. 'My name is Lan Yeung, and I am a very well-respected local business leader. Such is my standing in Hong Kong's industrial fastening industry that the ACOC has asked to write and deliver a speech at their upcoming quarterly dinner.'

'And how long would you like the speech to be, Mr. Yeung?' I enquired brightly.

'Oh, I think 20 minutes should be enough to provide a brief overview of the important work done by the department I run,' he replied. While the prospect of charging this puffed-up oaf for the three thousand or so words 20 minutes of verbiage would require was very enticing, a weekend spent feeding his gargantuan ego was anything but.

Throwing caution to the wind, I decided honesty was the best policy. 'Don't you think 20 minutes is a bit long, Mr. Yeung? I mean, have you ever had to actually sit in a room and listen to someone talking about something for that length of time – it's an absolute eternity! Why don't we look at the many interesting things I'm sure you have to say and then try to frame them in as engaging a fashion as possible. That way, there's no chance that the good burghers of the ACOC may find your speech – how can I put this – somehow less than riveting?'

Mr. Y fell silent as he considered the possibility that anyone might be less than enchanted by his self-aggrandizing views on the relative merits of battens, buttons, toggle bolts and treasury tags. Reluctantly, he conceded that 'shorter might just be the way to go'.

Discussing payment for jobs is always a tricky issue when you're a freelancer. Propose something akin to a realistic amount and you run the risk of either seriously under- or over-estimating just how much your client is willing to spend. Whenever possible, it's always advisable to try and let the client specify the budget for themselves.

After giving the man my email address so he could send his details over, I very politely asked Yeung how quickly he needed me to deliver his first draft and how much he was willing to pay. While it was now pushing 5:00 pm on Friday afternoon, it seemed Mr. Fast and Louche insisted on seeing the provisional speech 'first thing tomorrow'. Cue the unmistakable sound of pennies clanging down like girders in my head.

'Sorry, Mr. Yeung, but that's a pretty tight deadline you're setting there. Just how much are you willing to pay me for doing such a very, very high-profile job at such short notice?' I asked.

'Three hundred dollars,' came the reply.

'Three hundred US dollars is a little on the low side, but I'm sure we could work something out in terms of timing and number of permissible revisions...'

'No, no, Fuery, you misunderstand. I mean three hundred *Hong Kong* dollars! Three hundred

US dollars is far too much to expect me to pay for such a task!'

Faced with the prospect of wasting the next 48 hours pandering to the Territory's newly anointed Industrial Fastening King for the princely sum of around £25 I tried – and failed miserably – to stifle a dismissive snigger.

'What's so funny?' demanded Mr. Y 'I offer you a high-paying job' – more barely suppressed guffaws from the lobby of the AMC cinema – 'and all you can do is laugh. I don't think I care for your attitude, Fuery. Do you know what? While I would almost certainly have ended up rewriting large portions of your draft myself, had your work shown any promise, I would have given you two other very large jobs later on! Now I'm not only not going to pay you to help me write my speech, I'm not going to offer you the chance to write our company brochure or website either.'

'Sorry to hear that, Mr. Yeung. If it's any use, here's what I suggest we do next. Why don't you call back in a couple of hours, fill me in on the brief and budget for your brochure and website, and I'll do you the speech for free!'

Quelle surprise! Mr. Y didn't seem to have details of either the brochure or the website handy, so he was unable to collate and email them over. Instead, he merely contented himself with still more griping about my graceless reaction to a budget he felt was sufficient to allow me to start planning for my retirement.

Eager to get back to what was left of my movie, I was getting tired of talking to this waste of skin, organs, time and space. 'So sorry to hear that you think my attitude is bad, Mr. Yeung. If you've got a pen handy, I'll give you the contact details for a couple of other English freelance writers you might try.' I duly gave the Czar of the Structural Bolt a couple of names and numbers. Before 11:00 am the following morning, both writers had called to tell me to go screw myself for having the temerity to pass their details on to such a jerk.

* * *

Cast your mind back to your school and college days, and you'll eventually unearth long-buried memories of a classmate called Billy or Billi No-Mates. You know the one I mean. His (or her) sole joy in life was to rip apart everything anyone else discussed.

Of all the places I worked during my career, Hong Kong seemed to have far and away the largest concentration of these pedantic fuckwits. And what career path did these tiresome hair-splitters choose? Why, they became clients who liked nothing more than to remind you of just how much more they knew about everything than you did.

Irritatingly, their imagined superior insightfulness wouldn't just cover whatever product or service they were attempting to flog to the public. No, their relentless nit-picking even extended to their professional advisors' choice of words, sentence structure, and even art direction.

One of the most useful pieces of advice anyone ever gave me about working in advertising was: 'You're paid to say no twice.' After that, you unhesitatingly do whatever it is the client tells you to do – no matter how painfully you know they're about to shoot themselves in the foot.

I remember once attending a creative workshop hosted by legendary Asian adman Neil French. During the Q and A session at the end of Frenchy's talk, he picked out an arm from the audience. At the other end of said extremity lurked an annoyingly earnest American woman. 'Would,' the yankess asked Neil, 'your high professional standards allow you to work with a client who kept rejecting your ideas?' Not skipping a beat, Frenchy replied, 'Not a bit of it. If clients are stupid enough to piss their money up a wall, it might as well be my wall they're pissing it up against.'

During my time as a freelancer in Hong Kong, I had the misfortune to end up working for two real alpha examples of this particular type of client. The first gentleman, a 'Mr. Oh' (Oh, no, more like), oversaw the hosting of corporate events and loyalty trips for the big name operator of a local theme park. Each time the commissioning agency would send me over Mr. Oh's monthly draft copy for editing, my revisions would come back larded with tautologies such as 'solutions', 'situations', and 'events'.

In this particular client's world, 'meetings packages' became 'meetings package solutions', and 'emergencies' became 'emergency situations', or more confusingly still, 'emergency events'.

The best kind of client you can get as a free-lancer is one who pays you by the word or hour. As this was one of the rare clients who did, I should really have kept my trap shut and started stuffing my pockets while the going was good. But no. Cheesed off by Mr. Oh's arrogance, I took great pleasure in deleting any extraneous words from whatever rubbish he had written that month before returning my revisions. In sending back his amendments of my amendments, Mr Oh would then defiantly reinstate any superfluous words I'd struck out.

One day, I'd had enough and emailed the agency a message asking the client to explain how an 'emergency situation' differed from a good old vanilla 'emergency'. 'Is the former somehow less urgent because it takes twice as long to say?' I asked respectfully. Underwhelmed by my jocular 'copywriting solution', Mr. Oh immediately phoned the agency and implemented a 'sacking event'. Obviously now *persona non grata*, I have remained in an 'unemployed situation' in theme park advertising's outer darkness ever since.

Another massively annoying know-it-all I worked with during this time was a Thai gentleman who headed up one of Hong Kong's smaller financial institutions. After a long day of gouging his customers, 'Mr. Giinkii' liked nothing more than to jot down ideas for his bank's communications to existing and potential targets. Nothing really wrong with that in principle. Unfortunately, no one in the bank or its agency had the requisite balls to tell Mr. G that his grasp of English fell some distance short of whatever it was he wanted to say.

'To be born an Englishman', Cecil Rhodes once wrote, 'is to win the lottery of life.' To replace the word 'born' with 'speak and write' is to discover the stroke of good fortune that has literally propelled me around the world.

Of course, the biggest problem facing native English speakers travelling overseas is that almost everyone who loves Western culture sees you as a sounding board to improve their own English language skills. My attempts to learn other tongues having been suffocated in their crib as a result, I was in no position to sneer at someone whose English was far superior to my pidgin Thai.

Annoyingly, Mr. G's lack of proficiency in his second language was only surpassed only by his lack of marketing and communications nous. As a result, even the simplest business letter would come back time and time again.

What did I care? Mr. G was paying me for my services by the hour, so the more revisions he made, the more money I ended up getting paid. Eventually, of course, no amount of cash could even begin to compensate for the monotony of having to rewrite something for the seventh or eighth time. The big question was, given the many hours Mr. G was squandering on pointlessly butchering my copy, who was looking after the customers whose wealth he was supposed to 'protect and build'?

Each time Mr. G's agency e-mailed me his poorly structured and worded rewrites of my latest draft, I would chop and change his clumsy syntax into workable marketing English. Having been in the business long enough, I was confident my revisions would grab the attention of the type of targets Mr. G's bank was trying to reach.

Off would go my rewrite only for it to arrive back hideously eviscerated – usually at some ungodly hour when it was, of course, required 'urgently'. Back again would go my repairs, and so the dance would continue.

Eventually, Mr. G tired of the to-ing and fro-ing and announced to the agency AE that in future, he would write all his own marketing copy. I told the lady that I perfectly understood his decision. Before hanging up, I also recommended she move any money she had in Mr. G's bank elsewhere as he was spending more time playing copywriter than he was on safeguarding his customers' accounts.

Fortunately, the cavernous gap between Mr. G's willingness to pay handsomely for advice he was incapable of listening to didn't stop him from coughing up for my services for quite a long time. As the great Michael Caine neatly put it: 'To maintain a high standard of living, one is sometimes forced to accept a very low standard of job'.

I'm not sure what eventually became of Mr. G, as I didn't think about him again until about a year later when I mass emailed a list of lapsed past and potential future clients. With a reply rate of around three in a hundred generally considered encouraging, the fact that Mr. G's agency didn't answer my message was very much par for the course. What was intriguing was the fact that Googling his bank's HK URL simply succeeded in bringing up that dreaded '404 not found' error message.

* * *

With money tight and offers of work even tighter when I set up my freelancing stall, I made the beginner's mistake of being accessible for anyone who'd offered to pay for my services.

As a result, phoned queries regarding hopelessly arcane grammatical questions that weren't needed in a rush and could easily be dealt with via email soon became the bane of my life.

'Hi, John. It's Barbara. Sorry to disturb you, but I have a small question about ellipses that I need your help with. It'll only take a couple of minutes, so I'm sure you won't mind!'

'Mind' the hassle of serving as an unpaid Ernest Fowler English Language Usage guru, I most assuredly did. What I 'minded' with bells and ribbons, rounded off with a generous sprinkling of hundreds and thousands, plus a cherry on top, were idiotic requests that were called in rather than emailed. 'Why is "there" different from "their", and which one should I use and when?' went one typical exchange.

Sod's Law being Sod's Law, these enquiries almost always arrived at the most inopportune moments – usually while you were slaving over a complex task such as an annual report. There you'd be, trying to make sense of conflicting statements about the Hugely Prosperous Enterprise Group's corporate balance sheet, and *chirrup! chirrupl! chirrup!* would trill the phone. The moment you paused to pick it up, *cheerio! cheerio! cheerio!* would go your concentration.

As your freelance career starts to gain momentum, your time becomes an even more valuable commodity, and you quickly learn to refuse to accept phoned-in enquiries or participate in conference calls. The only exceptions to this rule are jobs that carry budgets so large it would be suicide not to speedily junk your principles and swiftly pick up the phone.

Then there were the 'urgent' jobs whose deadline was invariably always now; right this very minute.

When you're a freelancer, urgency ceases to have any real meaning as every client or agency staffer and his or her wife's job needs to be turned around in a frenzied, dervish-like rush. I soon hit on a novel way of handling callers who insisted that their tasks were somehow more deserving of my instant attention than those several places ahead of them in the queue.

What I did was to simply ask the caller to write down a series of numbers: 'Two, seven, three, four, eight, two, nine, seven. Got you! What's next?' After jotting down three or four sets of numbers in this fashion, callers would naturally start to query me as to why I was asking them to do so.

'Oh, these are just the numbers of people who called in their urgent jobs several hours ago and whom I'd like you to call and tell that your job is more important than theirs...'

Gratifyingly, many of those who got the numbers treatment almost always saw the funny side and never tried taking such liberties again. Of course, this might also have been because more than a few of them decided to start working with more 'compliant' writers.

In less time than it takes to say, 'The cheque's in the post,' the initial flurry of requests heading my way had mutated into a full-on blizzard. Never having had a great deal of time for mobile phones, it wasn't very long before I started doing everything possible to avoid calls altogether. While this policy has probably cost me dearly financially over the years, it has preserved what precious little remains of my sanity – not that there was a lot to begin with.

Then there were the rare occasions when I did actually deign to take calls. This normally happened with new clients who were pissed off with their existing writer because he or she hadn't been paying them – oh, the irony – sufficient attention. This perceived shortcoming was almost certainly due to the fact that the client wasn't paying them sufficient money or settling their invoices sufficiently quickly.

As I would eventually discover to my cost.

Any questions as to who was calling and what business they were in hopefully quickly dealt with, it was time to get down to brass tacks and identify what exactly needed to be done. A few maddening minutes of the initial call was usually enough to show that many clients simply didn't have the foggiest as to what they were trying to flog or to whom.

'I'm really not sure how to go about this, John.

Perhaps we could try press or outdoor. Maybe even radio or TV? Perhaps an online campaign or brochure...'

'OK, why don't we begin by narrowing down the list of options available to you? I generally find the easiest way of doing this is for you to give me an indication of what sort of money you want to spend on this marketing drive of yours.'

At this point in the proceedings, the client would usually utter a nervous little *mano-a-mano* laugh. 'Again, I'm really not sure. Perhaps *you* could suggest a figure...'

A good friend – and rival freelance writer – Colin Ruffell used to liken taking a brief from a client to a particularly clueless customer's going into a travel agent. The problem was, once there, our punter couldn't tell the agent where they wanted to go or how they'd like to get there.

Nor did they have any idea of how long they wanted to spend in their chosen destination. Or how and when they wanted to come back. Even the very gentlest enquiry as to how much they'd budgeted to pay for their package would be met with a horrified gasp at the extent of your nosiness.

Clients who instantly announce how much they 'adore' whatever you've written are another scourge of copywriter's lives – regardless of whether full-time agency staffers or freelancers. 'Hi, John, I'm just calling to say thanks for the terrific copy...' would come the client's invariably laid-on-with-a-trowel opening gambit.

'But' – and there it was, as sure as shit follows shinola, the inevitable 'but' – 'I still don't think we're' – note the use of the inclusive form here – 'quite there yet.'

'And what, pray, is "not quite there yet" about it? What do you suggest "*we*" do differently?' I would counter. These last words would be uttered through teeth ground so tightly my dentist would begin considering a full-spec BMW 7 Series upgrade rather than the entry-level 3 Series model he could previously ill afford.

The client would then emit a disappointed sigh followed by the words: 'I'm not sure, but I'll know it when I see it...'

* * *

The most fulfilling job I had while freelancing was for a man called Bill Kong at EDKO Pictures – then, as now, one of Asia's largest movie production houses and distributors. Having received one of the hundreds of business card mailers I used to routinely bung in the post in January each year, Kong bit and invited me in to discuss a job.

Ultimately, the film business is one ginormous sewer in which production houses view the offering of jobs to insignificant little Johnny-come-latelies such as myself as evidence of their boundless philanthropy. Lucky to be allowed into the industry's hallowed portals, one should shut up and happily accept whatever little money was being offered for however huge a task needed to be done. Not really giving a shit either way, I was determined my payment should reflect the amount of effort I expended on whatever crumbs of work I was thrown.

Rule One of making movies is apparently to never, ever follow in the footsteps of those incurably vain or stupid enough to invest their own money in films. As a result, every script – no matter how brilliantly or badly written – needs huge amounts of financial backing before it can secure sufficient funds to get greenlit for shooting.

In early 2004, I was asked to spin the base metal of a clumsily written and back-translated English script for a Chinese movie called *Riding Alone for Thousands of Miles (RAFTOM)* into 24-carat cinematic gold. While never written to be filmed, my English script would hopefully keep hard-nosed Western investors turning the pages and dashing off still more zeroes on their cheques as they turned.

The draft I was given to work on was about 150 A4 pages, or 27,000 words, long and would take me a solid couple of weeks of rewriting. My fee for all this? About US$4,000. While not exactly the princely sum one might expect for selling one's soul to the movie business, it seemed like a sound down payment.

When Kong read my rewrite, he was so pleased with my work that he asked me if I would 'like to go up to the set in China and shoot the EPK?'

Like 99.9999% of those of you reading this, I had little idea what an EPK was. Reluctant to make myself look dimmer than I was by accepting a challenge I had even less idea of how to accomplish, I asked for clarification.

'It's a kind of "making of" featurette to send out to TV stations, newspapers, and magazines,' I was told.

'OK. If you think I can do it, Bill, I'll happily take the job.'

My latest client rummaged around in his desk for a few seconds and passed me over an impressively thick folder. Inside was a list of the people behind the film – one of them was the renowned Chinese filmmaker Zhang Yimou, who'd directed *Raise the Red Lantern* and *House of Flying Daggers*. *RAFTOM*'s star was to be legendary Japanese actor Ken Takakura, who'd starred with Robert Mitchum (something of a cinematic hero of mine) in *The Yakuza* and Michael Douglas in Ridley Scott's *Black Rain*.

Until the day I first set foot on one, I always viewed film sets as being impossibly glamorous.

They're actually anything but. As Charlie Watts says in the Rolling Stones documentary *5 x 25*, 'It's just five minutes of filming followed by 25 minutes of hanging about.'

With electricians (sparks!), carpenters (chippies!), costume and make-up people (er, costume and make-up people), various camera operators and continuity persons, the set on a 'box office blockbuster' differs little from that for a TVC. The big difference here was that we were shooting our movie in the arse end of China's Yunnan Province and most of the cast and crew spoke little or no English. Having only ever been over the border once before, I waved goodbye to the lion's share of the budget and sub-contracted someone to handle the nuts and bolts involved in shooting there.

Whatever riches were percolating in big conurbations such as Beijing and Shanghai (as well as biggish but less well-known cities such as Chengdu and Chongqing), they certainly hadn't trickled down to Yunnan.

In addition to getting to drink in still – mercifully – largely unsullied scenery, the chance to meet unspoilt, take-us-as-you-find-us people remains one of the most rewarding aspects of travelling around the world's backwaters. In my 35-odd-year career, I was greatly touched by how frequently those with barely a pot to piss in happily welcomed me into their homes and shared what little they had.

Despite my lack of directorial skills and the obvious language problems – to this day, I have no idea why Kong commissioned me to handle the project – out EPK's shoot was going without a hitch. At least, it was until the end of my second and final visit, which coincided with the end of principal photography.

Neglecting to stock up on Western food or Imodium before flying up to our base in the tiny town of Buttafuk was my first big mistake. My second was to foolishly accept an invitation to share the local crew's catered last-day lunch.

Mercifully, I was back in my hotel room before the vague rumblings in my guts had mutated into a ceaseless spray of watery brown fluid gushing uncontrollably out of my back passage. Unwilling to appear stuck-up by failing to show my face at the post-shoot wrap party, I reluctantly boarded the bus and headed off to what I had been reassured was Buttafuk's top restaurant.

After half-heartedly shoving my food around my plate and barely denting my first beer (now that's what I call ill), I felt an overwhelming urge to visit the restaurant's ambitiously named 'comfort station'. Once safely bolted inside, I quickly resigned myself to spending the bulk of the evening bent double and talking out of my backside down the big white courtesy telephone.

Our location being several hundred miles away from the nearest eatery any Westerner might care to visit, there were, of course, no sit-down crappers. Squatting gingerly over the indeterminately stained ceramic-surrounded hole beneath me, I felt the earth move. Suddenly, the first of the evening's generous ladlefuls of what looked like thin Brown Windsor soup started squirting from my anus.

By the time the initial barrage had quelled, I was horrified to discover that hardly any of the sickly mess that had emerged from my nether regions had reached its intended target. The loo's walls, floor, and even the door were liberally slathered in shades and layers of pooey goo Jackson Pollock might have been moved to call 'Number Two'.

Having tried my hardest to clean everything up with rags from the floor, I hightailed it (literally) back to the hotel bedroom's more western-er-friendly WC. There, previously untapped bodily fluids that had probably been lurking in my system since I'd left the UK 23 years before began covering the cubicle in abstract expressionist masterpieces of their own. The only bright spot – and it certainly wasn't visible on the wall or floor– was there was nothing left to come out during our four-hour drive to the airport the next morning.

My Kermit the Frog-like greenish pallor and

demeanour weren't sufficient deterrents to stop Kong from buttonholing me on the plane back to Hong Kong. There was good news and bad news. The good news was that he was commissioning me to tighten up the script for a second film (eventually released as *Fearless*, starring Jet Li). The bad news was that I would have to work on the script in between what were likely to be lengthy sessions editing the hours of footage we'd shot for the *RAFTOM* EPK.

This time around, my involvement would be a bit more time-consuming. In addition to editing and tightening up the back-translated script, I'd also have to write a six-page treatment and a 30-page synopsis as a sort of sweetener for wavering financiers.

Despite my never having written one before, Mr. K gave me less than a week to write the *Fearless* treatment. For reasons that mystify me to this day, he omitted giving me samples of previous tasters for me to read so that I might produce work to a decent standard.

When he read my first draft, Kong quickly got on the blower to let me know how disappointed he was. A couple of months later, he showed me a treatment he'd had written by an experienced professional screenwriter in the States to give me a flavour of the sort of thing he expected. The fact that said screenwriter had had roughly eight times more time than he'd given me, a movie novice, seemed not to bother him in the slightest. But then, what did I know? Kong's career highs were measured in Academy Awards, while mine consisted of various gold, silver, bronze, and finalist honours from advertising award shows that 99.999999 per cent of the world didn't give a damn about.

Aside from my fee, the only thing I wanted for rewriting the *RAFTOM* script and writing, directing, and editing the EPK was a lobby poster autographed by Zhang Yimou and Ken Takakura. I didn't even ask Kong to have his company frame it. While I was too green to have the temerity to request one, Mr. Big-Shot Movie Producer even promised me an end credit for my work in getting the movie made and publicised.

Disappointingly, Kong never lifted a finger to get my souvenir poster signed. When *RAFTOM* finally emerged on DVD a few months later, I was sufficiently savvy to the ways of the movie business to buy a copy rather than wait for EDKO to send me one. Screen pumped up to maximum magnification, my then girlfriend and now wife Belle and I sat down to watch my tiny end credit on the movie roll by. Frustratingly, while the film's accountant and on-set drivers and caterers had – deservedly – got namechecks, my contribution had gone totally unrecognized.

Despite his apparent disregard for my efforts

on his behalf, Kong hadn't finished with me just quite yet. My all-too-brief movie career gave an audible death rattle when EDKO commissioned me to make sense of a messy back-translated script for a movie called *Dance, Subaru*. While the fee Kong was offering for my rewriting services had fallen off a cliff, his expectations of what I should achieve within the offered budget had been ratcheted up several notches. Despite my managing to pull together and tie off the myriad of loose ends in the original script, I again received no credit on the final movie.

Our initially promising relationship finally petered out when Kong emailed me that the original *Fearless* script, whose back translation I'd worked on several months before, had been heavily rewritten by the original writer.

Would I, he asked, help run through and edit the heavily revised script for the EDKO equivalent of 'mates' rates'? Faced with a 120-page script that would take me the best part of 10 days to recraft, I was anticipating a fee in the region of US$5,000. Kong, on the other hand, was expecting I should lock the door, unhook my phone, and do all of the work for fully 80 per cent less. When I pointed out that imdb.com was quoting *Fearless*'s budget as some US$10,000,000, Mr. K promptly elbowed his way to the top of the list of clients I'd never work with again.

While fascinating to be part of the gestation process for an – ahem – 'major motion picture', finding the time to get up to China was not easy. By that stage, I was working stupid hours – 10- or 12-hour days six and often seven days a week had long since become the norm. While I was admittedly earning literally obscene amounts of money, I rarely ever had sufficient time to enjoy spending it.

At my peak as a freelancer, I had three retainers. As a result, before crawling out of bed on the first morning of each month, I'd already earned more cash than I did in salary during my last full-time posting. The hassle was I'd ended up taking on more jobs and having to do more rounds of amends than I could keep track of.

Arriving home from the pub typically frayed around the edges one night, I found myself listening to a barely literate English script for a new TV from a leading Japanese electronics goods manufacturer. 'Jesus, who wrote this shit?' I wondered aloud to the long-suffering Belle.

Only when I caught sight of the brand's logo at the end of the TVC did enlightenment dawn. The script I'd just condemned was the putrefied remainder of something I'd written for a revision-happy client whose eloquence with words was akin to my adroitness with electronic engineering.

My biggest client at the time was a leading

insurance company who'd taken it into their heads to pay me to go and twiddle my thumbs in their office four afternoons a week. During my very first visit, I completed the few jobs given to me by the marketing director who'd hired me in well under an hour. When I suggested to her that slashing the amount of time I was contracted to spend on site might make economic sense, she reassured me that work would soon be 'flooding in'. Despite my sitting at a desk on the 17th floor of their office most afternoons for the next two and a half years, the anticipated deluge never did materialize.

What arrived instead was a mouthy lady called 'Julie Lomo', whose agency career had never really taken off for long enough to crash and burn. Appointed to oversee the company's corporate communications, Julie was determined to make her mark. While never an easy woman to work with, everything between the two of us seemed to be going reasonably well.

At least, it was until the afternoon I was tasked with writing some corporate, mission, and values statements. Positively *de rigueur* for every company trying to humanize itself, such similarly worded and structured statements remain the most patronising form of bullshit bingo ever.

Having taken Julie's brief, I dutifully skulked off to a quiet corner of the office to spend the next few days ~~banging out~~ crafting a raft of alternative statements in various styles and tones. Options duly finessed and categorized across a variety of directions – some matey, others corporate, and still more somewhere in between – I headed back to Ms. Lomo's office for a review.

Assuming Julie's agency background would have imbued her with a *soupçon* of irony, I made the mistake of reading the more straitlaced of the various alternatives in a less than serious voice. While everything I'd written was bang on brief, Ms. L's face had begun to resemble that of a zealot, the foundations of whose belief system a non-devotee has had the temerity to shake.

'John,' she said, 'I can't help but think that you may not be fully invested in anything you've written here...'

'In all honesty, Julie, why should I? Come to think of it, why should you? Having worked in agencies and done this sort of stuff a million and one times yourself, are you honestly trying to tell me that *you* seriously believe all of it?

'Let's be honest here, if the likes of you and I took every client we ever worked for at their word, our homes would be jam-packed with stuff we don't want and certainly don't need. Any agency or freelance writer who tries to persuade you any different is lying through their teeth.

'As you and I both know, writers – be they with agencies or freelancers like me – are asked to turn out three or four loads of copy like this every week.

'Ultimately, it's not my job – or indeed yours – to believe unquestioningly in the content we're asked to produce. We're paid to make other people believe what we've written or edited on our employer's behalf.'

Julie was horrified by my candour. 'Well, I have to admit I'm struggling with what you've just told me,' she said.

'How and why so?' I replied. 'Let's run through the brief you gave me and see if you can point out where there's anything wrong with any of the versions of the various statements I've given you.'

At this point, Ms. Lomo started to adopt the confused client default position of blustering incomprehension. She then started zooming down a road in which she ranted about what a wonderfully people-focused company she – and I – were fortunate enough to work for.

When asked whether she had such faith in her employer that she bought every life insurance product that the company marketed, Julie seemed strangely lost for words. She was equally unforthcoming when asked if she loved the company we worked for so much that she'd remain there until she retired or died. Apparently not. She eventually left the company a year or so after I headed off to 'pursue new opportunities' myself.

Day after day of similar hassles filled the whole of the next 13 years. As mentioned earlier, freelancing's biggest selling point is that, despite clients' best attempts to stop you, you are free to work almost anywhere you want. I decided to make the most of this liberty by scooting off to Europe for a month every December.

In addition to spending Christmas with my sister, Mary, and latterly her second husband, Reg, Belle and I would visit one European country we had never been to before. More importantly still, we would spend a weekend reconnecting with what remained of my family in Ireland.

Epilogue

This is where we came in

Of course, my freelance career didn't crash and burn the moment I told Julie that only a slack-jawed imbecile would believe even a smidgeon of what they were paid to write. To start taking everything clients wanted to say in ads and press releases and suchlike at face value? To paraphrase Shakespeare, 'that way, madness lay...'

Business – as businesses are wont to do – continued to trundle along nicely for a few years. Then, during one of my and Belle's annual trips back to Ireland, my brother-in-law, Reg, suggested we check out property prices by window-shopping at local estate agents.

A decade earlier, during what are now wryly referred to as Ireland's 'boom' years, Belle and I had already put a tentative toe on the lowest rung of the country's property ladder. Our collective gasts flabbered by the obscenely inflated prices even artists' impressions of houses not yet built were commanding, we fled, horror-struck, to the nearest pub.

Prohibitively expensive they might be, but apartment prices in Hong Kong at least reflect the territory's image as a global financial and trading powerhouse. As lovely as the town and its surrounding areas were (and are), Roscommon's property market and bloated house prices were then just scarily pumped-up bubbles waiting to burst.

By 2013, the Celtic Tiger of the early 2000s had long since become a tamed and tattered shadow of its former self. While financially – and in tragically way too many cases personally – cataclysmic for first-time buyers, the massive collapse in Ireland's property prices was good news for Belle and me.

Come spring 2013, we embarked on one last return journey to the Ireland my mum and dad always used to call 'home'.

During a week-long trip to Roscommon that March, we found and bought a beautiful four-bedroom dormer-style detached house with a huge garden. With the town about a mile to the left and some beautiful countryside and river scenery just a few hundred yards to the right, the quiet life with our dog and two cats has really suited us both. I wonder how differently things might have turned out had my parents – like so many Irish people before them and since – not been forced to try and build a life for themselves elsewhere.

When my folks were growing up, Ireland was a place where the boot of the Catholic Church was affixed firmly to the face of a cowed and poorly educated population. Their youth was lived in a land where fun was restricted to Saturday night dances whose price of admission also included a vituperative Sunday morning denunciation from the priestly pulpit.

Today, the country has transformed itself into a liberal hotbed that has finally shaken off the cold, dead hand with which the Church had been holding it back for far too long. Gay marriage and easier access to legal abortions are just two of the massive strides forward the country has taken these last few years. Having remained staunch Catholics in spite of the church-sanctioned intolerance of their youth, my parents would have been mortified.

Snug and warm at my desk on a nippy Roscommon morning, I can't help but think back to the day Belle and I first arrived in Ireland to live rather than just visit.

Horrified by the slate grey overcast skies, Belle seemed to be having second thoughts about moving so far away from the hotter, sunnier Asian climes of her childhood.

'Don't worry,' said the immigration officer who stamped our passports. 'It could well brighten up a bit later.'

He was right.

It not only could.

It did.

But then in Ireland it generally always does.

Acknowledgements

If this bit doesn't shift a few copies, Lord alone knows what will

In closing, I'd like to extend my heartfelt thanks to the many, many past and current friends and colleagues who've helped steer me to something approaching pensionable age in unfairly reasonable fettle. I'd almost certainly never have made it this far had you not told me to put down that 'last' drink, stub out the latest in my formerly endless chain of cigarettes and joints, or just 'shut the fuck up and piss off home'.

As they're largely responsible for getting this book to you: David Szabo (for the various covers and rather spiffy T-shirt), Mal Costain for his cheerful provision of excellent advice about this publishing lark (If you've not read it, Mal's own *Adlandia* is a must-read set of titillating advertising tales. He's also written a couple of books about running – although sadly not yet one called *Running to Fat* (for which I'll be first in the queue). On the editing front, warm thanks to my sister Mary and best friend Peter for giving this MS a last run through to spot what my tired eyes could not. Thanks also to Vanessa O'Laughlin at Inkwell Ireland and Sarah Jones and Jefferson at www.bookeditors.com for their editor's reports and proofings of my earlier drafts. To Nick and the guys at Word-2-Kindle for their excellent formatting of the various e-book and paperback editions.

The various friends, Romans and countrymen whose ears I've loaned and bent and whose names I've not shamefully forgotten include:

From my school, college and early UK career days: Pat Fox, John McManus, John Smith, Phil Bonner and Joe & Elaine Gallagher (from school); Paul Eden, Martin Foreman, George James, Hugh Selley, Richard Ford, Mick Toft, Pat Harkin, Martin Flynn (from Hull Uni); plus John Devaney, John Skidmore, Anne Marie Lennon, Jack Hassell and Jack Sparrow (from Manchester).

Moving on to the Middle East: John Livings, Mike Hawkins, Graeme Ead & David Madge Parker (RIP) and Mark Ridings (all Saudi); plus Rob & Debbie Dillon, Taher Konji, Jill & Jean Claude Beauvalet, Nick Bevens, Peter Welton, David Makinson, David Fox, Nick & Sharan Arnold, Dil Nawaz, Jim McEwan, Rob Buck, Kevin and Lyb Gieves, Clive and Stephanie Little, Donal Kilalea and Siobhan O'Shea, and Tony McIver (all Bahrain).

During my lengthy sojourn in Hong Kong & all-too-brief Vietnam *satori* & Kenyan safari: Anita & Larry Haynes, Tony Perone, Benny Cheng, Sue Carver, Lynda Lo, Jimmy Lam, Norman Cheong, Tom & Martine Kupcinas, David Szabo,

Matt Seddon, Paul Gordon, Colin Ruffell, Peter Brown & Brigid McGrath, Phil (RIP) and Shauna Brady, Darren Cornwall, Jimmy McIlveen, Gary and Marianne (RIP) Jones, George Berni, Peter Brannan, Robert Laird, Julie Hume, Kate Southam, DR and Levis Cupit, John Kittelson, Kievin Yim, Owen 'Oboe' Brown, Lee & Sashi Howard and Andy Duncan (RIP) (all from my first stint in HK); George McIntosh, Michael Canavan, Ron Badenhorst, Peter Sandor, Rose Lee, Louise Davidson, Quyen Phan, and watchman and friend extraordinaire, Mr. Tul *et famile* (all Vietnam); plus Sheena Round-Turner, Fred Afune, and Sam and David his fellow F1-wannabe taxi drivers (Kenya).

Also deserving of a mention are all those who gave Belle and me such a warm welcome when we moved back to my spiritual home in Roscommon: Chiefly my Uncle Jimmy and Aunties Mary (RIP) Coyle, Kitty Brennan, and Maura Killian; cousins, Betty Raftery, Eamon and Siobhan Fahy, Michelle Mulligan & Lee Newman, Noel and Evelyn Coyle; Deirdre and Dave Killian; plus friends Cathy and Con McAleavy, David Molloy, Jimmy McNeil. Let's also not forget our wonderful neighbours, Aetna Gavin & Pat Eadie, Sri, Padma, Ash and Laya, and Ted & Tina Lyons.

Last but not least, huge hugs and kisses to my sister, Mary, and her husband, Reg, plus my wife Belle, for their endlessly unfailing patience and good cheer in the face of my default bolshiness. Now there's a title for my next literary magnum opus/set of self-indulgent ramblings if I ever recover from writing this one...

Aside from the budgerigars mentioned in David 'Madge' Parker's anecdote in Chapter Three, no animals, birds or insects were harmed in the writing of this book.

Appendix One:

The 10 Commandments of expat life

1. ## Always get it in writing before you get on the plane...

   The number of supposedly smart and talented people who fail to get everything all nice and idiot-proofed in the legally-binding paperwork they sign before boarding planes to god-knows-where would knock you for six. Once stuck fast in whatever foreign hellhole they've signed up for, they spend their entire two- or three-year contract boo-hoo-hooing about how they've been gulled to the rapidly decreasing number of those who can be bothered to listen.

2. ## Always do your best to learn a few words of the local lingo...

   Colleagues, clients, taxi drivers, bar staff and – ahem – 'hostesses' will all positively adore you for your thoughtfulness in making such a pathetically transparent attempt to ingratiate yourself into their circle.

3. **Always get translations of your name checked out two or three times in countries where you need a business card...**

    Please see Chapter Six and the salutory tale of Bob Seaforth's name card for a timely reminder why this is such a good idea.

4. **Always cultivate a local taxi driver (or two or three) and treat and tip them well...**

    That way, you'll always have someone who'll be happy to pick you up and later get your pissed and sorry ass home safe and sound from the local pub. More importantly still, you'll always have an extra body to help you plead your case and fight your corner should you ever land in hot water with local crooks (never good news) or cops (invariably even worse).

5. **Always keep US$50 folded up and ready to accidentally 'fall out' of your passport before approaching immigration desks in the airports of especially corrupt Third World countries...**

    Many friends also swore by the practice

of keeping a similarly folded US$100 note handy should they ever be unfortunate enough to get pulled into the local cop shop. ('Good Lord, where on earth did *that* come from?') The decision to resort to such subterfuges in lawless Third World countries is, of course, entirely your own. As, needless to say, are any potential consequences you may suffer if unlucky/foolish enough to try bribing one of the few honest and upright public officials you may encounter in such backwaters. In other words, don't come running to me after you spend the next 20 years of your life trying to supplement your barely adequate prison diet with protein-rich lice from your cellmates' hair.

6. **Never count on getting any meaningful help from the British Consulate or Embassy...**

While you'd be an idiot not to call them to alert your family and friends back home, the best you can probably expect is a visit and a gentle urging not to rock the diplomatic boat. 'Strictly *entre nous*, old chep, this is very delicate time betwin arselves and INSERT NAME OF COUNTRY HERE, doncha know...'

7. **Never take home the local bar girls in a country where HIV/AIDS is rife...**

Sounds like common sense? Just wait until you're two and three-quarter sheets to the wind and a comely Nubian wench who looks like Halle Berry and Naomi Campbell rolled into one bats her eyes at you. When I lived in Kenya, I used to reward the local girls for *not* attempting to jump in the back of my taxis home.

8. **Never drink anything that doesn't come out of a can or bottle...**

Or boiled and poured before your eyes in the case of hot drinks. Ice cubes are another outwardly innocuous pleasure that are chock full of typhoid, E.coli and other equally unpleasant (and often potentially deadly) ailments. While the bacteria inside them won't harm the locals, they'll have you spending several days doubled-up in bed raving about how end times are upon us. On the bright side, if you *do* wind up catching something unspeakable, the chances you'll survive are probably far better than you might think. After being given the dread diagnosis he had bubonic plague, an expat friend in Vietnam was amazed when he learned he'd be right as rain after a course of antibiotics.

9. Never, ever become too attached to the places you work and/or whatever perks you may enjoy as a result of being an expat...

In his typically sniffy style, Noel Coward once airily disdained pre-war Singapore as 'a first-rate place ran by third rate people'. Anyone who didn't possess the gumption to make it quite that far were reviled as being 'FILTH' (Failed in London, Try Hong Kong). Those who wound up mired in Middle Eastern countries such as Saudi and Dubai were so far beneath contempt they weren't even deemed worthy of an acronym.

Overjoyed at being able to lord it over poorly-paid Filipino and Sri Lankan servants, this strand of expat ne'er do well is just too dense to comprehend the trap they've built for themselves. With skivvies paid just pennies to do all their fetching, carrying cooking, cleaning and everything in-between, such ignoramuses end up feathering nests they'll never, ever be able to leave.

The compounds of Jeddah are packed to the rafters with 'been-there, done-that, forget-your-old-friends and scream-at-the-maids and drivers' expats whose brains have been frazzled by too much time in the sun. Full of whiney old 'whenwes' whose sole topic of conversation seems to consist of how much better life was 'when we Europeans used to run everything', the bars of Asia are just as bad.

10. Always be very, very careful about who you piss off, and when and where you piss them off...

About 25 years ago, a guy I used to know (I'd hesitate to call him a friend) called Rick ended up being transferred from Hong Kong to Jakarta by his company. Whenever clients, colleagues or mates visited him on work or pleasure, Nick would take great delight in belittling Dismas, his 'terminally thick' company-provided driver. One night, Mr. Nick must have gone waaaaaaayyyyyyyyyy too far as Dismas apparently snapped and ended up stabbing him in excess of 40 times. Had Dismas driven his erstwhile boss to the hospital one supposes there might just have been a chance he could have been saved. Sadly,

ER doctors, nurses and crash carts were in short supply in the rat- and roach-infested alley where Dismas dumped his former tormentor's bloodied corpse.

Appendix Two:

The 10 most ridiculous things I've ever heard an ad agency client or colleague say...

1. **'You from the UK? London town, right? I have friend there, Mr. John Smith. Perhaps you know him, yes?'**

   Mr. and Mrs Smith's eldest? Yes, we've been BFFs since we were toddlers. I'll be sure to pass him along your best wishes the next time I get together with the other 7,500,000 people who live in 'London town'. The first question I was ever asked in my very first meeting in Saudi Arabia in June of 1981, this poser was subsequently repeated at pretty much every place I visited thereafter.

2. **'No, no, Hans, flying carpets are not real. The winners will be travelling to Istanbul aboard Turkish Airlines.'**

   Uttered by a Swiss hotelier in Jeddah when an underling jokingly remarked that the winners of an upcoming competition for return tickets would be flying to Turkey using a mode of transport now only found in the pages of *1,001 Arabian Nights*.

3. **'Cut some words from the script?**

Why can't we just tell the Voice Over (VO) talent to simply read everything a bit faster?'

Know how many words you can squeeze into the 30-second script for a radio or TV commercial before your voice talent starts sounding like the loony at the back of the bus? Leaving aside absurdly over-elaborate actual words such as floccinaucinihilipilification or rarely encountered (and hotly disputed) monickers such as the 189,819-character name for the protein titin, the answer is between 70 and 75. And the more words and syllables you attempt to pile on beyond that point, the more unhinged the VO – and by logical extension – your client will begin to sound.

Clients being clients, they refuse to either accept or have their creativity straitjacketed by Newton's Fourth Law of Physics (you know the one, it says 'you can't get two pounds of shit in a one pound bag.') My favourite example came in Vietnam when a rather lovely Vietnamese client called 'Ms. Phung' had commissioned us to do a 30-second TVC for the Japanese motorbikes her company agency-repped for. How was it, she asked me sweetly, our voice over talent was consistently failing to include the names, addresses and phone numbers of her company's 20 nationwide distributors in his script read throughs? When advised that just one seven-digit phone number would eat up around 10 per cent of her commercial's running-time, dear old Ms. P uttered the immortal words 'but can't he just squeeze everything in by reading the words a bit faster?'

4. 'Where's the footage of me I told you to include in my TVC?'

One of the first and most important of the – admittedly very few – lessons everyone working in advertising is ever taught is this instructive little rhyme.

Should the client criticise,
Make his logo twice the size.

Should said client still hesitate,
Bung in a shot of his factory's gate.

Only in the most desperate cases,
Ever show the client's faces.

5. *'I'd like the way the white space makes my product stand out from the layout much better if you padded it out with some of our other products.'*

Too many clients to mention – at least one at every agency in which I've ever worked.

6. **'I'm loving the look the reversed-out type gives our ad but the coupon doesn't seem to match...'**

Ever tried to write your name on a black piece of paper? Well, now you know why!

7. **'Don't worry, we'll easily sort that bad boy out in post-production.;.'**

As said by every AE at every agency I've ever worked at when a client sees something they're not happy with in a rough cut TVC. While some minor issues can indeed be 'fixed in post', doing so ain't as quick or cheap as the client might like – or have been soft-soaped – to believe. On one famous occasion, things the client wanted 'fixed' in post included the face of the main talent he himself had – against all agency advice – insisted on using before shooting commenced.

8. **'I'm something of a writer/illustrator/photographer myself. How about we save some money by letting me do the copywriting/art direction/photography?'**

Advertising agencies are probably the only service-centred businesses on earth where, rather than always being right, the customer is almost always totally and irredeemably wrong. This is especially true of the many clients who see ads in the papers or on TV and think 'I can do better than that.'

Sorry, mate, but as those piss-poor puns, crap cartoons and that Snappy Snaps bag of maladroitly framed and out-of-focus photos you've proudly dumped on the boardroom table prove, you really can't. So should you ever encounter a client who utters the dread words 'leave that bit to me', your only possible answer is to borrow from the late, great Frankie Howerd and say 'Nay, nay and thrice nay!'

9. **'I'll know what I want when I see it!'**

Yes, and before you know it, you'll be seeing stars, you fucking wazzock. My favourite story about this sort of comment dates back to the pre-computer days when every letter in every headline on every ad had to be painstakingly cut out from sheets of Letraset and meticulously rubbed onto a Daler artboard. Barely giving each layout a second thought, uncaring clients would pull out their pens and scribble their comments on boards in indelible ink.

Having lost count of the number of options he'd presented, an art director friend of mine in Manchester finally lost all patience with his indecisive client. Excusing himself from the meeting for a few moments, he returned to the creative department where he began cutting out individual characters from Xeroxed Letraset sheets and putting them in a bin bag.

Bag bulging with letters, numbers and all manner of punctuation in a multiplicity of sizes and types, he stormed back into the board room and dumped its contents over the client's head. Realising just how much of a dick he'd been, the client amazingly didn't call for my friend's sacking and was apparently 'a joy to work with' ever after.

10. **'I love the ad/script/TVC/radio commercial, but...'**

Every client in every agency in every country in the history of advertising.

Appendix Three:

Weasel words, and when – and more importantly still when not – to use them

Below is a list of useful, all-purpose weasel words all novice copywriters would be well advised to keep handy when asked to write an ad:

Advanced *(Ahd-vahnst)* i.e. Bog standard, normal.

'Advanced' is generally used to describe a humdrum piece of equipment or technique so yawnworthy that every one of your client's competitors will almost certainly already have and be using it. The fact that said item/practice has already been 'leveraged' by every other company in the field for several years before your client finally got around to purchasing and installing it? It matters not in the slightest.

SAMPLE: *'With the addition of an advanced widget system to its Shenzhen production facilities, BigCo has further underlined its leadership in Hong Kong's Asia's/the world's thingamajig industry.'*

Should your copy already have crossed the border into the land of over-the-top on the 'advanced' front, please feel free to substitute terms such as 'cutting-edge', 'state-of-the-art', 'ultra-advanced', 'ultra-modern', 'ultra-sophisticated', etc.

Almost *(Awl-mohst)*
See: QUALIFIERS

As little as *(As lit-tel as)*
As low as *(As loh as)*
　　See: QUALIFIERS

Attractive *(At-rack-tiv)*
　　See: 'COMPETITIVE'

Battle *(Bah-tul)*
　　See: QUALIFIERS

But *(Butt)* i.e. The three-letter single-syllable word that's sufficient to derail the many hours, weeks and months of work that went into creating your campaign. Whilst a qualifier, 'but' really does merit an entry all of its own.

SAMPLE: *'John, mate, the guys just adore your concepts!'* Fine words if only they were left right there. Disappointingly, such sentences inevitably herald the arrival of the word that leaves clients free to trample your cherished ideas into dust.

See also: YET

Combat (Kom-bat)

See: QUALIFIERS

Could (Kud)

See: QUALIFIERS

Committed (Kom-it-ted) i.e. Determined to make obscene profits for minimal effort.

SAMPLE: *'Adman, Adman and Bowtie Ltd. is committed to gouging its clients for every last cent of their marketing budgets.'*

Competitive *(Kom-pet-et-ive)* i.e. Similar to 'Advanced', 'Competitive' describes something that everyone in the business world bar the most indolent companies have already been providing since God donned his first pair of short trousers.

Typically sluggish, your client has finally realized that the features and benefits they're offering to potential customers/hires are all woefully lacking when compared to those of their rivals. It goes without saying that this dollop of information should be doled out in terms that make it sound as if your company is anything but behind the curve.

SAMPLE (Product): *'In underling the highly competitive nature of its business, the Tardy Watch Company has once again anticipated growing consumer demand and invested in...'*

SAMPLE (Recruitment): *'The successful applicant can look forward to a highly competitive remuneration package.'*

Cravenly hinting at rather than actually guaranteeing what it a potential hire **might** actually receive from the employer whose ad they are reading, 'look forward to' is, of course a useful assemblage of weasel words in its own right.

Coveted *(Kuh-veh-tid)* i.e. A worthless sop that will make zero discernible difference to the life of the clueless man or woman in the street who your client expects to mindlessly lap up their products or services.

Subsection 1 paragraph b, clause xxxxviii of Fuery's Copywriting Law number 5,237 states that **all** awards, baubles, trinkets, etc, must be described as 'coveted'. Any resultant prominence applies regardless of whether you, the writer, the client who has won them, or anyone bored enough to read awards announcement ads is aware of – or care two figs about – them.

SAMPLE: *'PolluShun Limited is delighted to announce it has just received the coveted Golden Turd Award for Environmental Sustainability.'*

Should you already have used the 'c' word earlier in your copy, feel free to insert vague and ultimately meaningless jargon such as 'enviable', 'high-profile', 'prestigious' or 'sought-after' (or better still, 'much sought after') in its place.

Determined (Dee-ter-minned)
>   See: COMMITTED

Dramatic *(Drah-mat-ik)* i.e. Ordinary, totally expected (if several years late).
>   See: DYNAMIC

Dynamic *(Die-nam-ik)*

　See: DRAMATIC

Essential: *(Eh-cent-shul)* i.e. Incredibly easy to live without.

After all, you've managed to live a long, fulfilling and perfectly happy life without having to moronically go out and snap up what's being advertised until now.

SAMPLE: *'RipOffCo's new skunk-scented deo-stick is an essential lifestyle accessory for those who have been summoned to appear before a Grand Jury and do not want their testimony subverted by an excess of underarm perspiration.'*

Far-sighted: *(Fah-sigh-tud)* i.e. Incapable of looking any further than the point at which it's possible to see what everyone else in your field is doing and then desperately trying to catch up.

SAMPLE: *'Bollocky Ltd. is one of the most far-sighted companies in the challenging field of testicular transplants.'*

See: FORWARD-THINKING, THINKING AHEAD, VISIONARY

Fight *(Fyte)*
See: QUALIFIERS

From just *(Frohm-jusd)*
See: QUALIFIERS

Forward-thinking *(Fore-wad thin-king)*
See: FAR-SIGHTED, THINKING AHEAD, VISIONARY

Gleaming *(Glee-ming)* i.e. A high-cost purchase such as a car or a property that could be said to be reasonably shiny and new. The term is equally apt when applied to newish items that have been 'previously loved' (or 'second hand' as folk used to say when I were a lad).

SAMPLE Property: *'With their gleaming, glass-clad frontage, Ranchman Properties' new multi-storey developments are full of homes you'll love to come home to!'*

SAMPLE Car: 'With its stylish aerodynamics and gleaming bodywork, Crash Co's new 1.6-litre Diana Tunnel model is a car that's sure to leave a lasting impression.'

Already blinded potential punters with your – ahem - 'gleaming' prose? Then don't hesitate to liberally sprinkle your ad with words such as 'glittering' or 'glossy.' When advertising shampoos, conditioners or hair gels, you can even up your cliché quotient a notch or three by dropping in impressive-sounding phrases such as 'luminous' and 'lustrous'.

Help *(Hell-puh)*

See: QUALIFIERS

Highly motivated *(Hy-lee moh-tiv-ate-ed)* i.e. Capable of getting out of bed in the morning on one's own without having to be chivvied along and have the buttons on one's clothes fastened by one's parents or partner.

This old recruitment standby really comes into its own when hiring companies want to convince readers that their ability to perform the simplest task without any external assistance somehow makes them a valuable commodity.

SAMPLE: *'Highly-motivated self-starter? Millgram Inc. will reward you with an attractive competitive salary for doing little else than walking around holding a clipboard and barking orders at those several pay grades below you.'*

Irresistible *(Ir-ruh-sist-ib-el)* i.e. Supposedly impossible to say no to

In actuality, the word generally describes something that is easily ignorable by anyone capable of exercising an ounce of self-restraint or willpower.

SAMPLE: *'If you're an easy mark for advertisers selling products you'll barely use once before you wonder why you bothered buying them, here's a simply irresistible offer!'*

Leveraged *(Leh-vuh-reg-duh)* i.e. A US$50 word that effectively means 'used'.

SAMPLE: *'In coming up with its latest hair regrowth formulation, Rooney & Co have leveraged an innovative blend of cow manure and magic beans harvested by Jack the Giant Killer.'*

Limited *(Lim-et-id)*

Limited edition *(Lim-et-id ed-ish-on)*

Limited time only *(Lim-et-id tyme-onlee)*

i.e. Limited to as few or as many units as the client can dump on the terminally gullible dickwads who believe advertising copy is some kind of holy writ.

SAMPLE: *'Pyroman's limited-edition set of Arsonists' Choice match boxes is sure to ignite some positively inflammatory discussions.'*

May *(Mey)*
May well *(Mey well)*
> See: QUALIFIERS

Measurably *(Mez-zyur-abli)*
> See: QUALIFIERS

Might *(Mite)*
Might just *(Mite juzt)*
> See: QUALIFIERS

Mouth-watering *(Mowth-waht-er-ing)* i.e. Every item of food ever advertised anywhere.

An old standby for ads aimed at those who regularly eat out or are dim enough to try creating 5-Star restaurant style meals in the comfort of their own home.

SAMPLE: *'This week's buffet at the Pavlov Bar and Grill features the usual mouth-watering array of tasty starters, delicious mains and to-die-for sweet treats.'*

Worried your target readers might be gagging after having ingested a surfeit of ads too liberally garnished with the word mouth-watering? Then why not top off with a jaunty garnish of alternatives such as 'Tasty', 'Delicious' and 'Moreish'?

Must-have *(muhst-av)*

    See: ESSENTIAL

Perhaps *(Purr-happs)*

    See: QUALIFIERS

Prevent *(Pree-vent)*

    See: QUALIFIERS

Possibly *(Poh-sib-lee)*

    See: QUALIFIERS

Probably (Proh-bab-lee)

    See: QUALIFIERS

Qualifiers i.e. Any word or phrase that automatically renders virtually meaningless the quasi-hyperbolic claim that appears immediately after it.

The undisputed Kings of the Advertising and Marketing Jungle, qualifiers are every copywriter's, agency's, and client's best friend. Got a claim you can't quite justify to whatever regulatory body you need to satisfy before you can get your ads or TVCs out there? Simple! Just bung a qualifier in front of your dubious boastings and Robert's your mother's brother.

You don't believe me? Then simply check out any oral hygiene product on TV and note the number of times old standby weasel words such as 'help', 'fight'/'battle' 'may well', 'might just' and 'up to' occur. While 'possibly'/'probably' and 'up to' are arguably (see how easily we emasculated those pesky potential objections in advance?) the greatest weasel words of them all, oral hygiene products deserve a special mention in despatches. After all, when was the last time you saw an ad for a toothbrush, toothpaste or fluoride rinse that didn't incorporate a vaguer or more meaningless qualifier than it came 'recommended by dentists'?

Covering increases of as little as (Congratulations! You're really starting to get the hang of this copywriting lark) 0.00000001th of some unit of time, weight or distance, 'measurably' is a particular favourite of mine. 'Almost' was another – particularly when it was appended in front of a far more definitive and forceful word such as 'invariably' as I once did on a Mercedes TVC. Too slow-witted to realize the two words are actually contradictory, the inattentive automatons at Hong Kong's Television and Entertainment Licencing Authority waved the script through without a second thought.

'From just/as little/low as' and 'up to' are other weasel words and phrases deserving of a worthy mention. Ultimately, each can be twisted to mean literally anything – and frequently are. If you really want to try and push your luck, even 0.000000000000001 can arguably be described as being 'up to 1,000.'

Airlines and travel companies are usually the worst offenders in using such semantic sleight of hand. You know the sort of thing I'm talking about – an airline that regularly offers 'flights to LA from just £9.99', say. It doesn't matter how inconvenient the reader might find the flight's point of origin/ departure time (Minsk at 0340 anyone?) It doesn't matter how byzantine the list of restrictions the airline has placed in the way of those hoping to take advantage of the fare (last call for one-legged transsexual grandparents who've not flown anywhere in the previous 23 years!) As long as said airline is offering at least one ticket at the absurdly low quoted price, it can quite legitimately make the claim the cornerstone of its TVCs, posters and press/radio ads. See you in Minsk, *tovarich*!

Still can't find anything positive to say about whatever it is you're being paid to advertise? Why not start rattling off a few 'no one tries harder than/nothing performs as well as' type lines? You'll never get pulled up on them as you're simply positing that your product/service is no better or worse than its competitors.

Self-starter *(Self-stah-tur)*

See: HIGHLY MOTIVATED

Scrumptious *(Scrump-chew-us)*

See: MOUTH-WATERING

Sumptous *(Sump-chew-us)* i.e. Lavish, opulent, highly desirable.

International Advertising Law states that all buffets must be 'sumptuous.' This is regardless of how stale the food or piss-poor the choice on offer may be for those desperate enough to try and satisfy their appetites at the advertiser's eaterie.

SAMPLE: *'The tables at Hotel Guantanamo's buffet are groaning beneath a sumptuous array of simply irresistible e-coli and salmonella-laden comestibles.'*

Buffet copy already stuffed to bursting point with sumptuous-type adjectives? Then why not top off your ad with glace cherry-type words or phrases such as 'enticing', 'exquisitely prepared and presented', 'melt-in-the-mouth' or 'tempting'.

Significantly *(Sig-nif-i-kant-lee)*

   See: QUALIFIERS

Targets *(Tah-getz)*

   See: QUALIFIERS

Thinking ahead *(Thin-king a-hed)*

   See: FAR-SIGHTED

Up to *(Uhp-too)*

See: QUALIFIERS

Virtually *(Vih-tu-allie)*
See: QUALIFIERS

Visionary *(Vih-zyun-ar-ee)*
See: FAR-SIGHTED

When it comes to... *(Wen-it-cums-tu)* i.e. A useful one-size fits all approach for when you're stuck for an opening for your press ads or TVC/radio scripts.

SAMPLE: *'When it comes to kicking off a piece of copy, what better way to start than by saying 'when it comes to'?'*

The advertising equivalent of movie teaser voice over talent's 'In a world where...', 'when it comes to...' is possibly the most widely-used opening gambit in advertising history. Tired and overused? Of course it is. And never more so than should you be unfortunate enough to have to jump-cut your way through the pages of the average copywriter's portfolio.

Yet *(Yett)* i.e. A useful qualifier when you are called upon to link two totally opposite characteristics, items or qualities to sell your product.

SAMPLE: *'Surprisingly compact on the outside, yet stylishly spacious in its passenger compartment, the new XYZ is a car that literally turns the laws of physics on their collective head.'*

Got a client who doesn't know what they want and/or a colleague in the client service department who's talking out of his or her arse (no surprises there then)?

The best way to make sense of, and accommodate, your clients' and colleagues' mutually conflicting requests? Be sure and liberally lard your copy with qualifying 'yets'.

Offhand yet oddly focused, timelessly classic yet up-to-the-minute casual, this approach is sure to satisfy everyone's desire for copy that is professional yet friendly, black yet white, short yet long.

Wait, come back! We're not finished yet!

If you've enjoyed *Good Morning, Mr. Sh*ttybottom,* please feel free to leave some suitably glowing praise on the Amazon Kindle review pages. If you've got any comments/criticisms or queries, or maybe ran into me at some point and would like to get back in touch, I'd also love to hear from you. So don't hesitate to drop me a line at

mailto:goodmorningmrsh1ttybottom@gmail.com

https://www.facebook.com/profile.php?id=100028516839568